D0078745

Logistics & Supply Chain Management

Prentice Hall

FINANCIAL TIMES

In an increasingly competitive world, we believe it's quality of thinking that gives you the edge – an idea that opens new doors, a technique that solves a problem, or an insight that simply makes sense of it all. The more you know, the smarter and faster you can go.

That's why we work with the best minds in business and finance to bring cutting-edge thinking and best learning practice to a global market.

Under a range of leading imprints, including *Financial Times Prentice Hall*, we create world-class print publications and electronic products, bringing our readers knowledge, skills and understanding, which can be applied whether studying or at work.

To find out more about Pearson Education publications, or tell us about the books you'd like to find, you can visit us at **www.pearsoned.co.uk**

PEARSON

MARTIN CHRISTOPHER

Logistics & Supply Chain Management

Fourth Edition

Financial Times
Prentice Hall
is an imprint of

PEARSON

Harlow, England • London • New York • Boston • San Francisco • Toronto • Sydney • Singapore • Hong Kong
Tokyo • Seoul • Taipei • New Delhi • Cape Town • Madrid • Mexico City • Amsterdam • Munich • Paris • Milan

PEARSON EDUCATION LIMITED

Edinburgh Gate
Harlow CM20 2JE
Tel: +44 (0)1279 623623
Fax: +44 (0)1279 431059
Website: www.pearsoned.co.uk

First published in Great Britain in 1992
Second edition 1998
Third edition 2005
Fourth edition 2011

ISBN: 978-0-273-73112-2

British Library Cataloguing-in-Publication Data
A catalogue record for this book is available from the British Library

Library of Congress Cataloging-in-Publication Data
Christopher, Martin.
  Logistics and supply chain management : creating value-adding networks / Martin
Christopher. -- 4th ed.
    p. cm.
  Includes index.
  ISBN 978-0-273-73112-2 (pbk.)
  1. Business logistics--Cost effectiveness. 2. Delivery of goods--Management. I.
Title.
  HD38.5.C46 2011
  658.5--dc22
                    2010033709

11 10 9 8 7 6 5 4 3
14 13 12 11

Typeset in Swiss Light 9.25 pt/12 pt by 30
Printed and bound in Great Britain by Henry Ling Limited, at the Dorset Press, Dorchester, DT1 1HD

About the author

Martin Christopher is Emeritus Professor of Marketing and Logistics at Cranfield School of Management in the United Kingdom. His work in the field of logistics and supply chain management has gained international recognition. He has published widely and his books have been translated into many languages. Martin Christopher co-founded the *International Journal of Logistics Management* and was its joint editor for 18 years. He is a regular contributor to conferences and workshops around the world.

In addition to working with many companies in an advisory capacity he is also a Visiting Professor at universities in the UK, Australia, Spain and Sweden.

Martin Christopher is an Emeritus Fellow of the Chartered Institute of Logistics and Transport. He is also a Fellow of the Chartered Institute of Purchasing and Supply and a Fellow of the Chartered Institute of Marketing. He is the recipient of the Distinguished Service Award of the USA Council of Supply Chain Management Professionals.

Contents

Preface

When the first edition of this book was published in 1992, supply chain management as an idea was still in its infancy and relatively few companies had made it a priority.

The same was true for logistics management, although its precursor, distribution management, was increasingly being recognised as important both in terms of cost and for its potential impact on sales.

In the intervening years from the first to the fourth edition, many things have happened. Firstly, there is now a much greater understanding of the role that supply chain management plays in creating competitive advantage. Whereas previously the focus was primarily tactical with a concern for optimising costs, now there is much more of a strategic focus with the emphasis on value creation and delivery. The second major change is the recognition that supply chain management is not just an extension of logistics management, but rather that it is about managing *relationships* across the complex networks that today's supply chains have become. A third significant change over that period is that the business environment has become a lot more volatile and hence less predictable. This transition from a relatively stable world to one that is much more turbulent requires supply chains to be capable of changing rapidly to meet changed circumstances.

These changes are reflected in the additional material included in this new edition. Thus complexity management and the challenge of making the transition from a forecast-driven to a demand-driven business model are given greater emphasis.

As ever, I have been greatly influenced in my thinking by the ideas and contributions of colleagues. I have had the privilege over the years to work with many academics and practitioners around the world who have provided me with inspiration as well as feedback on my ideas on how modern supply chains should be designed and managed. Long-standing collaborators include Alan Braithwaite, Chairman of LCP Consulting, Professor John Gattorna of Macquarie University, Australia, Professor Douglas Lambert of Ohio State University, USA and Professor Denis Towill of Cardiff University, UK.

More recently I have benefited greatly from sharing ideas with Dr Omera Khan of Manchester University, UK, Dr Matthias Holweg of Cambridge University, UK and Dr Janet Godsell and Dr Uta Jüttner, both colleagues at Cranfield University. I thank them all.

Finally I want to thank Tracy Stickells who has skilfully managed the production of the manuscript for this book – a complex logistics process in itself.

MARTIN CHRISTOPHER
EMERITUS PROFESSOR OF MARKETING & LOGISTICS
CENTRE FOR LOGISTICS AND SUPPLY CHAIN MANAGEMENT
CRANFIELD UNIVERSITY, UK

Publisher's Acknowledgements

We are grateful to the following for permission to reproduce copyright material:

Figures

Figure 1.7 from *Competitive Advantage*, The Free Press (Porter, M.E. 1985), Reprinted with the permission of The Free Press, a Division of Simon & Schuster, Inc., from COMPETETIVE ADVANTAGE: Creating and Sustaining Superior Performance by Michael E. Porter. Copyright © 1985, 1998 by Michael E. Porter. All rights reserved.; Figure 1.9 from Integrating the Supply Chain, *International Journal of Physical Distribution and Materials Management*, 19 (8) (Stevens, G.C. 1989), International Journal of Physical Distribution and Logistics Management by Scott, C. and Westbrook, R. Copyright 1991 by EMERALD GROUP PUBLISHING LIMITED. Reproduced with permission of EMERALD GROUP PUBLISHING LIMITED in the format Textbook via Copyright Clearance Center. ; Figure 2.2 from 'Stock-outs cause walkouts', *Harvard Business Review*, May (Corsten, D. and Gruen, T. 2004); Figure 3.10 from *Logistics – The Battleground of the 1990s*, A.T. Kearney (Hill, G.V.); Figure 3.11 from *Managing the Supply Chain: A Strategic Perspective*, Macmillan Press (Gattorna, J.L. and Walters, D.W. 1996); Figure 6.13 from 'New strategic tools for supply chain management', *International Journal of Physical Distribution of Logistics Management*, 21 (1) (Scott, C. and Westbrook, R. 1991), Emerald; Figure 9.3 from *Supply Chain Resilience, Report on behalf of the Department of Transport*, Cranfield School of Management (2003)

Tables

Table on page 74 from 'The Customer Profit Centre', *Focus*, 2 (2) (Hill, G.V. and Harland, D.V. 1983), Institute of Logistics and Distribution Management; Table 10.1 from *Supply Chains in a Vulnerable, Volatile World*, A.T. Kearney (2003)

Text

Quote on page 136 from *The Scotsman*, 14/02/2007; Extract on page 160 from *The Times*, 21/04/2010; Extract on page 186 from Disenchanted companies begin moving production back to UK, *The Times*, 30/12/2009; Article on page 195 from *Supply Chains in a Vulnerable, Volatile World* (A.T. Kearney 2003); Article on page 244 from 12,000-mile round trip to have seafood shelled, *Daily Telegraph*, 16/11/2006, © Telegraph Media Group Limited 2006; Extract on page 244 from *Mastering Carbon Management: Balancing Trade-Offs to Optimise Supply Chain Efficiencies*, IBM Global Services (Butner, K., Geuder, D. and Hittner, J. 2008), Reprint courtesy of International Business Machines Corporation, © 2008 International Business Machines Corporation; Extract on page 252 from *Supply Management*, 15 February 2007, www.supplymanagement.com; Extract on page 254 from 'Intelligent Transport Systems', *Postnote*, January, No. 322 (UK Parliamentary Office of Science and

Technology 2009), Crown Copyright material is reproduced with permission under the terms of the Click-Use Licence; Extract on page 260 from 'Global Trends in Energy', *The McKinsey Quarterly*, January 2007 (Bozon, I.J.H., Campbell, W.J. and Lindstrand, M.), Excerpt from "Global Trends in Energy", January 2007, McKinsey Quarterly, www. mckinseyquarterly.com. Copyright (c) 2010 McKinsey & Company. All rights reserved. Reprinted by permission. ; Article on page 261 from Web-savvy housewives sabotage efforts to save Japan's economy from stagnation, *The Times*, 02/04/2010

In some instances we have been unable to trace the owners of copyright material, and we would appreciate any information that would enable us to do so.

Logistics, the supply chain and competitive strategy

1

- Supply chain management is a wider concept than logistics

- Competitive advantage

- The supply chain becomes the value chain

- The mission of logistics management

- The supply chain and competitive performance

- The changing competitive environment

Logistics and supply chain management are not new ideas. From the building of the pyramids to the relief of hunger in Africa, the principles underpinning the effective flow of materials and information to meet the requirements of customers have altered little.

Throughout the history of mankind wars have been won and lost through logistics strengths and capabilities – or the lack of them. It has been argued that the defeat of the British in the American War of Independence can largely be attributed to logistics failure. The British Army in America depended almost entirely upon Britain for supplies. At the height of the war there were 12,000 troops overseas and for the most part they had not only to be equipped, but fed from Britain. For the first six years of the war the administration of these vital supplies was totally inadequate, affecting the course of operations and the morale of the troops. An organisation capable of supplying the army was not developed until 1781 and by then it was too late.[1]

In the Second World War logistics also played a major role. The Allied Forces' invasion of Europe was a highly skilled exercise in logistics, as was the defeat of Rommel in the desert. Rommel himself once said that '… before the fighting proper, the battle is won or lost by quartermasters'.

> It is only in the recent past that business organisations have come to recognise the vital impact that logistics management can have in the achievement of competitive advantage.

However, whilst the Generals and Field Marshals from the earliest times have understood the critical role of logistics, strangely it is only in the recent past that business organisations have come to recognise the vital impact that logistics management can have in the achievement of competitive advantage. Partly this lack of recognition springs from the relatively low level of understanding of the benefits of integrated logistics. As early as 1915, Arch Shaw pointed out that:

> *The relations between the activities of demand creation and physical supply …*
> *illustrate the existence of the two principles of interdependence and balance.*
> *Failure to co-ordinate any one of these activities with its group-fellows and also*
> *with those in the other group, or undue emphasis or outlay put upon any one*
> *of these activities, is certain to upset the equilibrium of forces which means*
> *efficient distribution.*
> *… The physical distribution of the goods is a problem distinct from the*
> *creation of demand … Not a few worthy failures in distribution campaigns*
> *have been due to such a lack of co-ordination between demand creation and*
> *physical supply …*
> *Instead of being a subsequent problem, this question of supply must be met*
> *and answered before the work of distribution begins.*[2]

It is paradoxical that it has taken almost 100 years for these basic principles of logistics management to be widely accepted.

What is logistics management in the sense that it is understood today? There are many ways of defining logistics but the underlying concept might be defined as:

> *Logistics is the process of strategically managing the procurement, move-*
> *ment and storage of materials, parts and finished inventory (and the related*
> *information flows) through the organisation and its marketing channels in*
> *such a way that current and future profitability are maximised through the*
> *cost-effective fulfilment of orders.*

This basic definition will be extended and developed as the book progresses, but it makes an adequate starting point.

Supply chain management is a wider concept than logistics

Logistics is essentially a planning orientation and framework that seeks to create a single plan for the flow of products and information through a business. Supply chain management builds upon this framework and seeks to achieve linkage and co-ordination between the *processes* of other entities in the pipeline, i.e. suppliers and customers, and the organisation itself. Thus, for example, one goal of supply chain management might be to reduce or eliminate the buffers of inventory that exist between organisations in a chain through the sharing of information on demand and current stock levels.

It will be apparent that supply chain management involves a significant change from the traditional arm's-length, even adversarial, relationships that so often typified buyer/supplier relationships in the past. The focus of supply chain management is on co-operation and trust and the recognition that, properly managed, the 'whole can be greater than the sum of its parts'.

The definition of supply chain management adopted in this book is:

The management of upstream and downstream relationships with suppliers and customers in order to deliver superior customer value at less cost to the supply chain as a whole.

Thus the focus of supply chain management is upon the management of *relationships* in order to achieve a more profitable outcome for all parties in the chain. This brings with it some significant challenges since there may be occasions when the narrow self-interest of one party has to be subsumed for the benefit of the chain as a whole.

Whilst the phrase 'supply chain management' is now widely used, it could be argued that it should really be termed '*demand chain management*' to reflect the fact that the chain should be driven by the market, not by suppliers. Equally the word 'chain' should be replaced by '*network*' since there will normally be multiple suppliers and, indeed, suppliers to suppliers as well as multiple customers and customers' customers to be included in the total system.

Figure 1.1 illustrates this idea of the firm being at the centre of a network of suppliers and customers.

Figure 1.1 The supply chain network

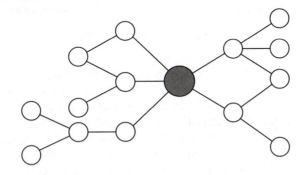

Extending this idea it has been suggested that a supply chain could more accurately be defined as:

A network of connected and interdependent organisations mutually and co-operatively working together to control, manage and improve the flow of materials and information from suppliers to end users.

SOURCE: J. AITKEN[3]

Competitive advantage

A central theme of this book is that effective logistics and supply chain management can provide a major source of competitive advantage – in other words a position of enduring superiority over competitors in terms of customer preference may be achieved through better management of logistics and the supply chain.

The foundations for success in the marketplace are numerous, but a simple model is based around the triangular linkage of the company, its customers and its competitors – the 'Three Cs'. Figure 1.2 illustrates the three-way relationship.

Figure 1.2 Competitive advantage and the 'Three Cs'

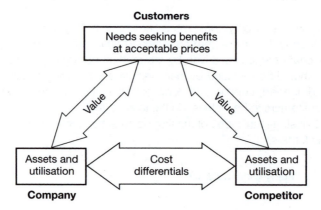

Source: Ohmae, K., *The Mind of the Strategist*, Penguin Books, 1983

The source of competitive advantage is found firstly in the ability of the organisation to differentiate itself, in the eyes of the customer, from its competition, and secondly by operating at a lower cost and hence at greater profit.

Seeking a sustainable and defensible competitive advantage has become the concern of every manager who is alert to the realities of the marketplace. It is no longer acceptable to assume that good products will sell themselves, neither is it advisable to imagine that success today will carry forward into tomorrow.

Let us consider the bases of success in any competitive context. At its most elemental, commercial success derives from either a cost advantage or a value advantage or, ideally, both. It is as simple as that – the most profitable competitor in any industry sector tends to be the lowest-cost producer or the supplier providing a product with the greatest perceived differentiated values.

Put very simply, successful companies either have a cost advantage or they have a value advantage, or – even better – a combination of the two. Cost advantage gives a lower cost profile and the value advantage gives the product or offering a differential 'plus' over competitive offerings.

Let us briefly examine these two vectors of strategic direction.

1 Cost advantage

In many industries there will typically be one competitor who will be the low-cost producer and often that competitor will have the greatest sales volume in the sector. There is substantial evidence to suggest that 'big is beautiful' when it comes to cost advantage. This is partly due to economies of scale, which enable fixed costs to be spread over a greater volume, but more particularly to the impact of the 'experience curve'.

The experience curve is a phenomenon with its roots in the earlier notion of the 'learning curve'. Researchers in the Second World War discovered that it was possible to identify and predict improvements in the rate of output of workers as they became more skilled in the processes and tasks on which they were working. Subsequent work by Boston Consulting Group, extended this concept by demonstrating that all costs, not just production costs, would decline at a given rate as volume increased (see Figure 1.3). In fact, to be precise, the relationship that the experience curve describes is between real unit costs and cumulative volume.

Figure 1.3 The experience curve

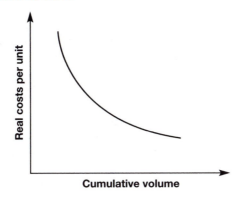

Traditionally it has been suggested that the main route to cost reduction was through the achievement of greater sales volume and in particular by improving market share. However, the blind pursuit of economies of scale through volume increases may not always lead to improved profitability – the reason being that in today's world much of the cost of a product lies outside the four walls of the business in the wider supply chain. Hence it can be argued that it is increasingly through better logistics and supply chain management that efficiency and productivity can be achieved leading to significantly reduced unit costs. How this can be achieved will be one of the main themes of this book.

> Logistics and supply chain management can provide a multitude of ways to increase efficiency and productivity and hence contribute significantly to reduced unit costs.

2 Value advantage

It has long been an axiom in marketing that 'customers don't buy products, they buy benefits'. Put another way, the product is purchased not for itself but for the promise of what it will 'deliver'. These benefits may be intangible, i.e. they relate not to specific product features but rather to such things as image or service. In addition, the delivered offering may be seen to outperform its rivals in some functional aspect.

Unless the product or service we offer can be distinguished in some way from its competitors there is a strong likelihood that the marketplace will view it as a 'commodity' and so the sale will tend to go to the cheapest supplier. Hence the importance of seeking to add additional values to our offering to mark it out from the competition.

What are the means by which such value differentiation may be gained? Essentially the development of a strategy based upon added values will normally require a more segmented approach to the market. When a company scrutinises markets closely it frequently finds that there are distinct 'value segments'. In other words, different groups of customers within the total market attach different importance to different benefits. The importance of such benefit segmentation lies in the fact that often there are substantial opportunities for creating differentiated appeals for specific segments. Take the car industry as an example. Most volume car manufacturers such as Toyota or Ford offer a range of models positioned at different price points in the market. However, it is increasingly the case that each model is offered in a variety of versions. Thus at one end of the spectrum may be the basic version with a small engine and two doors and at the other end, a four-door, high-performance version. In between are a whole variety of options, each of which seeks to satisfy the needs of quite different 'benefit segments'. Adding value through differentiation is a powerful means of achieving a defensible advantage in the market.

Equally powerful as a means of adding value is service. Increasingly it is the case that markets are becoming more service-sensitive and this of course poses particular challenges for logistics management. There is a trend in many markets towards a decline in the strength of the 'brand' and a consequent move towards 'commodity' market status. Quite simply this means that it is becoming progressively more difficult to compete purely on the basis of brand or corporate image. Additionally, there is increasingly a convergence of technology within product categories, which means that it is often no longer possible to compete effectively on the basis of product differences. Thus the need to seek differentiation through means other than technology. Many companies have responded to this by focusing upon service as a means of gaining a competitive edge. Service in this context relates to the process of developing relationships with customers through the provision of an augmented offer. This augmentation can take many forms including delivery service, after-sales services, financial packages, technical support and so forth.

Seeking the high ground

In practice what we find is that the successful companies will often seek to achieve a position based upon both a cost advantage and a value advantage. A useful way of examining the available options is to present them as a simple matrix. Let us consider these options in turn.

Figure 1.4 Logistics and competitive advantage

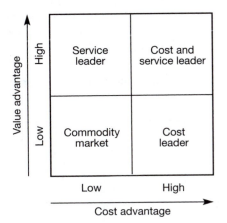

For companies who find themselves in the bottom left-hand corner of our matrix (Figure 1.4) the world is an uncomfortable place. Their products are indistinguishable from their competitors' offerings and they have no cost advantage. These are typical commodity market situations and ultimately the only strategy is either to move to the right of the matrix, i.e. to cost leadership, or upwards towards service leadership. Often the cost leadership route is simply not available. This particularly will be the case in a mature market where substantial market share gains are difficult to achieve. New technology may sometimes provide a window of opportunity for cost reduction but in such situations the same technology is often available to competitors.

Cost leadership strategies have traditionally been based upon the economies of scale gained through sales volume. This is why market share is considered to be so important in many industries. However, if volume is to be the basis for cost leadership then it is preferable for that volume to be gained early in the market life cycle. The 'experience curve' concept, briefly described earlier, demonstrates the value of early market share gains – the higher your share relative to your competitors the lower your costs should be. This cost advantage can be used strategically to assume a position of price leader and, if appropriate, to make it impossible for higher-cost competitors to survive. Alternatively, price may be maintained, enabling above-average profit to be earned, which potentially is available to further develop the position of the product in the market.

However, an increasingly powerful route to achieving a cost advantage comes not necessarily through volume and the economies of scale but instead through logistics and supply chain management. In many industries, logistics costs represent such a significant proportion of total costs that it is possible to make major cost reductions through fundamentally re-engineering logistics processes. The means whereby this can be achieved will be returned to later in this book.

The other way out of the 'commodity' quadrant of the matrix is to seek a strategy of differentiation through service excellence. We have already commented on the fact that markets have become more 'service-sensitive'. Customers in all industries are seeking greater responsiveness and reliability from suppliers; they are looking for reduced lead times, just-in-time delivery and value-added services that enable them to do a better job of serving their customers. In Chapter 2 we will examine the specific ways in which superior service strategies, based upon enhanced logistics management, can be developed.

Figure 1.5 The challenge to logistics and supply chain management

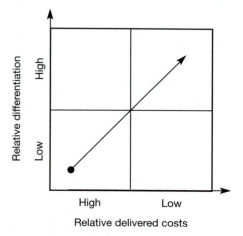

Relative delivered costs

One thing is certain: there is no middle ground between cost leadership and service excellence. Indeed the challenge to management is to identify appropriate logistics and supply chain strategies to take the organisation to the top right-hand corner of the matrix. Companies who occupy that position have offers that are distinctive in the value they deliver and are also cost competitive. Clearly it is a position of some strength, occupying 'high ground' that is extremely difficult for competitors to attack. Figure 1.5 clearly presents the challenge: it is to seek out strategies that will take the business away from the 'commodity' end of the market towards a securer position of strength based upon differentiation and cost advantage.

Logistics management, it can be argued, has the potential to assist the organisation in the achievement of both a cost advantage and a value advantage. As Figure 1.6 suggests, in the first instance there are a number of important ways in which productivity can be enhanced through logistics and supply chain management. Whilst these possibilities for leverage will be discussed in detail later in the book, suffice it to say that the opportunities for better capacity utilisation, inventory reduction and closer integration with suppliers at a planning level are considerable. Equally the prospects for gaining a value advantage in the marketplace through superior customer service should not be underestimated. It will be argued later that the way we service the customer has become a vital means of differentiation.

Figure 1.6 Gaining competitive advantage

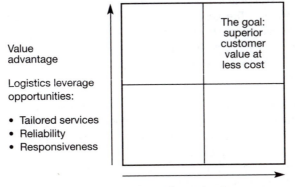

Value
advantage

Logistics leverage
opportunities:

• Tailored services
• Reliability
• Responsiveness

The goal:
superior
customer
value at
less cost

Cost advantage
Logistics leverage opportunities:

• Capacity utilisation
• Asset turn
• Synchronous supply

To summarise, those organisations that will be the leaders in the markets of the future will be those that have sought and achieved the twin peaks of excellence: they have gained both cost leadership and service leadership.

The underlying philosophy behind the logistics and supply chain concept is that of planning and co-ordinating the materials flow from source to user as an integrated system rather than, as was so often the case in the past, managing the goods flow as a series of independent activities. Thus under this approach the goal is to link the marketplace, the distribution network, the manufacturing process and the procurement activity in such a way that customers are serviced at higher levels and yet at lower cost. In other words the goal is to achieve competitive advantage through both cost reduction and service enhancement.

The supply chain becomes the value chain

Of the many changes that have taken place in management thinking over the last 30 years or so perhaps the most significant has been the emphasis placed upon the search for strategies that will provide superior value in the eyes of the customer. To a large extent the credit for this must go to Michael Porter, the Harvard Business School professor, who through his research and writing[4] has alerted managers and strategists to the central importance of competitive relativities in achieving success in the marketplace.

One concept in particular that Michael Porter has brought to a wider audience is the 'value chain':

> *Competitive advantage cannot be understood by looking at a firm as a whole. It stems from the many discrete activities a firm performs in designing, producing, marketing, delivering, and supporting its product. Each of these activities can contribute to a firm's relative cost position and create a basis for differentiation … The value chain disaggregates a firm into its strategically relevant activities in order to understand the behaviour of costs and the existing and potential sources of differentiation. A firm gains competitive advantage by performing these strategically important activities more cheaply or better than its competitors.[5]*

Value chain activities (shown in Figure 1.7) can be categorised into two types – primary activities (inbound logistics, operations, outbound logistics, marketing and sales, and service) and support activities (infrastructure, human resource management, technology development and procurement). These activities are integrating functions that cut across the traditional functions of the firm. Competitive advantage is derived from the way in which firms organise and perform these activities within the value chain. To gain competitive advantage over its rivals, a firm must deliver value to its customers by performing these activities more efficiently than its competitors or by performing the activities in a unique way that creates greater differentiation.

Figure 1.7 The value chain

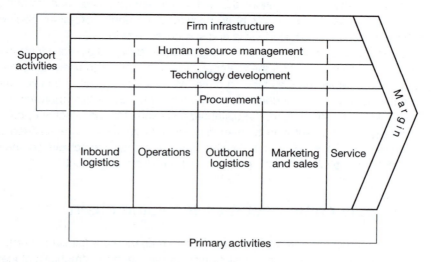

Source: Porter, M.E., *Competitive Advantage*, The Free Press, 1985

The implication of Michael Porter's thesis is that organisations should look at each activity in their value chain and assess whether they have a real competitive advantage in the activity. If they do not, the argument goes, then perhaps they should consider outsourcing that activity to a partner who can provide that cost or value advantage. This logic is now widely accepted and has led to the dramatic upsurge in outsourcing activity that can be witnessed in almost every industry.

Whilst there is often a strong economic logic underpinning the decision to outsource activities that may previously have been performed in-house, such decisions may add to the complexity of the supply chain. Because there are by definition more interfaces to be managed as a result of outsourcing, the need for a much higher level of relationship management increases.

The effect of outsourcing is to extend the value chain beyond the boundaries of the business. In other words, the supply chain becomes the value chain. Value (and cost) is not just created by the focal firm in a network, but by all the entities that connect to each other. This 'extended enterprise', as some have termed it, becomes the vehicle through which competitive advantage is gained – or lost.

The mission of logistics management

It will be apparent from the previous comments that the mission of logistics management is to plan and co-ordinate all those activities necessary to achieve desired levels of delivered service and quality at lowest possible cost. Logistics must therefore be seen as the link between the marketplace and the supply base. The scope of logistics spans the organisation, from the management of raw materials through to the delivery of the final product. Figure 1.8 illustrates this total systems concept.

> The scope of logistics spans the organisation, from the management of raw materials through to the delivery of the final product.

Figure 1.8 Logistics management process

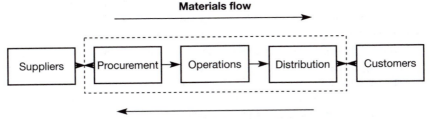

LOGISTICS, THE SUPPLY CHAIN AND COMPETITIVE STRATEGY   **11**

Logistics management, from this total systems viewpoint, is the means whereby the needs of customers are satisfied through the co-ordination of the materials and information flows that extend from the marketplace, through the firm and its operations and beyond that to suppliers. To achieve this company-wide integration clearly requires a quite different orientation than that typically encountered in the conventional organisation.

For example, for many years marketing and manufacturing have been seen as largely separate activities within the organisation. At best they have coexisted, at worst there has been open warfare. Manufacturing priorities and objectives have typically been focused on operating efficiency, achieved through long production runs, minimised set-ups and change-overs and product standardisation. On the other hand, marketing has sought to achieve competitive advantage through variety, high service levels and frequent product changes.

In today's more turbulent environment there is no longer any possibility of manufacturing and marketing acting independently of each other. The internecine disputes between the 'barons' of production and marketing are clearly counter-productive to the achievement of overall corporate goals.

It is no coincidence that in recent years both marketing and manufacturing have become the focus of renewed attention. Marketing as a concept and a philosophy of customer orientation now enjoys a wider acceptance than ever. It is now generally accepted that the need to understand and meet customer requirements is a prerequisite for survival. At the same time, in the search for improved cost competitiveness, manufacturing management has been the subject of a massive revolution. The last few decades have seen the introduction of flexible manufacturing systems (FMS), of new approaches to inventory based on materials requirements planning (MRP) and just-in-time (JIT) methods and, perhaps most important of all, a sustained emphasis on total quality management (TQM).

Equally there has been a growing recognition of the critical role that procurement plays in creating and sustaining competitive advantage as part of an integrated logistics process. Leading-edge organisations now routinely include supply-side issues in the development of their strategic plans. Not only is the cost of purchased materials and supplies a significant part of total costs in most organisations, but there is a major opportunity for leveraging the capabilities and competencies of suppliers through closer integration of the buyers' and suppliers' logistics processes.

In this scheme of things, logistics is therefore essentially an integrative concept that seeks to develop a system-wide view of the firm. It is fundamentally a *planning* concept that seeks to create a framework through which the needs of the marketplace can be translated into a manufacturing strategy and plan, which in turn links into a strategy and plan for procurement. Ideally there should be a 'one-plan' mentality within the business which seeks to replace the conventional stand-alone and separate plans of marketing, distribution, production and procurement. This, quite simply, is the mission of logistics management.

The supply chain and competitive performance

Traditionally most organisations have viewed themselves as entities that exist independently from others and indeed need to compete with them in order to survive. However, such a philosophy can be self-defeating if it leads to an unwillingness to co-operate in order to compete. Behind this seemingly paradoxical concept is the idea of supply chain integration.

The supply chain is the network of organisations that are involved, through upstream and downstream linkages, in the different processes and activities that produce value in the form of products and services in the hands of the ultimate consumer. Thus, for example, a shirt manufacturer is a part of a supply chain that extends upstream through the weavers of fabrics to the manufacturers of fibres, and downstream through distributors and retailers to the final consumer. Each of these organisations in the chain are dependent upon each other by definition and yet, paradoxically, by tradition do not closely co-operate with each other.

Supply chain management is not the same as 'vertical integration'. Vertical integration normally implies ownership of upstream suppliers and downstream customers. This was once thought to be a desirable strategy but increasingly organisations are now focusing on their 'core business' – in other words the things they do really well and where they have a differential advantage. Everything else is 'outsourced' – in other words it is procured outside the firm. So, for example, companies that perhaps once made their own components now only assemble the finished product, e.g. automobile manufacturers. Other companies may also sub-contract the manufacturing as well, e.g. Nike in footwear and sportswear. These companies have sometimes been termed 'virtual' or 'network' organisations.

Clearly this trend has many implications for supply chain management, not the least being the challenge of integrating and co-ordinating the flow of materials from a multitude of suppliers, often offshore, and similarly managing the distribution of the finished product by way of multiple intermediaries.

GANT: creating value across a virtual network

A good example of a virtual organisation is the Swedish clothing brand GANT. At the centre of the network is Pyramid Sportswear AB, which directly employs fewer than ten people. Pyramid contracts with designers, identifies trends, uses contract manufacturers, develops the retailer network and creates the brand image through marketing communications. Through its databases, Pyramid closely monitors sales, inventories and trends. Its network of closely co-ordinated partners means it can react quickly to changes in the market. The network itself changes as requirements change, and it will use different designers, freelance photographers, catalogue producers, contract manufacturers and so on as appropriate.

SOURCE: CHRISTOPHER, M., PAYNE, A. AND BALLANTYNE, D., *RELATIONSHIP MARKETING: CREATING STAKEHOLDER VALUE*, BUTTERWORTH HEINNEMANN, 2002

In the past it was often the case that relationships with suppliers and downstream customers (such as distributors or retailers) were adversarial rather than co-operative. It is still the case today that some companies will seek to achieve cost reductions or profit improvement at the expense of their supply chain partners. Companies such as these do not realise that simply transferring costs upstream or downstream does not make them any more competitive. The reason for this is that ultimately all costs will make their way to the final marketplace to be reflected in the price paid by the end user. The leading-edge companies recognise the fallacy of this conventional approach and instead seek to make the supply chain as a whole

Figure 1.9 Achieving an integrated supply chain

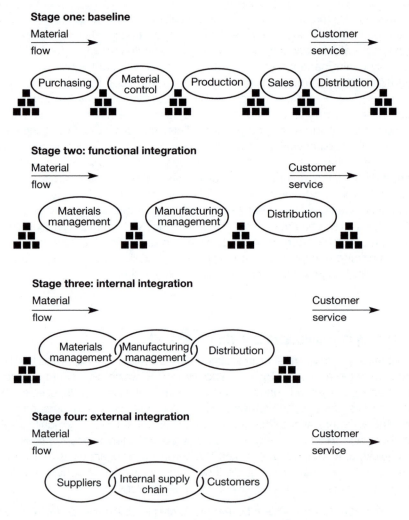

Source: Stevens, G.C., 'Integrating the Supply Chain', *International Journal of Physical Distribution and Materials Management*, Vol. 19, No. 8, 1989

more competitive through the value it adds and the costs that it reduces overall. They have realised that the real competition is not company against company but rather supply chain against supply chain.

It must be recognised that the concept of supply chain management, whilst relatively new, is in fact no more than an extension of the logic of logistics. Logistics management is primarily concerned with optimising flows within the organisation, whilst supply chain management recognises that internal integration by itself is not sufficient. Figure 1.9 suggests that there is in effect an evolution of integration from the stage 1 position of complete functional independence where each business function such as production or purchasing does its own thing in complete isolation from the other business functions. An example would be where production seeks to optimise its unit costs of manufacture by long production runs without regard for the build-up of finished goods inventory and heedless of the impact it will have on the need for warehousing space and the impact on working capital.

Stage 2 companies have recognised the need for at least a limited degree of integration between adjacent functions, e.g. distribution and inventory management or purchasing and materials control. The natural next step to stage 3 requires the establishment and implementation of an 'end-to-end' planning framework that will be fully described later in this book.

Stage 4 represents true supply chain integration in that the concept of linkage and co-ordination that is achieved in stage 3 is now extended upstream to suppliers and downstream to customers. There is thus a crucial and important distinction to be made between *logistics* and *supply chain management*.

The changing competitive environment

As the competitive context of business continues to change, bringing with it new complexities and concerns for management generally, it also has to be recognised that the impact on logistics and supply chain management of these changes can be considerable. Indeed, of the many strategic issues that confront the business organisation today, perhaps the most challenging are in the area of logistics and supply chain management.

Much of this book will be devoted to addressing these challenges in detail but it is useful at this stage to highlight what are perhaps the most pressing currently. These are:

- The new rules of competition
- Globalisation of industry
- Downward pressure on price
- Customers taking control

The new rules of competition

We are now entering the era of 'supply chain competition'. The fundamental difference from the previous model of competition is that an organisation can no longer act as an isolated and independent entity in competition with other similarly 'stand-alone' organisations. Instead, the need to create value delivery systems that are more responsive to fast-changing markets and are much more consistent and reliable in the delivery of that value requires that the supply chain as a whole be focused on the achievement of these goals.

In the past the ground rules for marketing success were obvious: strong brands backed up by large advertising budgets and aggressive selling. This formula now appears to have lost its power. Instead, the argument is heard, companies must recognise that increasingly it is through their *capabilities* and *competencies* that they compete.[6]

Essentially, this means that organisations create superior value for customers and consumers by managing their *core processes* better than competitors manage theirs. These core processes encompass such activities as new product development, supplier development, order fulfilment and customer management. By performing these fundamental activities in a more cost-effective way than competitors, it is argued, organisations will gain the advantage in the marketplace. This principle is powerfully expressed in the words of Jorma Ollila, the past Chairman and CEO of Nokia:

> *Our experienced and unique way of operating is what we see as increasingly putting us ahead of the competition. As we move forward in this complex industry, winning will be less about what we do and more about the way we do it.*

For example, one capability that is now regarded by many companies as fundamental to success in the marketplace is supply chain agility. As product life cycles shorten, as customers adopt just-in-time practices and as sellers' markets become buyers' markets then the ability of the organisation to respond rapidly and flexibly to demand can provide a powerful competitive edge. This is a theme to which we will return in Chapter 5.

A major contributing factor influencing the changed competitive environment has been the trend towards 'commoditisation' in many markets. A commodity market is characterised by perceived product equality in the eyes of customers resulting in a high preparedness to substitute one make of product for another. Research increasingly suggests that consumers are less loyal to specific brands but instead will have a portfolio of brands within a category from which they make their choice. In situations such as this actual product availability becomes a major determinant of demand. There is evidence that more and more decisions are being taken at the point of purchase and if there is a gap on the shelf where Brand X should be, but Brand Y is there instead, then there is a strong probability that Brand Y will win the sale.

It is not only in consumer markets that the importance of logistics process excellence is apparent. In business-to-business and industrial markets it seems that product or technical features are of less importance in winning orders than issues such as delivery lead times and flexibility. This is not to suggest that product or technical features are unimportant – rather it is that they are taken as a 'given' by the customer. Quite simply, in today's marketplace the order-winning criteria are more likely to be service-based than product-based.

> In today's marketplace the order-winning criteria are more likely to be service-based than product-based.

A parallel development in many markets is the trend towards a concentration of demand. In other words customers – as against consumers – are tending to grow in size whilst becoming fewer in number. The retail grocery industry is a good example in that in most northern European countries a handful of large retailers account for over 50 per cent of all sales in any one country. This tendency to the concentration of buying power is being accelerated as a result of global mergers and acquisitions. The impact of these trends is that these more powerful customers are becoming more demanding in terms of their service requirements from suppliers.

At the same time as the power in the distribution channel continues to shift from supplier to buyer, there is also a trend for customers to reduce their supplier base. In other words they want to do business with fewer suppliers and often on a longer-term basis. The successful companies in the coming years will be those that recognise these trends and seek to establish strategies based upon establishing closer relationships with key accounts. Such strategies will focus upon seeking innovative ways to create more value for these customers.

Building competitive platforms that are grounded in this idea of value-based growth will require a much greater focus on managing the core processes that we referred to earlier. Whereas the competitive model of the past relied heavily on *product* innovation this will have to be increasingly supplemented by *process* innovation. The basis for competing in this new era will be:

Competitive advantage = Product excellence × Process excellence

Figure 1.10 suggests that traditionally for many companies the investment has mainly been on product excellence and less on process excellence. This is not to suggest that product innovation should be given less emphasis – far from it – but rather that more emphasis needs to be placed on developing and managing processes that deliver greater value for key customers.

Figure 1.10 Investing in process excellence yields greater benefits

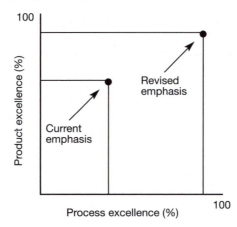

We have already commented that product life cycles are getting shorter. What we have witnessed in many markets is the effect of changes in technology and consumer demand combining to produce more volatile markets where a product can be obsolete almost as soon as it reaches the market. There are many current examples of shortening life cycles but perhaps the personal computer symbolises them all. In this particular case we have seen rapid developments in technology that have first created markets where none existed before and then almost as quickly have rendered themselves obsolete as the next generation of product is announced.

Such shortening of life cycles creates substantial problems for logistics and supply chain management. In particular, shorter life cycles demand shorter lead times – indeed our definition of lead time may well need to change. Lead times are traditionally defined as the elapsed period from receipt of customer order to delivery. However, in today's environment there is a wider perspective that needs to be taken. The real lead time is the time taken from the drawing board, through procurement, manufacture and assembly to the end market. This is the concept of strategic lead time and the management of this time span is the key to success in managing logistics operations.

There are already situations arising where the life cycle is shorter than the strategic lead time. In other words the life of a product on the market is less than the time it takes to design, procure, manufacture and distribute that same product! The implications of this are considerable both for planning and operations. In a global context the problem is exacerbated by the longer transportation times involved.

Ultimately, therefore, the means of achieving success in such markets is to accelerate movement through the supply chain and to make the entire logistics system far more flexible and thus responsive to these fast-changing markets.

Globalisation of industry

A further strategic issue that provides a challenge for logistics management is the continued trend towards globalisation.

A global company is more than a multinational company. In the global business materials and components are sourced worldwide and products may be manufactured offshore and sold in many different countries, perhaps with local customisation.

Such is the trend towards globalisation that it is probably safe to forecast that before long most markets will be dominated by global companies. The only role left for national companies will be to cater for specific and unique local demands, for example in the food industry.

For global companies like Hewlett Packard, Philips and Caterpillar, the management of the logistics process has become an issue of central concern. The difference between profit and loss for an individual product can hinge upon the extent to which the global pipeline can be optimised, because the costs involved are so great. The global company seeks to achieve competitive advantage by identifying world markets for its products and then to develop a manufacturing and logistics strategy to support its marketing strategy. So a company like Caterpillar, for example, has dispersed assembly operations to key overseas markets and uses global logistics channels to supply parts to offshore assembly plants and after-markets. Where appropriate, Caterpillar will use third-party companies to manage distribution and even final finishing. So, for example, in the US a third-party company in addition to providing parts inspection and warehousing attaches options to fork lift trucks. Wheels, counterweights, forks and masts are installed as specified by Caterpillar. Thus local market needs can be catered for from a standardised production process.

Globalisation also tends to lengthen supply chains as companies increasingly move production offshore or source from more distant locations. The impetus for this trend, which in recent years has accelerated dramatically, is the search for lower labour costs. However, one implication of these decisions is that 'end-to-end' pipeline times may increase significantly. In time-sensitive markets, longer lead times can be fatal.

'Time-based competition' is an idea that will be returned to many times in later chapters. Time compression has become a critical management issue. Product life cycles are shorter than ever, customers and distributors require just-in-time deliveries and end users are ever more willing to accept a substitute product if their first choice is not instantly available.

The globalisation of industry, and hence supply chains, is inevitable. However, to enable the potential benefits of global networks to be fully realised, a wider supply chain perspective must be adopted. It can be argued that for the global corporation competitive advantage will increasingly derive from excellence in managing the complex web of relationships and flows that characterise their supply chains.

Downward pressure on price

Whilst the trend might not be universal there can be no doubting that most markets are more price competitive today than they were a decade ago. Prices in the high streets and the shopping malls continue to fall in many countries.

Whilst some of this price deflation can be explained as the result of normal cost reduction through learning and experience effects, the rapid fall in the price of many consumer goods has other causes. Figure 1.11 shows the comparative rate at which VCR and DVD player prices fell in the UK market. The striking feature is that whilst it took 20 years for a VCR to fall in price from £400 to just over £40, it took only five years for a DVD player to fall by the same amount, and at the time of writing a DVD player can be bought in the UK for £20! The same phenomenon is apparent in markets as diverse as clothing, home furnishings and air travel.

A fundamental change in the global competitive landscape is driving prices to levels that in real terms are as low as they have ever been. A number of causal factors have contributed to this new market environment.

Firstly, there are new global competitors who have entered the marketplace supported by low-cost manufacturing bases. The dramatic rise of China as a major producer of quality consumer products is evidence of this. Secondly, the removal of barriers to trade and the deregulation of many markets has accelerated this trend, enabling new players to rapidly gain ground. One result of this has been

Figure 1.11 Price deflation in consumer electronics (UK high street prices)

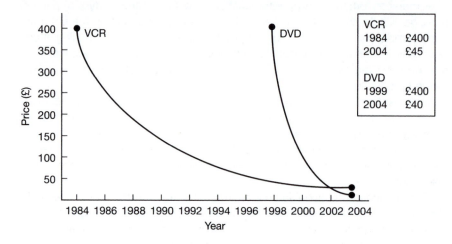

overcapacity in many industries. Overcapacity implies an excess of supply against demand and hence leads to further downward pressure on price.

A further cause of price deflation, it has been suggested, is the Internet, which makes price comparison so much easier. The Internet has also enabled auctions and exchanges to be established at industry-wide levels, which have also tended to drive down prices.

In addition, there is evidence that customers and consumers are more value conscious than has hitherto been the case. Brands and suppliers that could once command a price premium because of their perceived superiority can no longer do so as the market recognises that equally attractive offers are available at significantly lower prices. The success of many retailers' own-label products or the inroads made by low-cost airlines proves this point.

Against the backdrop of a continued downward pressure on price, it is self-evident that, in order to maintain profitability, companies must find a way to bring down costs to match the fall in price.

The challenge to the business is to find new opportunities for cost reduction when, in all likelihood, the company has been through many previous cost-reduction programmes. It can be argued that the last remaining opportunity of any significance for major cost reduction lies in the wider supply chain rather than in the firm's own internal operations.

This idea is not new. Back in 1929 Ralph Borsodi expressed it in the following words:

> In 50 years between 1870 and 1920 the cost of distributing necessities and luxuries has nearly trebled, while production costs have gone down by one-fifth ... What we are saving in production we are losing in distribution.[7]

The situation that Borsodi describes can still be witnessed in many industries today. For example, companies which thought they could achieve a leaner operation by moving to just-in-time (JIT) practices often only shifted costs elsewhere in the supply chain by forcing suppliers or customers to carry that inventory. The car industry, which to many is the home of lean thinking and JIT practices, has certainly exhibited some of those characteristics. One analysis of the western European automobile industry[8] showed that whilst car assembly operations were indeed very lean with minimal inventory, the same was not true upstream and downstream of those operations. Figure 1.12 shows the profile of inventory through the supply chain from the tier 1 suppliers down to the car dealerships.

Figure 1.12 Inventory profile of the automotive supply chain

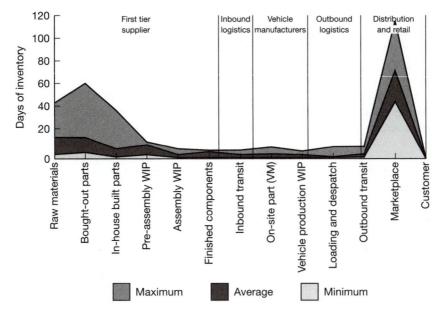

Source: Holweg, M. and Pil, F.K., *The Second Century*, MIT Press, 2004

In this particular case the paradox is that most inventory is being held when it is at its most expensive, i.e. as a finished product. The true cost of this inventory to the industry is considerable. Whilst inventory costs will vary by industry and by company, it will be suggested in Chapter 3 that the true cost of carrying inventory is rarely less than 25 per cent per year of its value. In the conditions in which the automobile industry currently finds itself, this alone is enough to make the difference between profit and loss.

This example illustrates the frequently encountered failure to take a wider view of cost. For many companies their definition of cost is limited only to those costs that are contained within the four walls of their business entity. However, as has been suggested earlier, since today's competition takes place not between companies but between supply chains the proper view of costs has to be 'end-to-end' since all costs will ultimately be reflected in the price of the finished product in the final marketplace.

The need to take a supply chain view of cost is further underscored by the major trend that is observable across industries worldwide towards outsourcing. For many companies today, most of their costs lie outside their legal boundaries; activities that used to be performed in-house are now outsourced to specialist service providers. The amazing growth of contract manufacturing in electronics bears witness to this trend. If the majority of an organisation's costs lie outside the business then it follows that the biggest opportunities for improvement in their cost position will also be found in that wider supply chain.

The customers take control

So much has been written and talked about service, quality and excellence that there is no escaping the fact that the customer in today's marketplace is more demanding, not just of product quality, but also of service.

As more and more markets become in effect 'commodity' markets, where the customer perceives little technical difference between competing offers, the need is for the creation of differential advantage through added value. Increasingly a prime source of this added value is through customer service.

> The customer in today's marketplace is more demanding, not just of product quality, but also of service.

Customer service may be defined as the consistent provision of time and place utility. In other words, products don't have value until they are in the hands of the customer at the time and place required. There are clearly many facets of customer service, ranging from on-time delivery through to after-sales support. Essentially the role of customer service should be to enhance 'value-in-use', meaning that the product becomes worth more in the eyes of the customer because service has added value to the core product. In this way significant differentiation of the total offer (that is the core product plus the service package) can be achieved.

Those companies that have achieved recognition for service excellence, and thus have been able to establish a differential advantage over their competition, are typically those companies where logistics management is a high priority. Companies like Xerox, Zara and Dell are typical of such organisations. The achievement of competitive advantage through service comes not from slogans or expensive so-called customer care programmes, but rather from a combination of a carefully thought-out strategy for service, the development of appropriate delivery systems and commitment from people, from the chief executive down.

The attainment of service excellence in this broad sense can only be achieved through a closely integrated logistics strategy. In reality, the ability to become a market leader depends as much upon the effectiveness of one's operating systems as it does upon the presentation of the product, the creation of images and the influencing of consumer perceptions. In other words, the success of McDonald's, WalMart or any of the other frequently cited paragons of service excellence is due not to their choice of advertising agency, but rather to their recognition that managing the logistics of service delivery on a consistent basis is the crucial source of differential advantage.

Managing the '4Rs'

As we move rapidly into the era of supply chain competition a number of principles emerge to guide the supply chain manager. These can be conveniently summarised as the '4Rs' of responsiveness, reliability, resilience and relationships.

1 Responsiveness

In today's just-in-time world the ability to respond to customers' requirements in ever-shorter time-frames has become critical. Not only do customers want shorter lead times, they are also looking for flexibility and increasingly customised solutions. In other words, the supplier has to be able to meet the precise needs of customers in less time than ever before. The key word in this changed environment is *agility*. Agility implies the ability to move quickly and to meet customer demand sooner. In a fast-changing marketplace agility is actually more important than long-term planning in its traditional form. Because future demand patterns are uncertain, by definition this makes planning more difficult and, in a sense, hazardous.

In the future, organisations must be much more *demand-driven* than *forecast-driven*. The means of making this transition will be through the achievement of agility, not just within the company but across the supply chain. Responsiveness also implies that the organisation is close to the customer, hearing the voice of the market and quick to interpret the demand signals it receives.

2 Reliability

One of the main reasons why any company carries safety stock is because of uncertainty. It may be uncertainty about future demand or uncertainty about a supplier's ability to meet a delivery promise, or about the quality of materials or components. Significant improvements in reliability can only be achieved through re-engineering the processes that impact performance. Manufacturing managers long ago discovered that the best way to improve product quality was not by quality control through inspection but rather to focus on process control. The same is true for logistics reliability.

One of the keys to improving supply chain reliability is through reducing process *variability*. In recent years there has been a considerable increase in the use of so-called 'six sigma' methodologies. The concept of six sigma will be discussed in more detail in Chapter 10 but in essence these tools are designed to enable variability in a process to be reduced and controlled. Thus, for example, if there is variability in order processing lead times then the causes of that variability can be identified and where necessary the process can be changed and brought under control through the use of six sigma tools and procedures.

3 Resilience

Today's marketplace is characterised by higher levels of turbulence and volatility. The wider business, economic and political environments are increasingly subjected to unexpected shocks and discontinuities. As a result, supply chains are vulnerable to disruption and, in consequence, the risk to business continuity is increased.

Whereas in the past the prime objective in supply chain design was probably cost minimisation or possibly service optimisation, the emphasis today has to be upon resilience. Resilience refers to the ability of the supply chain to cope with unexpected disturbances. There is evidence that the tendencies of many companies to seek out low-cost solutions because of pressure on margins may have led to leaner, but more vulnerable, supply chains.

Resilient supply chains may not be the lowest-cost supply chains but they are more capable of coping with the uncertain business environment. Resilient supply chains have a number of characteristics, of which the most important is a business-wide recognition of where the supply chain is at its most vulnerable. Managing the critical nodes and links of a supply chain, to be discussed further in Chapter 10, becomes a key priority. Sometimes these 'critical paths' may be where there is dependence on a single supplier, or a supplier with long replenishment lead times, or a bottleneck in a process.

Other characteristics of resilient supply chains are their recognition of the importance of strategic inventory and the selective use of spare capacity to cope with 'surge' effects.

4 Relationships

The trend towards customers seeking to reduce their supplier base has already been commented upon. In many industries the practice of 'partnership sourcing' is widespread. It is usually suggested that the benefits of such practices include improved quality, innovation sharing, reduced costs and integrated scheduling of production and deliveries. Underlying all of this is the idea that buyer/supplier relationships should be based upon partnership. Increasingly companies are discovering the advantages that can be gained by seeking mutually beneficial, long-term relationships with suppliers. From the suppliers' point of view, such partnerships can prove formidable barriers to entry for competitors. The more that processes are linked between the supplier and the customer the more the mutual dependencies increase and hence the more difficult it is for competitors to break in.

Supply chain management by definition is about the management of relationships across complex networks of companies that, whilst legally independent, are in reality interdependent. Successful supply chains will be those that are governed by a constant search for win-win solutions based upon mutuality and trust. This is not a model of relationships that has typically prevailed in the past. It is one that will have to prevail in the future as supply chain competition becomes the norm.

These four themes of responsiveness, reliability, resilience and relationships provide the basis for successful logistics and supply chain management. They are themes that will be explored in greater detail later in this book.

References

1. Bowler, R.A., *Logistics and the Failure of the British Army in America 1775–1783*, Princeton University Press, 1975.
2. Shaw, A.W., *Some Problems in Market Distribution*, Harvard University Press, 1915.
3. Aitken, J., *Supply Chain Integration within the Context of a Supplier Association*, Cranfield University, Ph.D. thesis, 1998.
4. Porter, M.E.,*Competitive Strategy*, The Free Press, 1980.
5. Porter, M.T.,*Competitive Advantage*, The Free Press, 1985, p.33.
6. Stalk, G., Evans, P. and Shulman, L.E., 'Competing on capabilities: the new rule of corporate strategy', *Harvard Business Review*, March–April 1992; Prahalad, C. and Hamel, G., 'The core competence of the corporation', *Harvard Business Review*, May–June 1990.
7. Borsodi, R., *The Distribution Age*, D. Appleton & Co, 1929.
8. Holweg, M. and Pil, F.K., *The Second Century*, MIT Press, 2004.

Logistics and customer value

- The marketing and logistics interface

- Delivering customer value

- What is customer service?

- The impact of out-of-stock

- Customer service and customer retention

- Market-driven supply chains

- Defining customer service objectives

- Setting customer service priorities

- Setting service standards

Earlier in Chapter 1 the mission of logistics management was defined simply in terms of providing the means whereby customers' service requirements are met at lowest cost. In other words the ultimate purpose of any logistics system is to satisfy customers. It is a simple idea that is not always easy to recognise if you are a manager involved in activities such as production scheduling or inventory control which may seem to be some distance away from the marketplace. The fact is of course that everybody in the organisation has a stake in customer service. Indeed many successful companies have started to examine their internal service standards in order that everyone who works in the business understands that they must service someone – if they don't, why are they on the payroll?

The objective should be to establish a chain of customers that links people at all levels in the organisation directly or indirectly to the marketplace.[1] Xerox is a company that has worked hard to implement the idea of the internal customer. They have even extended the idea to the point of linking bonuses to an index of customer satisfaction. In organisations like Xerox, managing the customer service chain through the business and onwards is the central concern of logistics management.

The marketing and logistics interface

Even though the textbooks describe marketing as the management of the 'Four Ps' – product, price, promotion and place – it is probably true to say that, in practice, most of the emphasis has always been placed on the first three. 'Place', which might better be described in the words of the old cliché, 'the right product in the right place at the right time', was rarely considered part of mainstream marketing.

There are signs that this view is rapidly changing, however, as the power of customer service as a potential means of differentiation is increasingly recognised. In more and more markets the power of the brand has declined and customers are more willing to accept substitutes; even technology differences between products have been reduced so that it is harder to maintain a competitive edge through the product itself. In situations like this it is customer service that can provide the distinctive difference between one company's offer and that of its competitors.

Two factors have perhaps contributed more than anything else to the growing importance of customer service as a competitive weapon. One is the continual increase in customer expectations; in almost every market the customer is now more demanding, more 'sophisticated' than he or she was, say, 30 years ago. Likewise, in industrial purchasing situations we find that buyers expect higher levels of service from vendors, particularly as more companies convert to just-in-time logistics systems.

The second factor is the slow but inexorable transition towards 'commodity' type markets. By this is meant that increasingly the power of the 'brand' is diminishing as the technologies of competing products converge, thus making product differences difficult to perceive – at least to the average buyer. Take, for example, the current state of the personal computer market. There are many competing models which in reality are substitutable as far as most would-be purchasers are concerned.

Faced with a situation such as this the customer may be influenced by price or by 'image' perceptions but overriding these aspects may well be 'availability' – in other words, is the product in stock, can I have it now? Since availability is clearly an aspect of customer service, we are in effect saying that the power of customer service is paramount in a situation such as this. This trend towards the *service-sensitive* customer is as apparent in industrial markets as it is in consumer markets. Hence companies supplying the car industry, for example, must be capable of providing just-in-time deliveries direct to the assembly line; similarly a food manufacturer supplying a large supermarket chain must have an equivalent logistics capability, enabling it to keep the retail shelf filled whilst minimising the amount of inventory in the system. The evidence from across a range of markets suggests that the critical determinant of whether orders are won or lost, and hence the basis for becoming a preferred supplier, is customer service. Time has become a far more critical element in the competitive process. Customers in every market want ever shorter lead times; product availability will overcome brand or supplier loyalty – meaning that if the customer's preferred brand is not available and a substitute is, then the likelihood is a lost sale.

Delivering customer value

Ultimately the success or failure of any business will be determined by the level of customer value that it delivers in its chosen markets. Customer value can be defined quite simply as the difference between the perceived benefits that flow from a purchase or a relationship and the total costs incurred. Another way of expressing the idea is:

$$\text{Customer value} = \frac{\text{Perceptions of benefits}}{\text{Total cost of ownership}}$$

'Total cost of ownership' rather than 'price' is used here because in most transactions there will be costs other than the purchase price involved. For example, inventory carrying costs, maintenance costs, running costs, disposal costs and so on. In business-to-business markets particularly, as buyers become increasingly sophisticated, the total costs of ownership can be a critical element in the purchase decision. 'Life-cycle costs', as they are referred to in the military and defence industries, have long been a critical issue in procurement decisions in those markets. Figure 2.1 shows the 'iceberg' effect of total costs of ownership where the immediate purchase price is the only aspect of cost that is visible, whereas below the surface of the water are all the costs that will arise as a result of the purchase decisions.

Figure 2.1 The total cost of ownership

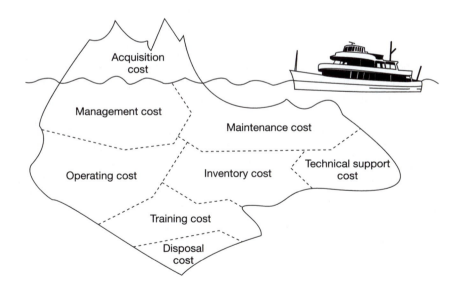

In the same way that the total cost of ownership is greater than the initial purchase price so too the benefits that are perceived to flow from the purchase or the relationship will often be greater than the tangible product features or functionality. For example, there may be little difference between two competitive products in terms of technical performance, but one may be superior to the other in terms of the customer support that is provided.

One way to define 'competitive advantage' is simply that the successful companies will generally be those that deliver more customer value than their competitors. In other words, their ratio of benefits to costs is superior to other players in that market or segment.

Logistics management is almost unique in its ability to impact both the numerator and the denominator of the customer value ratio. This point becomes clearer if we expand the ratio as follows:

$$\text{Customer value} = \frac{\text{Quality} \times \text{Service}}{\text{Cost} \times \text{Time}}$$

Source: Johansson, H.J., McHugh, P., Pendlebury, A.J. and Wheeler, W.A., *Business Process Reengineering*, John Wiley & Sons, 1993.

Each of the four constituent elements can briefly be defined as follows:

Quality: The functionality, performance and technical specification of the offer.

Service: The availability, support and commitment provided to the customer.

Cost: The customer's transaction costs including price and life cycle costs.

Time: The time taken to respond to customer requirements, e.g. delivery lead times.

Each of these four elements requires a continuous programme of improvement, innovation and investment to ensure continued competitive advantage.

One company that has built a global leadership position in its markets is Caterpillar, marketing machines and diesel engines for the construction and mining industries. Caterpillar has for many years focused on developing not just its manufacturing capabilities and innovative products but also its customer support and responsiveness. Underpinning these initiatives has been a continuing emphasis on creating superior logistics and supply chain management capabilities. Caterpillar has developed a world-class reputation for customer support, in particular its guarantee to provide 48-hour availability of parts no matter how remote the location. In the industries where Caterpillar's equipment is used, the cost of 'down-time' can be significant, hence the importance of responsive service. Through close partnership with its worldwide network of dealers and distributors and through advanced inventory and information management systems, Caterpillar offers levels of customer support – and thus customer value – that few companies in any industry can match.

What is customer service?

It has been suggested that the role of customer service is to provide 'time and place utility' in the transfer of goods and services between buyer and seller. Put another way, there is no value in the product or service until it is in the hands of the customer or consumer. It follows that making the product or service 'available' is what, in essence, the distribution function of the business is all about. 'Availability' is in itself a complex concept, impacted upon by a galaxy of factors which together constitute customer service. These factors might include delivery frequency and reliability, stock levels and order cycle time, for example. Indeed it could be said that ultimately customer service is determined by the interaction of all those factors that affect the process of making products and services available to the buyer.

In practice, we see that many companies have varying views of customer service. LaLonde and Zinszer[2] in a major study of customer service practices suggested that customer service could be examined under three headings:

1 Pre-transaction elements
2 Transaction elements
3 Post-transaction elements

The pre-transaction elements of customer service relate to corporate policies or programmes, e.g. written statements of service policy, adequacy of organisational structure and system flexibility. The transaction elements are those customer service variables directly involved in performing the physical distribution function, e.g. product and delivery reliability. The post-transaction elements of customer service are generally supportive of the product while in use, for instance, product warranty, parts and repair service, procedures for customer complaints and product replacement.

Table 2.1 indicates some of the many elements of customer service under these three headings.

Table 2.1 The components of customer service

Pre-transaction elements

For example:
• *Written customer service policy*
  (Is it communicated internally and externally? Is it understood? Is it specific and quantified where possible?)
• *Accessibility*
  (Are we easy to contact/do business with? Is there a single point of contact?)
• *Organisation structure*
  (Is there a customer service management structure in place? What level of control do they have over their service process?)
• *System flexibility*
  (Can we adapt our service delivery systems to meet particular customer needs?)

▶

► **Table 2.1** Continued

Transaction elements

For example:
- *Order cycle time*
  (What is the elapsed time from order to delivery? What is the reliability/variation?)
- *Inventory availability*
  (What percentage of demand for each item can be met from stock?)
- *Order fill rate*
  (What proportion of orders are completely filled within the stated lead time?)
- *Order status information*
  (How long does it take us to respond to a query with the required information? Do we inform the customer of problems or do they contact us?)

Post-transaction elements

For example:
- *Availability of spares*
  (What are the in-stock levels of service parts?)
- *Call-out time*
  (How long does it take for the engineer to arrive and what is the 'first call fix rate'?)
- *Product tracing/warranty*
  (Can we identify the location of individual products once purchased? Can we maintain/extend the warranty to customers' expected levels?)
- *Customer complaints, claims, etc.*
  (How promptly do we deal with complaints and returns? Do we measure customer satisfaction with our response?)

In any particular product/market situation, some of these elements will be more important than others and there may be factors other than those listed above which have a significance in a specific market. Indeed the argument that will be developed later is that it is essential to understand customer service in terms of the differing requirements of different market segments and that no universally appropriate list of elements exists; each market that the company services will attach different importance to different service elements.

It is because of the multivariate nature of customer service and because of the widely differing requirements of specific markets that it is essential for any business to have a clearly identified policy towards customer service. It is surprising perhaps that so few companies have defined policies on customer service, let alone an organisation flexible enough to manage and control that service, when it is considered that service can be the most important element in the company's marketing mix. A considerable body of evidence exists that supports the view that if the product or service is not available at the time the customer requires it and a close substitute is available then the sale will be lost to the competition. Even in markets where brand loyalty is strong a stock-out might be sufficient to trigger brand switching.

> It is because of the multivariate nature of customer service and because of the widely differing requirements of specific markets that it is essential for any business to have a clearly identified policy towards customer service.

The impact of out-of-stock

One study[3] identified that a significant cost penalty is incurred by both manufacturers and retailers when a stock-out occurs on the shelf. The research found that on a typical day a shopper in the average supermarket will face stock-outs on 8 per cent of items in the categories studied. The reaction of customers when faced with a stock-out was highlighted by the same study. As Figure 2.2 illustrates, over a quarter of shoppers bought a different brand and 31 per cent said they would shop elsewhere for that product. This represents bad news for both the manufacturer and the retailer. Even worse, other research[4] has suggested that over two-thirds of shopping decisions are made at the point of purchase, i.e. the purchase is triggered by seeing the product on the shelf. If the product is not on the shelf then the purchase will not be triggered. Persistent stock-outs can also drive customers away from the brand and/or the store permanently. The potential loss of business for both manufacturers and retailers caused by out-of-stock situations is clearly significant.

Figure 2.2 Shopper behaviour when faced with a stock-out

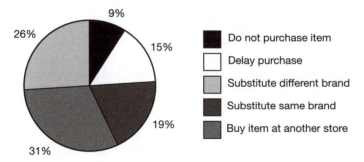

Source: Corsten, D. and Gruen, T., 'Stock-outs cause walkouts', *Harvard Business Review*, May 2004

In industrial markets, too, the same pressures on purchasing source loyalty seem to be at work. It is perhaps not surprising that as more and more companies adopt 'just-in-time' strategies, with minimal inventories, they require even higher levels of response from suppliers. The demand is for ever shorter delivery lead times and reliable delivery. The pressure on suppliers is further increased as these same customers seek to rationalise their supplier base and to do business with fewer suppliers. Becoming a preferred supplier in any industry today inevitably means that a high priority must be placed on delivering superior customer service.

Many companies have suffered in this new competitive environment because in the past they have focused on the traditional aspects of marketing – product development, promotional activities and price competition. However, whilst these are still necessary dimensions of a successful marketing strategy they are not sufficient. Equally damaging has been the focus on cost reduction that has driven many companies' operational and logistics strategy – particularly as a result of recession. Cost reduction is a worthy goal as long as it is not achieved at the expense of value creation. Low-cost strategies may lead to *efficient* logistics but not to *effective* logistics. More often than not today the order winning criteria are those elements of the offer that have a clearly identifiable positive impact upon the customers' own value-creating processes.

One powerful way of highlighting the impact that customer service and logistics management can have on marketing effectiveness is outlined in Figure 2.3. The suggestion here is that customer service impacts not only on the ultimate end user but also on intermediate customers such as distributors. Traditionally marketing has focused on the end customer – or consumer – seeking to promote brand values and to generate a 'demand pull' in the marketplace for the company's products. More recently we have come to recognise that this by itself is not sufficient. Because of the swing in power in many marketing channels away from manufacturers and towards the distributor (e.g. the large concentrated retailers) it is now vital to develop the strongest possible relations with such intermediaries – in other words to create a customer franchise as well as a consumer franchise.

Figure 2.3 The impact of logistics and customer service on marketing

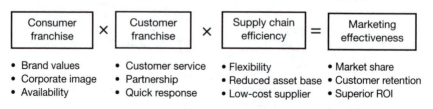

The impact of both a strong consumer franchise and a customer franchise can be enhanced or diminished by the efficiency of the supplier's logistics system. It is only when all three components are working optimally that marketing effectiveness is maximised. To stress the interdependence of these three components of competitive performance it is suggested that the relationship is multiplicative. In other words the combined impact depends upon the product of all three.

Customer service and customer retention

It will be apparent from what has been said that organisations that compete only on the product's features will find themselves at a severe disadvantage to those companies that augment the basic product with added-value services. It was one of the leading thinkers in marketing, Theodore Levitt, who first said that 'people don't buy products, they buy benefits'.[5] The idea behind this statement is that it is the totality of the 'offer' that delivers customer value. A simple example would be that a finished product in a warehouse is the same as a finished product in the hands of the customer in terms of its tangible features. Clearly, however, the product in the hands of the customer has far more value than the product in the warehouse. Distribution service in this case has been the source of added value. Figure 2.4 develops this idea with the concept of the 'service surround'.

Figure 2.4 Using service to augment the core product

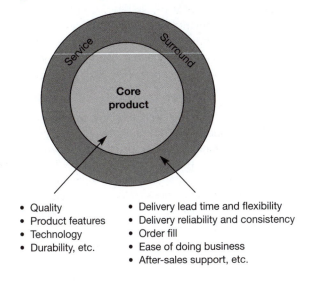

- Quality
- Product features
- Technology
- Durability, etc.

- Delivery lead time and flexibility
- Delivery reliability and consistency
- Order fill
- Ease of doing business
- After-sales support, etc.

At the centre is the core product, which is the basic product as it leaves the factory. The outer 'halo' represents all the added value that customer service and logistics provide. Clearly it is not only customer service and logistics activity that add value; in many cases advertising, branding and the packaging can all enhance the perceived value of the product to the customer. However, it is increasingly evident, as we have seen, that it takes more than branding to differentiate the product.

This idea underpins the current emphasis on seeking to create strategies that focus on 'servitisation', i.e. converting a product into a service. The example of Rolls-Royce aero engines, highlighted below, provides powerful support for this idea.

Power by the hour

Rolls-Royce Group plc is a UK-based manufacturer of gas turbines and is one of the major suppliers of engines to the aviation and energy industries. Typically these engines will cost several million pounds and require periodic and expensive maintenance and upgrading. In the past most airlines having bought an engine would assume responsibility for the servicing of that engine and holding the necessary inventory of spare parts. Clearly the cost of this was significant and also the unpredictability meant that a global service and repair capability was required.

Realising that what their customers really wanted was not the engine *per se* but rather the guarantee of *performance* led Rolls-Royce to develop the idea of 'power by the hour'. Under this arrangement Rolls-Royce takes responsibility for remotely monitoring the 'health' of the engine throughout its working life and providing all the necessary service and support wherever it is needed around the world. For this 'Total Care' package the customer pays Rolls-Royce by the flying hour.

One of the classic definitions of marketing is that it is concerned with 'getting and keeping customers'. In practice, if we look at where most organisations' marketing efforts focus, it is on the 'getting' of customers, rather than on the 'keeping' of them. Thus an examination of the typical marketing plan will show a bias towards increasing market share rather than towards customer retention. Whilst new customers are always welcome in any business it has to be realised that an existing customer can provide a higher profit contribution and has the potential to grow in terms of the value and frequency of purchases.

The importance of customer retention is underlined by the concept of the 'lifetime value' of a customer. The lifetime value of a customer is calculated as follows:

Lifetime value = Average transaction value × Yearly frequency of purchase × Customer 'life expectancy'

Clearly if customers can be persuaded to remain loyal to a supplier, their lifetime value can be significantly increased. A further benefit comes from the fact that the longer the customer stays with an organisation the more profitable they become. A study by consulting company Bain and Co.[6] found higher customer retention rates correlated strongly with profitability. The reasons for this are that a retained customer typically costs less to sell to and to service. Also as the relationship develops there is an increased likelihood that they will give a greater part of their business to a supplier whom they are prepared to treat as a partner. This is the idea of 'share of wallet', whereby the goal is to increase the total spend that is captured by the company. Furthermore, satisfied customers tell others and thus the chance increases that further business from new customers will be generated through this source.

A simple measure of customer retention is to ask the question: 'How many of the customers that we had 12 months ago do we still have today?' This measure is the real test of customer retention. It can be extended to include the value of purchases made by the retained customer base to assess how successful the company has been in increasing the level of purchasing from these accounts (see Figure 2.5).

Figure 2.5 Customer retention indicators

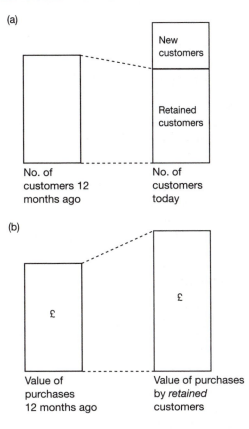

(a)

New customers

Retained customers

No. of customers 12 months ago

No. of customers today

(b)

£

£

Value of purchases 12 months ago

Value of purchases by *retained* customers

A prime objective of any customer service strategy should be to enhance customer retention. Whilst customer service obviously also plays a role in winning new customers it is perhaps the most potent weapon in the marketing armoury for the keeping of customers.

There is rapidly emerging a new focus in marketing and logistics on the creation of 'relationships' with customers. The idea is that we should seek to create such a level of satisfaction with customers that they do not feel it necessary even to consider alternative offers or suppliers. Many markets are characterised by a high level of 'churn' or 'promiscuity' amongst the customer base. In these markets customers will buy one brand on one occasion and then are just as likely to buy another on the next occasion.

The principle behind 'relationship marketing' is that the organisation should consciously strive to develop marketing strategies to maintain and strengthen customer loyalty.[7] So, for example, an airline might develop a frequent-flyer programme, or a credit card company might award points based upon the value of purchases made with the card that can then be redeemed for cash or awards. At the other extreme, a company like IBM will consciously seek to develop long-term relationships with its customers through training programmes, client seminars, frequent customer communication and so on.

Market-driven supply chains

Most traditional supply chains were designed to optimise the internal operations of the supplying company. Thus a manufacturer might be motivated to establish supply and distribution arrangements that would enable production efficiencies to be maximised. Typically this would entail manufacturing in large batches, shipping in large quantities and buffering the factory, both upstream and downstream, with inventory. In this way the goal of becoming a 'low-cost producer' could be achieved.

Whilst this approach was fine from the perspective of the manufacturing organisation, it clearly did not come anywhere close to being 'customer-centric', in the sense of designing the supply chain around the needs of the customer. With the continuing transfer of power in the distribution channel from the producer to the consumer, this conventional philosophy has become less and less appropriate. Now, instead of designing supply chains from the 'factory outwards' the challenge is to design them from the 'customer backwards'.

This new perspective sees the consumer not at the end of the supply chain but at its start. In effect this is the philosophical difference between supply chain management and what more properly might be called 'demand chain management'.

As one author has suggested:

> Managing demand chains is … fundamentally different to managing supply chains. It requires turning the supply chain on its head, and taking the end user as the organization's point of departure and not its final destination.

SOURCE: S. BAKER[8]

Figure 2.6 suggests an appropriate sequence of actions to create a market-driven supply chain.

This sequence begins with an understanding of the value that customers seek in the market in which the company competes. This customer insight will enable the identification of the real market segmentation, i.e. the clusters of customers who share the same value preferences. The Spanish fashion chain Zara provides an excellent example of how market understanding and supply chain excellence can create real value for its target customers.

ZARA: linking supply chain processes to the value proposition

Zara is one of world's most successful clothing manufacturers and retailers. They have achieved this leadership position through creating a value proposition around the idea of 'Fast Fashion'. Almost uniquely they have developed supply chain processes that enable them to capture ideas and trends in the apparel market and to translate them into products in amazingly short lead times. Zara's target time to take an idea from design to store is between three and four weeks.

To achieve this quick response capability Zara have developed an agile network of closely integrated company-owned and independent manufacturing facilities that have the flexibility to produce in small batches at short notice. Whilst this is not the cheapest way to make a garment, it ensures that they achieve their value proposition.

Figure 2.6 Linking customer value to supply chain strategy

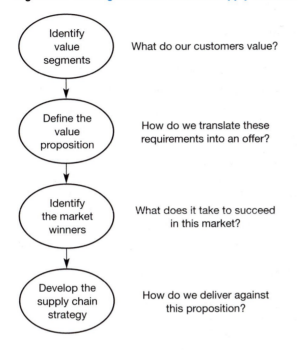

Identify value segments — What do our customers value?

Define the value proposition — How do we translate these requirements into an offer?

Identify the market winners — What does it take to succeed in this market?

Develop the supply chain strategy — How do we deliver against this proposition?

Identifying customers' service needs

It is important to remember that no two customers will ever be exactly the same in terms of their service requirements. However, it will often be the case that customers will fall into groups or 'segments' that are characterised by a broad similarity of service needs. These groupings might be thought of as 'service segments'. The logistics planner therefore needs to know just what the service issues are that differentiate customers. Market research can be of great assistance in understanding this service segmentation and it is often surprising to see how little formal research is conducted in this crucial area.

How might such a research programme be implemented?

The first point to emphasise is that customer service is perceptual. Whatever our own 'hard' internal measures of service might say our service performance is, perceptions are the reality. We might use measures which, whilst providing useful measures of productivity, do not actually reflect the things the customer values. For example, whilst 'stock availability' is a widespread internal measure of performance, a more appropriate external measure from the customer's viewpoint could be 'on-time delivery'. Hence it is critical that we develop a set of service criteria that are meaningful to customers.

The approach to service segmentation suggested here follows a three-step process:

1 Identify the key components of customer service as seen by customers themselves.

2 Establish the relative importance of those service components to customers.

3 Identify 'clusters' of customers according to similarity of service preferences.

1 Identifying the key components of customer service

A common failing in business is to assume that 'we know what our customers want'. However, the truth is that it is easy to become divorced from the reality of the marketplace when management is consumed with the day-to-day pressures of running a business. How should we know which aspects of service are most highly rated by the customer? Given the complexity of the market that the typical company serves how might it better understand the segmentation of those markets in terms of service requirements? What does it take for a company to become the supplier of choice?

Clearly it is important to develop an understanding of the service needs of customers through detailed research.

The first step in research of this type is to identify the key sources of influence upon the purchase decision. If, for example, we are selling components to a manufacturer, who will make the decision on the choice of supplier? This is not always an easy question to answer as in many cases there will be several people involved. The purchasing manager of the company to which we are selling may only be acting as an agent for others within the firm. In other cases his or her influence will be much greater. Alternatively if we are manufacturing products for sale through retail outlets, is the decision to stock made centrally or by individual store managers? The answers can often be supplied by the sales force. The sales representative should know from experience who the decision makers are.

Given that a clear indication of the source of decision-making power can be gained, the customer service researcher at least knows who to research. The question remains as to which elements of the vendor's total marketing offering have what effect upon the purchase decision.

Ideally once the decision-making unit in a specific market has been identified, an initial, small-scale research programme should be undertaken based upon personal interviews with a representative sample of buyers. The purpose of these interviews is to elicit, in the language of the customers, firstly, the importance they attach to customer service vis-à-vis the other marketing mix elements such as price, product quality, promotion, etc., and secondly, the specific importance they attach to the individual components of customer service.

The importance of this initial step in measuring customer service is that relevant and meaningful measures of customer service are generated by the customers themselves. Once these dimensions are defined we can identify the relative importance of each one and the extent to which different types of customer are prepared to trade off one aspect of service for another.

2 Establishing the relative importance of customer service components

One of the simplest ways of discovering the importance a customer attaches to each element of customer service is to take the components generated by means of the process described in step 1 and to ask a representative sample of customers to rank order them from the 'most important' to the 'least important'. In practice this is difficult, particularly with a large number of components, and would not give any insight into the relative importance of each element. Alternatively a form of rating scale could be used. For example, the respondents could be asked to place a weight from 1 to 10 against each component according to how much importance they attached to each element. The problem here is that respondents will tend to rate most of the components as highly important, especially since those components were generated on the grounds of importance to customers in the first place. A partial solution is to ask the respondent to allocate a total of 100 points amongst all the elements listed, according to perceived importance. However, this is a fairly daunting task for the respondent and can often result in an arbitrary allocation.

Fortunately a relatively recent innovation in consumer research technology now enables us to evaluate very simply the implicit importance that a customer attaches to the separate elements of customer service. The technique is based around the concept of trade-off and can best be illustrated by an example from everyday life. In considering, say, the purchase of a new car we might desire specific attributes, e.g. performance in terms of speed and acceleration, economy in terms of petrol consumption, size in terms of passenger and luggage capacity and, of course, low price. However, it is unlikely that any one car will meet all of these requirements so we are forced to trade off one or more of these attributes against the others.

The same is true of the customer faced with alternative options of distribution service. The buyer might be prepared to sacrifice a day or two of lead time in order to gain delivery reliability, or to trade off order completeness against improvements in order entry, etc. Essentially the trade-off technique works by presenting the respondent with feasible combinations of customer service elements and asking for a rank order of preference for those combinations. Computer analysis then determines the implicit importance attached by the respondent to each service element.[9]

Whatever technique is used it is important to understand which are the 'qualifiers' and which are the 'order winners' amongst the different customer groups. This understanding must then drive the design of the supply chain processes that will enable success in the marketplace.

3 Identifying customer service segments

Now that we have determined the importance attached by different respondents to each of the service attributes previously identified, the final step is to see if any similarities of preference emerge. If one group of respondents, for example, has a clearly distinct set of priorities from another then it would be reasonable to think of them both as different service segments.

How can these customer service segments be identified? One technique that has been successfully used in this connection is cluster analysis. Cluster analysis is a computer-based method for looking across a set of data and seeking to 'match' respondents across as many dimensions as possible. Thus if two respondents completed the step 2 trade-off analysis in a similar way their importance scores on the various service dimensions would be similar and hence the cluster analysis would assign them to the same group.

One study in an industrial market suggested that the traditional way of segmenting customers according to 'Standard Industrial Classification' (SIC) had little relevance to purchasing behaviour. The classic categorisation of customers according to industry sector did not correlate with the attributes they sought from suppliers. Instead it seemed that some companies were very time-sensitive in terms of delivery reliability – a 'just-in-time' segment – regardless of the industry they were in. In the same way there was a very clear 'price' segment, which also cut across conventional industrial classifications. A further segment was much more responsive to a 'relationship' approach, valuing technical support and close supplier liaison much more highly. As a result of this research the supplier was better able to focus its marketing efforts and to re-engineer its supply chain strategy to achieve a better match with customer requirements.

The challenge to logistics management is to create appropriate supply chain solutions to meet the needs of these different value segments. More than likely there will be the need for multiple supply chain solutions since 'one size will not fit all'. This issue will be dealt with in detail in Chapter 5 where the concept of supply chain agility is discussed.

Defining customer service objectives

The whole purpose of supply chain management and logistics is to provide customers with the level and quality of service that they require and to do so at less cost to the total supply chain. In developing a market-driven logistics strategy the aim is to achieve 'service excellence' in a consistent and cost-effective way.

> The whole purpose of supply chain management and logistics is to provide customers with the level and quality of service that they require and to do so at less cost to the total supply chain.

The definition of appropriate service objectives is made easier if we adopt the concept of the *perfect order*. The perfect order is achieved when the customer's service requirements are met in full. Clearly such a definition is specific to individual customers, but it is usually possible to group customers into segments and then to identify, along the lines described earlier, the key service needs of those segments. The perfect order is achieved only when each of those service needs is met to the customer's satisfaction.

The measure of service is therefore defined as the percentage of occasions on which the customer's requirements are met in full. Normally this percentage would be measured across all customers over a period of time. However, it can also be used to measure service performance at the individual customer level and indeed at any level, e.g. segment, country or by distribution centre.

One frequently encountered measure of the perfect order is 'on-time, in-full' (OTIF). An extension of this is on-time, in-full and error-free. This latter element relates to documentation, labelling and damage to the product or its packaging. To calculate the actual service level using the perfect order concept requires performance on each element to be monitored and then the percentage achievement on each element to be multiplied together.

For example, if the actual performance across all orders for the last 12 months was as follows:

On-time : **90%**

In-full : **80%**

Error-free : **70%**

the actual perfect order achievement would be:

$$90\% \times 80\% \times 70\% = 50.4\%$$

In other words the likelihood that a perfect order was achieved during the period under review was only 50.4 per cent!

The cost benefit of customer service

All companies have to face a basic fact: there will be significant differences in profitability between customers. Not only do different customers buy different quantities of different products, but the cost to service these customers will typically vary considerably. This issue will be explored more fully in Chapter 3.

The 80/20 rule will often be found to hold: 80 per cent of the profits of the business come from 20 per cent of the customers. Furthermore, 80 per cent of the total costs to serve will be generated from 20 per cent of the customers (but probably not the same 20 per cent!). Whilst the proportion may not be exactly 80/20 it will generally be in that region. This is the so-called Pareto Law, named after a nineteenth century Italian economist.

The challenge to customer service management therefore is, firstly, to identify the real profitability of customers and then, secondly, to develop strategies for service that will improve the profitability of all customers. What has to be recognised is that there are costs as well as benefits in providing customer service and that therefore the appropriate level and mix of service will need to vary by customer type.

The basic relationship between the level of service and the cost is often depicted as a steeply rising curve (Figure 2.7).

The curve assumes that demand for the item is 'normally' distributed, i.e. it takes on the classic bell-shape. A feature of the normal distribution is that once its two key parameters, the mean ($\bar{x}$) and standard deviation (σ), are known, the probability of a given value occurring can be easily calculated. Thus, as Figure 2.8 shows, if the distribution depicted describes daily sales for a particular product, it can be calculated that on approximately 68 per cent of occasions total demand would be within plus or minus one standard deviation either side of the mean; on approximately 95 per cent of occasions total demand would lie within plus or minus two standard deviations either side of the mean and on 99 per cent of occasions three standard deviations either side of the mean.

Figure 2.7 The costs of service

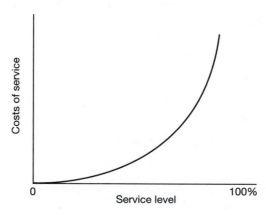

Figure 2.8 Probability of level of sales being within given limits

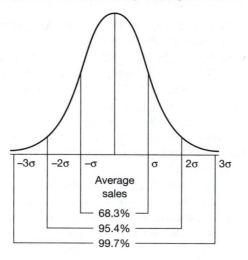

In calculating how much safety stock is required the inventory manager is only concerned with those occasions when demand is greater than average. If sales are approximately normally distributed, demand will be lower than average approximately 50 per cent of the time, and thus a 50 per cent service level would be maintained with no safety stock. It is on those occasions when demand exceeds the average that safety stock is required. In other words we must focus attention on the area of the curve to the right of the mean. Thus, by setting a stock level one standard deviation greater than the mean, the manager can achieve a service level of approximately 84 per cent. By setting the level two standard deviations greater than the mean the service level would be approximately 98 per cent and with three standard deviations it would be 99.9 per cent (Figure 2.9).

Figure 2.9 Service levels and the normal distribution

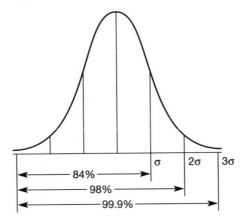

What this highlights is that, as the desired service level rises, it takes a disproportionate investment in inventory to achieve small incremental improvements in availability. The table below illustrates this effect:

Inventory level	Service level
$\bar{x}$	50%
$\bar{x} + \sigma$	84%
$\bar{x} + 2\sigma$	98%
$\bar{x} + 3\sigma$	99,9%

- If inventory equivalent to average expected daily demand ($\bar{x}$) is held then the service level would be 50 per cent.
- If safety stock equivalent to one standard deviation of demand (σ) is held then the service level would be 84 per cent, etc.

However, if it is possible to find alternative service strategies for servicing customers, say, for example, by speeding up the flow of information about customer requirements and by using faster modes of transport, then the same level of service can be achieved with less inventory – in effect pushing the curve to the right (Figure 2.10). This is the idea of substituting information and responsiveness for inventory. In other words if we can gain earlier warning of customer requirements and our lead times are short, then we can reduce our reliance on inventory.

Figure 2.10 Shifting the costs of service

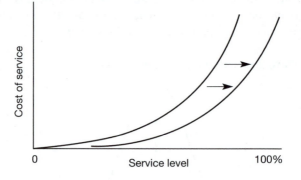

Setting customer service priorities

Whilst it should be the objective of any logistics system to provide all customers with the level of service that has been agreed or negotiated, it must be recognised that there will inevitably need to be service priorities. In this connection the Pareto Law, or 80/20 rule, can provide us with the basis for developing a more cost-effective service strategy. Fundamentally, the service issue is that since not all our customers are equally profitable nor are our products equally profitable, should not the highest service be given to key customers and key products? Since we can assume that money spent on service is a scarce resource then we should look upon the service decision as a resource allocation issue.

Figure 2.11 shows how a typical company might find its profits varying by customer and by product.

Figure 2.11 The 'Pareto' or 80/20 rule

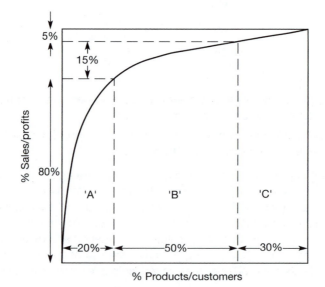

The curve is traditionally divided into three categories: the top 20 per cent of products and customers by profitability are the 'A' category; the next 50 per cent or so are labelled 'B'; and the final 30 per cent are category 'C'. The precise split between the categories is arbitrary as the shape of the distribution will vary from business to business and from market to market.

The appropriate measure should be profit rather than sales revenue or volume. The reason for this is that revenue and volume measures might disguise considerable variation in costs. In the case of customers this cost is the 'cost to serve', and we will later suggest an approach to measuring customer profitability. In the case of product profitability we must also be careful that we are identifying the appropriate service-related costs as they differ by product. One of the problems here is that conventional accounting methods do not help in the identification of these costs.

What we should be concerned to do at this stage in the analysis is to identify the contribution to profit that each product (at the individual stock keeping unit (SKU) level) makes. By contribution we mean the difference between total revenue accruing and the directly attributable costs that attach as the product moves through the logistics system.

Looking first at differences in product profitability, what use might be made of the A,B,C categorisation? Firstly it can be used as the basis for classic inventory control whereby the highest level of service (as represented by safety stock) is provided for the 'A' products, a slightly lower level for the 'B' products and lower still for the 'Cs'. Thus we might seek to follow the stock holding policy shown below:

Product category	Stock availability
A	99%
B	97%
C	90%

Alternatively, and probably to be preferred, we might differentiate the stock holding by holding the 'A' items as close as possible to the customer and the 'B' and 'C' items further up the supply chain. The savings in stock holding costs achieved by consolidating the 'B' and 'C' items as a result of holding them at fewer locations would normally cover the additional cost of despatching them to the customer by a faster means of transportation (e.g. overnight delivery).

Perhaps the best way to manage product service levels is to take into account both the profit contribution and the individual product demand.

We can bring both these measures together in the form of a simple matrix in Figure 2.12. The matrix can be explained as follows.

Figure 2.12 Managing product service levels

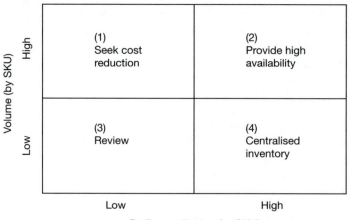

Quadrant 1: Seek cost reductions

Because these products have high volume it would suggest that they are in frequent demand. However, they are also low in profit contribution and the priority should be to re-examine product and logistics costs to see if there is any scope for enhancing profit.

Quadrant 2: Provide high availability

These products are frequently demanded and they are more profitable. We should offer the highest level of service on these items by holding them as close to the customer as possible and with high availability. Because there will be relatively few of these items we can afford to follow such a strategy.

Quadrant 3: Review

Products in this category should be regularly appraised with a view to deletion from the range. They do not contribute to profits (or at least only marginally) and they are slow movers from a sales point of view. Unless they play a strategic role in the product portfolio of the firm then there is probably a strong case for dropping them.

Quadrant 4: Centralised inventory

Because these products are highly profitable but only sell at a relatively slow rate they are candidates for centralised management. In other words, they should be kept in some central location, as far back up the supply chain as possible in order to reduce the total inventory investment, and then shipped by express transport direct to customers.

This concept of service prioritisation by product can be extended to include customer priorities. Because the same 80/20 rule applies to customers as it does to products, it makes sense to focus resources on key accounts as well as key products.

Figure 2.13 shows that if the 80/20 rule applies both to products and customers then all businesses are actually very dependent upon a very few customers buying a few high profit lines. Indeed the arithmetic is easy:

20% of customers buying 20% of the products
= 4% of all customer/product transactions

Which provides:

80% of 80% of total profit = 64%

In other words, just 4 per cent of transactions (measured order line by order line) gives us 64 per cent of all our profit!

Figure 2.13 Customer service and the 80/20 rule

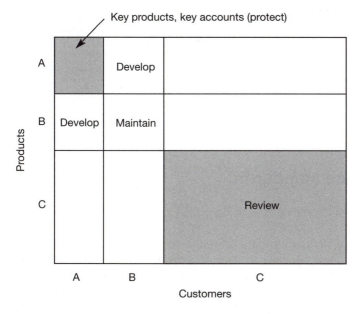

How can we make use of this important fact? The first thing is obviously to offer the highest levels of service and availability to key customers ordering key products. At the other end of the spectrum we should constantly review the less profitable customers and the less profitable products. In between there is scope for a degree of pragmatism, perhaps based upon the 'critical value' of an item to the customer. This is particularly relevant when developing a service strategy for spare parts. The idea is that if certain items are essential for, say, the operation of a machine where the downtime costs are high then those parts would be accorded a high critical value. If appropriate a 'weight' could be assigned on the basis of criticality and the 80/20 ranking based on profit could be adjusted accordingly. Table 2.2 provides an example.

Table 2.2 Critical value analysis

Products	Profitability rank order	Critical value to customers			Rank × Critical value	Order of priority for service
		1	2	3		
C	1			X	3	1
P	2		X		4	2 =
R	3		X		6	5
B	4	X			4	2 =
X	5	X			5	4
Y	6			X	18	8
Z	7		X		14	7
H	8	X			8	6
J	9			X	27	10
K	10		X		20	9

Critical values: 1 = Sale lost
                 2 = Slight delay acceptable
                 3 = Longer delay acceptable

Setting service standards

Obviously if service performance is to be controlled then it must be against predetermined standards.

Ultimately the only standard to be achieved is 100 per cent conformity to customer expectations. This requires a clear and objective understanding of the customers' requirements and at the same time places an obligation upon the supplier to shape those expectations. In other words there must be a complete match between what the customer expects and what we are willing and able to provide. This may require negotiation of service standards since clearly it is in neither party's interest to provide service levels that would lead to a long-term deterioration in profitability – either for the supplier or the customer.

What are the customer service elements for which standards should be set?

To be effective these standards must be defined by the customers themselves. This requires customer research and competitive benchmarking studies to be conducted so that an objective definition of customer service for each market segment may be identified.

However, for the moment we can indicate some of the key areas where standards are essential:

- Order cycle time
- Stock availability
- Order-size constraints
- Ordering convenience
- Frequency of delivery
- Delivery reliability
- Documentation quality
- Claims procedure
- Order completeness
- Technical support
- Order status information

Let us examine each of these in turn.

Order cycle time

This is the elapsed time from customer order to delivery. Standards should be defined against the customer's stated requirements.

Stock availability

This relates to the percentage of demand for a given line item (stock keeping unit, or SKU) that can be met from available inventory.

Order-size constraints

More and more customers seek just-in-time deliveries of small quantities. Do we have the flexibility to cope with the range of customer demands likely to be placed upon us?

Ordering convenience

Are we accessible and easy to do business with? How are we seen from the customers' viewpoint? Do our systems talk to their systems?

Frequency of delivery

A further manifestation of the move to just-in-time is that customers require more frequent deliveries within closely specified time windows. Again it is flexibility of response that should be the basis for the performance standard.

Delivery reliability

What proportion of total orders are delivered on time? It is a reflection not just of delivery performance but also of stock availability and order processing performance.

Documentation quality

What is the error rate on invoices, delivery notes and other customer communications? Is the documentation 'user friendly'? A surprisingly large number of service failures are from this source.

Claims procedure

What is the trend in claims? What are their causes? How quickly do we deal with complaints and claims? Do we have procedures for 'service recovery'?

Order completeness

What proportion of orders do we deliver complete, i.e. no back orders or part shipments?

Technical support

What support do we provide customers with after the sale? If appropriate do we have standards for call-out time and first-time fix rate on repairs?

Order status information

Can we inform customers at any time on the status of their order? Do we have 'hotlines' or their equivalent? Do we have procedures for informing customers of potential problems on stock availability or delivery?

All of these issues are capable of quantification and measurement against customer requirements. Similarly they are all capable of comparison against competitive performance.

It must be recognised that from the customer's perspective there are only two levels of service – either 100 per cent or 0 per cent. In other words either the customer gets exactly what they ordered at the time and place required or they don't. It must also be remembered that 100 per cent order fill rates are extremely difficult to achieve – the laws of probability see to that! If there are ten items on a particular order and each item is carried in stock at the 95 per cent level of availability then the probability that the complete order can be filled is $(0.95)^{10}$, which is 0.599. In other words, just over a 50/50 chance that we can satisfy the complete order.

Table 2.3 shows how the probability of order fill diminishes as the number of items on the customer order increases.

Table 2.3 Probability of a complete order

Number of lines in order	Line item availability			
	90%	92%	94%	95%
1	0.900	0.920	0.940	0.950
2	0.810	0.846	0.884	0.903
3	0.729	0.779	0.831	0.857
4	0.656	0.716	0.781	0.815
5	0.590	0.659	0.734	0.774
6	0.531	0.606.	0.690	0.735
7	0.478	0.558	0.648	0.698
8	0.430	0.513	0.610	0.663
9	0.387	0.472	0.573	0.630
10	0.348	0.434	0.538	0.599
11	0.314	0.399	0.506	0.569
12	0.282	0.368	0.476	0.540
14	0.225	0.311	0.400	0.488
15	0.206	0.286	0.395	0.463
16	0.195	0.263	0.372	0.440
17	0.167	0.243	0.349	0.418
18	0.150	0.223	0.328	0.397
19	0.135	0.205	0.309	0.377
20	0.122	0.185	0.290	0.358

Ideally organisations should establish standards and monitor performance across a range of customer service measures. For example, using the pre-transaction, transaction and post-transaction framework, the following measures provide valuable indicators of performance:

Pre-transaction

- Stock availability
- Target delivery dates
- Response times to queries

Transaction

- Order fill rate
- On-time delivery
- Back orders by age
- Shipment delays
- Product substitutions

Post-transaction

- First call fix rate
- Customer complaints
- Returns/claims
- Invoice errors
- Service parts availability

It is possible to produce a composite index based upon multiple service measures and this can be a useful management tool, particularly for communicating service performance internally. Such an index is shown in Table 2.4 where the weight attached to each service element reflects the importance that the customers attach to those elements.

Table 2.4 Composite service index

Service element	Importance weight (i)	Performance level (ii)	Weighted score (i) × (ii)
Order fill rate	30%	70%	0.21
On-time delivery	25%	60%	0.15
Order accuracy	25%	80%	0.20
Invoice accuracy	10%	90%	0.09
Returns	10%	95%	0.095
		Index =	0.745

Customer service is one of the most powerful elements available to the organisation in its search for competitive advantage and yet it is often the least well managed. The key message of this chapter has been that the quality of customer service performance depends in the main upon the skill with which the logistics system is designed and managed. Put very simply, the output of all logistics activity is customer service.

References

1. Schonberger, R.J., *Building a Chain of Customers*, The Free Press, 1990.
2. LaLonde, B.J. and Zinszer, P.H., *Customer Service: Meaning and Measurement*, National Council of Physical Distribution Management, Chicago, 1976.
3. Corsten, D. and Gruen, T., 'Stock-outs cause walkouts', *Harvard Business Review*, May 2004.
4. Bayle, M., 'Brand killers', *Fortune*, 11 August 2003, pp. 51–56.
5. Levitt, T. *The Marketing Mode*, McGraw Hill, 1969.
6. Reichheld, F.A., 'Loyalty and the renaissance of marketing', *Marketing Management*, Vol. 2, No. 4, 1994, pp. 10–21.
7. Christopher, M., Payne, A. and Ballantyne, D., *Relationship Marketing: Creating Stakeholder Value*, Butterworth-Heinemann, 2002.
8. Baker, S., *New Consumer Marketing*, John Wiley & Sons, 2003.
9. Christopher, M. and Peck, H., *Marketing Logistics*, 2nd edition, Butterworth-Heinemann, 2003.

Measuring logistics costs and performance

3

- Logistics and the bottom line

- Logistics and shareholder value

- Logistics cost analysis

- The concept of total cost analysis

- Principles of logistics costing

- Customer profitability analysis

- Direct product profitability

- Cost drivers and activity-based costing

The costs of satisfying customer demand can be significant and yet, surprisingly, they are not always fully understood by organisations. One reason for this is that traditional accounting systems tend to be focused around understanding *product* costs rather than *customer* costs. Whilst logistics costs will vary by company and by industry, across the economy as a whole the total cost of logistics as a proportion of gross domestic product is estimated to be close to 10 per cent in the US[1] and in other countries costs of similar magnitudes will be encountered.

However, logistics activity does not just generate cost, it also generates revenue through the provision of availability – thus it is important to understand the profit impact of logistics and supply chain decisions. At the same time logistics activity requires resources in the form of fixed capital and working capital and so there are financial issues to be considered when supply chain strategies are devised.

Logistics and the bottom line

Today's turbulent business environment has produced an ever greater awareness amongst managers of the financial dimension of decision making. 'The bottom line' has become the driving force which, perhaps erroneously, determines the direction of the company. In some cases this has led to a limiting, and potentially dangerous, focus on the short term. Hence we find that investment in brands, in R&D and in capacity may well be curtailed if there is no prospect of an immediate payback.

Just as powerful an influence on decision making and management horizons is cash flow. Strong positive cash flow has become as much a desired goal of management as profit.

The third financial dimension to decision making is resource utilisation and specifically the use of fixed and working capital. The pressure in most organisations is to improve the productivity of capital – 'to make the assets sweat'. In this regard it is usual to utilise the concept of return on investment (ROI). Return on investment is the ratio between the net profit and the capital that was employed to produce that profit, thus:

$$ROI = \frac{Profit}{Capital\ employed}$$

This ratio can be further expanded:

$$ROI = \frac{Profit}{Sales} \times \frac{Sales}{Capital\ employed}$$

It will be seen that ROI is the product of two ratios: the first, profit/sales, being commonly referred to as the margin and the second, sales/capital employed, termed capital turnover or asset turn. Thus to gain improvement on ROI one or other, or both, of these ratios must increase. Typically many companies will focus their main attention on the margin in their attempt to drive up ROI, yet it can often be more effective to use the leverage of improved capital turnover to boost ROI. For example, many successful retailers have long since recognised that very small net margins can lead to excellent ROI if the productivity of capital is high, e.g. limited inventory, high sales per square foot, premises that are leased rather than owned and so on.

Figure 3.1 illustrates the opportunities that exist for boosting ROI through either achieving better margins or higher assets turns or both. Each 'iso-curve' reflects the different ways the same ROI can be achieved through specific margin/asset turn combination. The challenge to logistics management is to find ways of moving the iso-curve to the right.

The ways in which logistics management can impact on ROI are many and varied. Figure 3.2 highlights the major elements determining ROI and the potential for improvement through more effective logistics management.

Figure 3.1 The impact of margin and asset turn on ROI

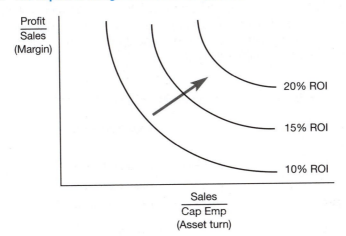

Figure 3.2 Logistics impact on ROI

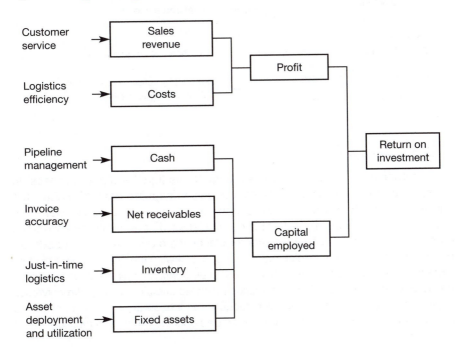

Logistics and the balance sheet

As well as its impact on operating income (revenue less costs) logistics can affect the balance sheet of the business in a number of ways. In today's financially challenging business environment improving the shape of the balance sheet through better use of assets and resources has become a priority.

Once again better logistics management has the power to transform performance in this crucial area. Figure 3.3 summarises the major elements of the balance
sheet and links to each of the relevant logistics management components.

By examining each element of the balance sheet in turn it will be seen how
logistics variables can influence its final shape.

Figure 3.3 Logistics management and the balance sheet

Balance sheet	Logistics variable
Assets	
Cash	Order cycle time
	Order completion rate
Receivables	Invoice accuracy
Inventories	Inventory
Property, plant and equipment	Distribution facilities and equipment
	Plant and equipment
Liabilities	
Current liabilities	Purchase order quantities
Debt	Financing options for inventory, plant and equipment
Equity	

Cash and receivables

This component of current assets is crucial to the liquidity of the business. In
recent years its importance has been recognised as more companies become
squeezed for cash. It is not always recognised, however, that logistics variables
have a direct impact on this part of the balance sheet. For example, the shorter the
order cycle time, from when the customer places the order to when the goods are
delivered, the sooner the invoice can be issued. Likewise the order completion rate
can affect the cash flow if the invoice is not issued until after all the goods are des-
patched. One of the less obvious logistics variables affecting cash and receivables
is invoice accuracy. A customer who receives an inaccurate invoice is unlikely to
pay and the payment lead time will be extended until the problem is rectified.

Inventories

Fifty per cent or more of a company's current assets will often be tied up in
inventory. Logistics is concerned with all inventory within the business from raw
materials, sub-assembly or bought-in components, through work-in-progress to
finished goods. The company's policies on inventory levels and stock locations
will clearly influence the size of total inventory. Also influential will be the extent to

which inventory levels are monitored and managed, and beyond that the extent to which strategies are in operation that minimise the need for inventory.

Property, plant and equipment

The logistics system of any business will usually be a heavy user of fixed assets. The plant, depots and warehouses that form the logistics network, if valued realistically on a replacement basis, will represent a substantial part of total capacity employed (assuming that they are owned rather than rented or leased). Materials handling equipment, vehicles and other equipment involved in storage and transport can also add considerably to the total sum of fixed assets. Many companies have outsourced the physical distribution of their products partly to move assets off their balance sheet. Warehouses, for example, with their associated storage and handling equipment represent a sizeable investment and the question should be asked: 'Is this the most effective way to deploy our assets?'

Current liabilities

The current liabilities of the business are debts that must be paid in cash within a specified period of time. From the logistics point of view the key elements are accounts payable for bought-in materials, components, etc. This is an area where a greater integration of purchasing with operations management can yield dividends. The traditional concepts of economic order quantities can often lead to excessive levels of raw materials inventory as those quantities may not reflect actual manufacturing or distribution requirements. The phasing of supplies to match the total logistics requirements of the system can be achieved through the twin techniques of materials requirement planning (MRP) and distribution requirements planning (DRP). If premature commitment of materials can be minimised this should lead to an improved position on current liabilities.

Debt/equity

Whilst the balance between debt and equity has many ramifications for the financial management of the total business, it is worth reflecting on the impact of alternative logistics strategies. More companies are leasing plant facilities and equipment and thus converting a fixed asset into a continuing expense. The growing use of 'third-party' suppliers for warehousing and transport instead of owning and managing these facilities in-house is a parallel development. These changes obviously affect the funding requirements of the business. They may also affect the means whereby that funding is achieved, i.e. through debt rather than equity. The ratio of debt to equity, usually referred to as 'gearing' or 'leverage', will influence the return on equity and will also have implications for cash flow in terms of interest payments and debt repayment.

Logistics and shareholder value

One of the key measures of corporate performance today is shareholder value. In other words, what is the company worth to its owners? Increasingly senior management within the business is being driven by the goal of enhancing shareholder value. There are a number of complex issues involved in actually calculating shareholder value but at its simplest it is determined by the net present value of future cash flows. These cash flows may themselves be defined as:

Net operating income

less

Taxes

less

Working capital investment

less

Fixed capital investment

=

After-tax free cash flow

More recently there has been a further development in that the concept of economic value added (EVA) has become widely used and linked to the creation of shareholder value. The term EVA originated with the consulting firm Stern Stewart,[2] although its origins go back to the economist Alfred Marshall who, over 100 years ago, developed the concept of 'economic income'.

Essentially EVA is the difference between operating income after taxes less the true cost of capital employed to generate those profits. Thus:

Economic value added (EVA)
= Profit after tax − True cost of capital employed

It will be apparent that it is possible for a company to generate a negative EVA. In other words, the cost of capital employed is greater than the profit after tax. The impact of a negative EVA, particularly if sustained over a period of time, is to erode shareholder value. Equally improvements in EVA will lead to an enhancement of shareholder value. If the net present value of expected future EVAs were to be calculated this would generate a measure of wealth known as market value added (MVA), which is a true measure of what the business is worth to its shareholders. A simple definition of MVA is:

Stock price × Issued shares

less

Book value of total capital invested

=

Market value added

and, as we have already noted,

$$\text{MVA} = \text{Net present value of expected future EVA}$$

Clearly, it will be recognised that there are a number of significant connections between logistics performance and shareholder value. Not only the impact that logistics service can have upon net operating income (profit) but also the impact on capital efficiency (asset turn). Many companies have come to realise the effect that lengthy pipelines and highly capital-intensive logistics facilities can have on EVA and hence shareholder value. As a result they have focused on finding ways in which pipelines can be shortened and, consequently, working capital requirements reduced. At the same time they have looked again at their fixed capital deployment of distribution facilities and vehicle fleets and in many cases have moved these assets off the balance sheet through the use of third-party logistics service providers.

The drivers of shareholder value

The five basic drivers of enhanced shareholder value are shown in Figure 3.4. They are revenue growth, operating cost reduction, fixed capital efficiency, working capital efficiency and tax minimisation. All five of these drivers are directly and indirectly affected by logistics management and supply chain strategy.

Figure 3.4 The drivers of shareholder value

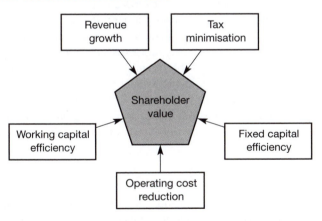

Revenue growth

The critical linkage here is the impact that logistics service can have on sales volume and customer retention. Whilst it is not generally possible to calculate the exact correlation between service and sales there have been many studies that have indicated a positive causality.

It can also be argued that superior logistics service (in terms of reliability and responsiveness) can strengthen the likelihood that customers will remain loyal to a supplier. In Chapter 2 it was suggested that higher levels of customer retention lead to greater sales. Typically this occurs because satisfied customers are more likely to place a greater proportion of their purchases with that supplier.

Operating cost reduction

The potential for operating cost reduction through logistics and supply chain management is considerable. Because a large proportion of costs in a typical business are driven by logistics decisions and the quality of supply chain relationships, it is not surprising that in the search for enhanced margins many companies are taking a new look at the way they manage the supply chain.

It is not just the transportation, storage, handling and order processing costs within the business that need to be considered. Rather a total pipeline view of costs on a true 'end-to-end' basis should be taken. Often the upstream logistics costs can represent a significant proportion of total supply chain costs embedded in the final product.

There is also a growing recognition that time compression in the supply chain not only enhances customer service but can also reduce costs through the reduction of non-value-adding activities. This is an issue that we shall return to in Chapter 6.

Fixed capital efficiency

Logistics by its very nature tends to be fixed asset 'intensive'. Trucks, distribution centres and automated handling systems involve considerable investment and, consequently, will often depress return on investment. In conventional multi-echelon distribution systems, it is not unusual to find factory warehouses, regional distribution centres and local depots, all of which represent significant fixed investment.

One of the main drivers behind the growth of the third-party logistics service sector has been the desire to reduce fixed asset investment. At the same time the trend to lease rather than buy has accelerated. Decisions to rationalise distribution networks and production facilities are increasingly being driven by the realisation that the true cost of financing that capital investment is sometimes greater than the return it generates.

Working capital efficiency

Supply chain strategy and logistics management are fundamentally linked to the working capital requirement within the business. Long pipelines by definition generate more inventory; order fill and invoice accuracy directly impact accounts receivable and procurement policies also affect cash flow. Working capital requirements can be dramatically reduced through time compression in the pipeline and subsequently reduced order-to-cash cycle times.

Surprisingly few companies know the true length of the pipeline for the products they sell. The 'cash-to-cash' cycle time (i.e. the elapsed time from procurement of materials/components through to sale of the finished product) can be six months or longer in many manufacturing industries. By focusing on eliminating non-value-adding time in the supply chain, dramatic reduction in working capital can be achieved. So many companies have lived with low inventory turns for so long that they assume that it is a feature of their industry and that nothing can be done. They are also possibly not motivated to give working capital reduction a higher priority because an unrealistically low cost of capital is often used in decision making.

Tax minimisation

In today's increasingly global economy, organisations have choices as to where they can locate their assets and activities. Because tax regimes are different country by country, location decisions can have an important impact on after-tax free cash flow. It is not just corporate taxes on profits that are affected, but also property tax and excise duty on fuel. Customs regulations, tariffs and quotas become further considerations, as do rules and regulation on transfer pricing. For large global companies with production facilities in many different countries and with dispersed distribution centres and multiple markets, supply chain decisions can significantly affect the total tax bill and hence shareholder value.

The role of cash flow in creating shareholder value

There is general agreement with the view of Warren Buffet[3] that ultimately the value of a business to its owners is determined by the net present value of the free cash flow occurring from its operations over its lifetime. Thus the challenge to managers seeking to enhance shareholder value is to identify strategies that can directly or indirectly affect free cash flow. Srivastava *et al.*[4] have suggested that the value of any strategy is inherently driven by:

1 an acceleration of cash flows because risk and time adjustments reduce the value of later cash flows;

2 an increase in the level of cash flows (e.g. higher revenues and/or lower costs, working capital and fixed investment);

3 a reduction in risk associated with cash flows (e.g. through reduction in both volatility and vulnerability of future cash flows) and hence, indirectly, the firm's cost of capital; and

4 the residual value of the business (long-term value can be enhanced, for example, by increasing the size of the customer base).

In effect, what Srivastava *et al.* are suggesting is that strategies should be evaluated in terms of how they either *enhance* or *accelerate* cash flow. Those strategic objectives can be graphically expressed as a cumulative distribution of free cash flow over time (see Figure 3.5) with the objective of building a greater cumulative cash flow, sooner. Obviously the sooner cash is received and the greater the amount then the greater will be the net present value of those cash flows.

In recent years a number of studies have been conducted which highlight the connection between supply chain excellence and financial performance. A study by Accenture[5] in 2003 in collaboration with INSEAD Business School in France and

Figure 3.5 Changing the cash flow profile

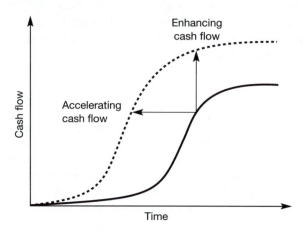
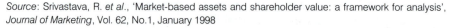

Source: Srivastava, R. *et al.*, 'Market-based assets and shareholder value: a framework for analysis', *Journal of Marketing*, Vol. 62, No.1, January 1998

Stanford University in the US analysed the financial performance of 636 companies in 24 industries and found that those companies classed as supply chain leaders also tended to be above average in terms of sustained profitability. More recently AMR Research[6] has conducted an annual survey of the top 25 supply chains, drawing on a combination of published financial data and peer group evaluation. It is probably no coincidence that most of those companies ranked in the top 25 are also above average in terms of market value added (MVA). For example, in the 2009 ranking Apple, Procter & Gamble, Dell and Wal-Mart were amongst the highest ranked companies.

Logistics cost analysis

After a century or more of reliance upon traditional cost accounting procedures to provide an often unreliable insight into profitability, managers are now starting to question the relevance of these methods.[7] The accounting frameworks still in use by the majority of companies today rely upon arbitrary methods for the allocation of shared and indirect costs and hence frequently distort the true profitability of both products and customers. Indeed, as we shall see, these traditional accounting methods are often quite unsuited for analysing the profitability of customers and markets since they were originally devised to measure product costs.

Because logistics management is a flow-oriented concept with the objective of integrating resources across a pipeline which extends from suppliers to final customers, it is desirable to have a means whereby costs and performance of that pipeline flow can be assessed.

Because logistics management is a flow-oriented concept with the objective of integrating resources across a pipeline which extends from suppliers to final customers, it is desirable to have a means whereby costs and performance of that pipeline flow can be assessed.

Probably one of the main reasons why the adoption of an integrated approach to logistics and distribution management has proved so difficult for many companies is the lack of appropriate cost information. The need to manage the total distribution activity as a complete system, having regard for the effects of decisions taken in one cost area upon other cost areas, has implications for the cost accounting systems of the organisation. Typically, conventional accounting systems group costs into broad, aggregated categories which do not then allow the more detailed analysis necessary to identify the true costs of servicing customers buying particular product mixes. Without this facility to analyse aggregated cost data, it becomes impossible to reveal the potential for cost trade-offs that may exist within the logistics system.

Generally the effects of trade-offs are assessed in two ways: from the point of view of their impact on total costs and their impact on sales revenue. For example, it may be possible to trade off costs in such a way that total costs increase, yet because of the better service now being offered, sales revenue also increases. If the difference between revenue and costs is greater than before, the trade-off may be regarded as leading to an improvement in cost effectiveness. However, without an adequate logistics-oriented cost accounting system it is extremely difficult to identify the extent to which a particular trade-off is cost-beneficial.

The concept of total cost analysis

Many problems at the operational level in logistics management arise because all the impacts of specific decisions, both direct and indirect, are not taken into account throughout the corporate system. Too often decisions taken in one area can lead to unforeseen results in other areas. Changes in policy on minimum order value, for example, may influence customer ordering patterns and lead to additional costs. Similarly, changes in production schedules that aim to improve production efficiency may lead to fluctuations in finished stock availability and thus affect customer service.

The problems associated with identifying the total system impact of distribution policies are immense. By its very nature logistics cuts across traditional company organisation functions with cost impacts on most of those functions. Conventional accounting systems do not usually assist in the identification of these company-wide impacts, frequently absorbing logistics-related costs in other cost elements. The cost of processing orders, for example, is an amalgam of specific costs incurred in different functional areas of the business which generally prove extremely difficult to bring together. Figure 3.6 outlines the various cost elements involved in the complete order processing cycle, each of these elements having a fixed and variable cost component which will lead to a different total cost for any one particular order.

Figure 3.6 Stages in the order-to-collection cycle

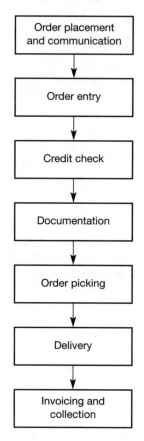

Accounting practice for budgeting and standard-setting has tended to result in a compartmentalisation of company accounts; thus budgets tend to be set on a functional basis. The trouble is that policy costs do not usually confine themselves within the same watertight boundaries. It is the nature of logistics that, like a stone thrown into a pond, the effects of specific policies spread beyond their immediate area of impact.

A further feature of logistics decisions that contributes to the complexity of generating appropriate cost information is that they are usually taken against a background of an existing system. The purpose of total cost analysis in this context is to identify the change in costs brought about by these decisions. Cost must therefore be viewed in incremental terms – the change in total costs caused by the change to the system. Thus the addition of an extra warehouse to the distribution network will bring about cost changes in transport, inventory investment and communications. It is the incremental cost difference between the two options that is the relevant accounting information for decision making in this case. Figure 3.7 shows how total logistics costs can be influenced by the addition, or removal, of a depot from the system.

Figure 3.7 **The total costs of a distribution network**

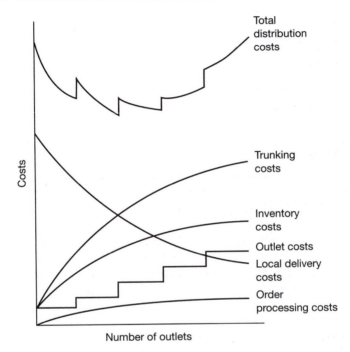

The cost of holding inventory

As we noted, there are many costs incurred in the total logistics process of converting customer orders into cash. However, one of the largest cost elements is also the one that is perhaps least well accounted for and that is inventory. It is probably the case that many managers are unaware of what the true cost of holding inventory actually is. If all the costs that arise as a result of holding inventory are fully accounted for, then the real holding cost of inventory is probably in the region of 25 per cent per annum of the book value of the inventory.

This figure is as high as it is because there are a number of costs to be included. The largest cost element will normally be the cost of capital. The cost of capital comprises the cost to the company of debt and the cost of equity. It is usual to use the *weighted cost of capital* to reflect this. Hence, even though the cost of borrowed money might be low, the expectation of shareholders as to the return they are looking for from the equity investment could be high.

The other costs that need to be included in the inventory holding cost are the costs of storage and handling, obsolescence, deterioration and pilferage, as well as insurance and all the administrative costs associated with the management of the inventory (see box).

The true cost of inventory

- Cost of capital
- Storage and handling
- Obsolescence
- Damage and deterioration
- Pilferage/shrinkage
- Insurance
- Management costs

Principles of logistics costing

It will be apparent from the previous comments that the problem of developing an appropriate logistics-oriented costing system is primarily one of focus. That is, the ability to focus upon the output of the distribution system, in essence the provision of customer service, and to identify the unique costs associated with that output. Traditional accounting methods lack this focus, mainly because they were designed with something else in mind.

One of the basic principles of logistics costing, it has been argued, is that the system should mirror the materials flow, i.e. it should be capable of identifying the costs that result from providing customer service in the marketplace. A second principle is that it should be capable of enabling separate cost and revenue analyses to be made by customer type and by market segment or distribution channel. This latter requirement emerges because of the dangers inherent in dealing solely with averages, e.g. the average cost per delivery, since they can often conceal substantial variations either side of the mean.

To operationalise these principles requires an 'output' orientation to costing. In other words, we must first define the desired outputs of the logistics system and then seek to identify the costs associated with providing those outputs. A useful concept here is the idea of 'mission'. In the context of logistics and supply chain management, a mission is a set of customer service goals to be achieved by the system within a specific product/market context. Missions can be defined in terms of the type of market served, by which products and within what constraints of service and cost. A mission by its very nature cuts across traditional company lines. Figure 3.8 illustrates the concept and demonstrates the difference between an 'output' orientation based upon missions and the 'input' orientation based upon functions.

Figure 3.8 Missions that cut across functional boundaries

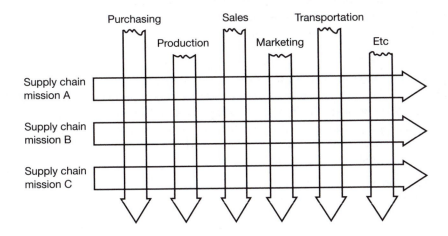

The successful achievement of defined mission goals involves inputs from a large number of functional areas and activity centres within the firm. Thus an effective costing system must seek to determine the total systems cost of meeting desired mission objectives (the 'output' of the system) and the costs of the various inputs involved in meeting these outputs.

Figure 3.9 illustrates how three supply chain missions may make a differential impact upon activity centre/functional area costs and, in so doing, provide a logical basis for costing within the company. As a cost or budgeting method,

Figure 3.9 The programme budget (£'000)

	Functional area/ Activity centre 1	Functional area/ Activity centre 2	Functional area/ Activity centre 3	Functional area/ Activity centre 4	Total mission cost
Mission A	100	90	20	80	290
Mission B	50	70	200	20	340
Mission C	70	30	50	70	220
Activity centre inputs	220	190	270	170	850

mission costing is the reverse of traditional techniques: under this scheme a functional budget is determined now by the demands of the missions it serves. Thus in Figure 3.9 the cost per mission is identified horizontally and from this the functional budgets may be determined by summing vertically.

Given that the logic of mission costing is sound, how might it be made to work in practice? This approach requires firstly that the activity centres associated with a particular distribution mission be identified, e.g. transport, warehousing, inventory, etc., and secondly that the incremental costs for each activity centre incurred as a result of undertaking that mission must be isolated. Incremental costs are used because it is important not to take into account 'sunk' costs or costs that would still be incurred even if the mission were abandoned. We can make use of the idea of 'attributable costs'[8] to operationalise the concept:

Attributable cost is a cost per unit that could be avoided if a product or function were discontinued entirely without changing the supporting organisation structure.

In determining the costs of an activity centre, e.g. transport, attributable to a specific mission, the question should be asked: 'What costs would we avoid if this customer/ segment/channel were no longer serviced?' These avoidable costs are the true incremental costs of servicing the customer/segment/channel. Often they will be substantially lower than the average cost because so many distribution costs are fixed and/or shared.

This approach becomes particularly powerful when combined with a customer revenue analysis, because even customers with low sales offtake may still be profitable in incremental costs terms if not on an average cost basis. In other words the company would be worse off if those customers were abandoned.

Such insights as this can be gained by extending the mission costing concept to produce profitability analyses for customers, market segments or distribution channels. The term 'customer profitability accounting' describes any attempt to relate the revenue produced by a customer, market segment or distribution channel to the costs of servicing that customer/segment/channel.

Customer profitability analysis

One of the basic questions that conventional accounting procedures have difficulty answering is: 'How profitable is this customer compared to another?' Usually customer profitability is only calculated at the level of gross profit – in other words the net sales revenue generated by the customer in a period, less the cost of goods sold for the actual product mix purchased. However, there are still many other costs to take into account before the real profitability of an individual customer can be exposed. The same is true if we seek to identify the relative profitability of different market segments or distribution channels.

The significance of these costs that occur as a result of servicing customers can be profound in terms of how logistics strategies should be developed. Customer profitability analysis will often reveal a proportion of customers who make a negative contribution, as in. Figure 3.10. The reason for this is very simply that the costs of servicing a customer can vary considerably – even between two customers who may make equivalent purchases from us.

Figure 3.10 Customer profitability analysis

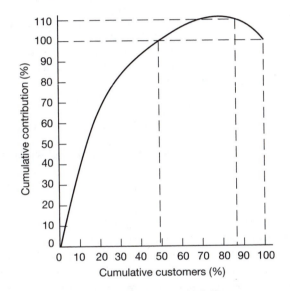

Source: Hill, G.V., *Logistics – The Battleground of the 1990s*, A.T. Kearney

If we think of all the costs that a company incurs from when it captures an order from a customer to when it collects the payment, is will be apparent that the total figure could be quite high. It will also very likely be the case that there will be significant differences in these costs customer by customer. At the same time, different customers will order a different mix of products so the gross margin that they generate will differ.

As Table 3.1 highlights, there are many costs that need to be identified if customer profitability is to be accurately measured.

The best measure of customer profitability is to ask the question: 'What costs would I avoid and what revenues would I lose if I lost this customer?' This is the concept of 'avoidable' costs and incremental revenue. Using this principle helps circumvent the problems that arise when fixed costs are allocated against individual customers.

Table 3.1 The customer profit and loss account

Revenues Less	• Net sales value
Costs (attributable costs only)	• Cost of sales (actual product mix) • Commissions • Sales calls • Key account management time • Trade bonuses and special discount • Order processing costs • Promotional costs (visible and hidden) • Merchandising costs • Non-standard packaging/unitisation • Dedicated inventory holding costs • Dedicated warehouse space • Materials handling costs • Transport costs • Documentation/communications costs • Returns/refusals • Trade credit (actual payment period)

The average customer A study by the consulting company A.T. Kearney suggested that the significance of customer-oriented costs is not their average value, but specifically how they vary by customer, by order size, by type of order and other key factors. Whilst the average cost per customer may be easily calculated, there may be no customer that incurs the average cost to serve. The need is to be aware of the customers at the extremes of the cost range because, on the one hand, profits may be eroded by serving them and, on the other, although high profit is being generated, the business is vulnerable to competitive price-cutting. The table below shows an example of the range of values of some customer-oriented costs expressed as a percentage of net sales. This illustrates how misleading the use of averages can be.

Customer costs as a percentage of net sales

	Low	Average	High
Order processing	0.2	2.6	7.4
Inventory carrying	1.1	2.6	10.2
Picking and shipping	0.3	0.7	2.5
Outbound freight	2.8	7.1	14.1
Commissions	2.4	3.1	4.4

Source: Hill, G.V. and Harland, D.V., 'The customer profit centre', *Focus*, Institute of Logistics and Distribution Management, Vol. 2, No. 2, 1983

What sort of costs should be taken into account in this type of analysis? Figure 3.11 presents a basic model that seeks to identify only those customer-related costs that are avoidable (i.e. if the customer did not exist, these costs would not be incurred).

The starting point is the gross sales value of the order from which is then subtracted the discounts that are given on that order to the customer. This leaves the net sales value from which must be taken the direct production costs or cost of goods sold. Indirect costs are not allocated unless they are fully attributable to that customer. The same principle applies to sales and marketing costs as attempts to allocate indirect costs, such as national advertising, can only be done on an arbitrary and usually misleading basis. The attributable distribution costs can then be assigned to give customer gross contribution. Finally any other customer-related costs, such as trade credit, returns, etc., are subtracted to give a net contribution to overheads and profit. Often the figure that emerges as the 'bottom line' can be revealing as shown, in Table 3.2.

Table 3.2 Analysis of revenue and cost for a specific customer

	£	£
Gross sales value		100,000
Less Discount	10,000	
Net sales value		90,000
Less Direct cost of goods sold	20,000	
Gross contribution		70,000
Less Sales and marketing costs:		
Sales calls	3,000	
Co-operative promotions	1,000	
Merchandising	3,000	
	7,000	
		63,000
Less Distribution costs:		
Order processing	500	
Storage and handling	600	
Inventory financing	700	
Transport	2,000	
Packaging	300	
Refusals	500	
	4,600	
Customer gross contribution		58,400
Less Other customer-related costs:		
Credit financing	1,500	
Returns	500	
	2,000	
Customer net contribution		56,400

Figure 3.11 Customer profitability analysis: a basic model

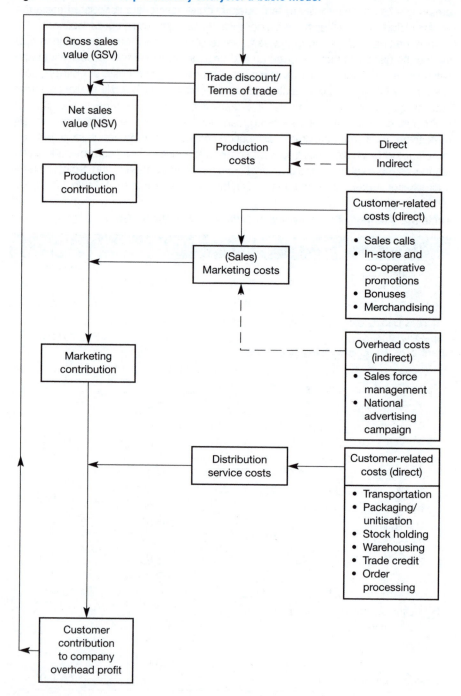

Source: Gattorna, J.L. and Walters, D.W., *Managing the Supply Chain: A Strategic Perspective*, Macmillan Press, 1996

In this case a gross contribution of £70,000 becomes a net contribution of £56,400 as soon as the costs unique to this customer are taken into account. If the analysis were to be extended by attempting to allocate overheads (a step not to be advised because of the problems usually associated with such allocation), what might at first seem to be a profitable customer could be deemed to be the reverse. However, as long as the net contribution is positive and there is no 'opportunity cost' in servicing that customer the company would be better off with the business than without it.

The value of this type of exercise can be substantial. The information could be used, firstly, when the next sales contract is negotiated and, secondly, as the basis for sales and marketing strategy in directing effort away from less profitable types of account towards more profitable business. More importantly it can point the way to alternative strategies for managing customers with high servicing costs. Ideally we require all our customers to be profitable in the medium to long term and where customers currently are profitable we should seek to build and extend that profitability further.

Figure 3.12 represents a simple categorisation of customers along two dimensions: their total net sales value during the period and their cost-to-serve. The suggestion is that there could be a benefit in developing customer-specific solutions depending upon which box of the matrix they fall into. Possible strategies for each of the quadrants are suggested below.

Figure 3.12 Customer profitability matrix

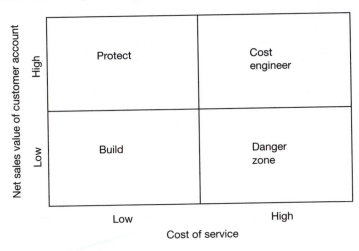

Build

These customers are relatively cheap to service but their net sales value is low. Can volume be increased without a proportionate increase in the costs of service? Can our sales team be directed to seek to influence these customers' purchases towards a more profitable sales mix?

Danger zone

These customers should be looked at very carefully. Is there any medium- to long-term prospect either of improving net sales value or of reducing the costs of service? Is there a strategic reason for keeping them? Do we need them for their volume even if their profit contribution is low?

Cost engineer

These customers could be more profitable if the costs of servicing them could be reduced. Is there any scope for increasing drop sizes? Can deliveries be consolidated? If new accounts in the same geographic area were developed would it make delivery more economic? Is there a cheaper way of gathering orders from these customers, e.g. the Internet?

Protect

The high net sales value customers who are relatively cheap to service are worth their weight in gold. The strategy for these customers should be to seek relationships which make the customer less likely to want to look for alternative suppliers. At the same time we should constantly seek opportunities to develop the volume of business that we do with them whilst keeping strict control of costs.

Ideally the organisation should seek to develop an accounting system that would routinely collect and analyse data on customer profitability. Unfortunately most accounting systems are product focused rather than customer focused. Likewise cost reporting is traditionally on a functional basis rather than a customer basis. So, for example, we know the costs of the transport function as a whole or the costs of making a particular product but what we do not know are the costs of delivering a specific mix of products to a particular customer.

There is a pressing need for companies to move towards a system of accounting for customers and market segments as well as accounting for products. As has often been observed, it is customers who make profits, not products!

Direct product profitability

An application of logistics cost analysis that has gained widespread acceptance, particularly in the retail industry, is a technique known as direct product profitability – or more simply 'DPP'. In essence it is somewhat analogous to customer profitability analysis in that it attempts to identify all the costs that attach to a product or an order as it moves through the distribution channel.

The idea behind DPP is that in many transactions the customer will incur costs other than the immediate purchase price of the product. Often this is termed the *total cost of ownership*. Sometimes these costs will be hidden and often they can be substantial – certainly big enough to reduce or even eliminate net profit on a particular item.

For the supplier it is important to understand DPP inasmuch as his/her ability to be a low-cost supplier is clearly influenced by the costs that are incurred as that product moves through their logistics system. Similarly, as distributors and retailers are now very much more conscious of an item's DPP, it is to the advantage of the supplier equally to understand the cost drivers that impact upon DPP so as to seek to influence it favourably.

Table 3.3 describes the steps to be followed in moving from a crude gross margin measure to a more precise DPP.

Table 3.3 Direct product profit (DPP)

	The net profit contribution from the sales of a product after allowances are added and all costs that can be rationally allocated or assigned to an individual product are subtracted = direct product profit
	Sales
−	Cost of goods sold
=	Gross margin
+	Allowances and discounts
=	Adjusted gross margin
−	Warehouse costs 　　Labour (labour model – case, cube, weight) 　　Occupancy (space and cube) 　　Inventory (average inventory)
−	Transportation costs (cube)
−	Retail costs 　　Stocking labour 　　Front end labour 　　Occupancy 　　Inventory
=	Direct product profit

The importance to the supplier of DPP is based on the proposition that a key objective of customer service strategy is 'to reduce the customer's costs of ownership'. In other words the supplier should be looking at his products and asking the question: 'How can I favourably influence the DPP of my customers by changing either the characteristics of the products I sell, or the way I distribute them?'

From pack design onwards there are a number of elements that the manufacturer or supplier may be able to vary in order to influence DPP/square metre in a positive way, for example, changing the case size, increasing the delivery frequency, direct store deliveries, etc.

Cost drivers and activity-based costing

As we indicated earlier in this chapter there is a growing dissatisfaction with conventional cost accounting, particularly as it relates to logistics management. Essentially these problems can be summarised as follows:

- There is a general ignorance of the true costs of servicing different customer types/channels/market segments.
- Costs are captured at too high a level of aggregation.
- Full cost allocation still reigns supreme.
- Conventional accounting systems are functional in their orientation rather than output oriented.
- Companies understand product costs but not customer costs.

The common theme that links these points is that we seem to suffer in business from a lack of visibility of costs as they are incurred through the logistics pipeline. Ideally what logistics management requires is a means of capturing costs as products and orders flow towards the customer.

To overcome this problem it is necessary to change radically the basis of cost accounting away from the notion that all expenses must be allocated (often on an arbitrary basis) to individual units (such as products) and, instead, to separate the expenses and match them to the activities that consume the resources. One approach that can help overcome this problem is 'activity-based costing'.[9] The key to activity-based costing (ABC) is to seek out the 'cost drivers' along the logistics pipeline that cause costs because they consume resources. Thus, for example, if we are concerned to assign the costs of order picking to orders then in the past this may have been achieved by calculating an average cost per order. In fact an activity-based approach might suggest that it is the number of lines on an order that consume the order picking resource and hence should instead be seen as the cost driver.

The advantage of using activity-based costing is that it enables each customer's unique characteristics in terms of ordering behaviour and distribution requirements to be separately accounted for. Once the cost attached to each level of activity is identified (e.g. cost per line item picked, cost per delivery, etc.) then a clearer picture of the true cost-to-serve will emerge. Whilst ABC is still strictly a cost allocation method it uses a more logical basis for that allocation than traditional methods.

There are certain parallels between activity-based costing and the idea of *mission costing* introduced earlier in this chapter. Essentially mission costing seeks to identify the unique costs that are generated as a result of specific logistics/ customer service strategies aimed at targeted market segments. The aim is to establish a better matching of the service needs of the various markets that the company addresses with the inevitably limited resources of the company. There is little point in committing incremental costs where the incremental benefits do not justify the expenditure.

There are four stages in the implementation of an effective mission costing process:

1 *Define the customer service segment*

Use the methodology described in Chapter 2 to identify the different service needs of different customer types. The basic principle is that because not all customers share the same service requirements and characteristics they should be treated differently.

2 *Identify the factors that produce variations in the cost of service*

This step involves the determination of the service elements that will directly or indirectly impact upon the costs of service, e.g. the product mix, the delivery characteristics such as drop size and frequency or incidence of direct deliveries, merchandising support, special packs and so on.

3 *Identify the specific resources used to support customer segments*

This is the point at which the principles of activity-based costing and mission costing coincide. The basic tenet of ABC is that the activities that generate cost should be defined and the specific cost drivers involved identified. These may be the number of lines on an order, the people involved, the inventory support or the delivery frequency.

4 *Attribute activity costs by customer type or segment*

Using the principle of 'avoidability' the incremental costs incurred through the application of a specific resource to meeting service needs are attributed to customers. It must be emphasised that this is not cost allocation but cost attribution. In other words it is because customers use resources that the appropriate share of cost is attributed to them.

Clearly to make this work there is a prerequisite that the cost coding system in the business be restructured. In other words, the coding system must be capable of gathering costs as they are incurred by customers from the point of order generation through to final delivery, invoicing and collection.

The basic purpose of logistics cost analysis is to provide managers with reliable information that will enable a better allocation of resources to be achieved. Given that the purpose of logistics and supply chain management, as we have observed, ultimately is concerned to meet customer service requirements in the most cost-effective way, then it is essential that those responsible have the most accurate and meaningful data possible.

References

1. *State of Logistics Report,* Council for Supply Chain Management Professionals. (Annually)
2. Stewart, G.B., *The Quest for Value*, Harper Business, 1991 (EVA is a registered trademark of Stern Stewart & Co.).
3. Buffet, W., *Annual Report*, Berkshire Hathaway Corporation, 1994.
4. Srivastava, R. *et al.*, 'Market-based assets and shareholder value: a framework for analysis', *Journal of Marketing,* Vol. 62, No. 1, January 1998,
5. *Creating and Sustaining the High-Performance Business*, Accenture, 2003.

6. O'Marah, K. and Hofman, D., 'Top 25 supply chains', *Supply Chain Management Review*, October 2009.
7. Johnson, H.T. and Kaplan, R.S., *Relevance Lost: The Rise and Fall of Management Accounting,* Harvard Business School Press, 1987.
8. Shillinglow, G., 'The concept of attributable cost', *Journal of Accounting Research*, Vol. 1, No. 1, Spring 1963.
9. Cooper, R. and Kaplan, R.S., 'Profit priorities from activity-based costing', *Harvard Business Review,* May–June 1991.

Matching supply and demand

- The lead-time gap

- Improving the visibility of demand

- The supply chain fulcrum

- Forecast for capacity, execute against demand

- Demand management and planning

- Collaborative planning, forecasting and replenishment

Reduced to its basic essence, the goal of supply chain management is very simple – to try to match supply and demand. However, what makes this seemingly simple task so difficult in reality is the presence of uncertainty. In other words, for most organisations, on both the supply side and the demand side, there can be no certainty what tomorrow will bring. This uncertainty brings with it a serious challenge to the classic practice of running a business on the basis of a forecast. The levels of volatility and turbulence that typify today's business environment add to the problem. It will be apparent that in conditions of stability – and hence lower uncertainty – forecast accuracy should generally be high. Equally the converse will be true, i.e. as uncertainty increases so too will the forecast accuracy reduce.

All forecasts are prone to error and the further ahead the forecast horizon is, the greater the error. Figure 4.1 shows how forecast error increases more than proportionally over time.

The lead-time gap

Most organisations face a fundamental problem: the time it takes to procure, make and deliver the finished product to a customer is longer than the time the customer is prepared to wait for it.

This is the basis of the lead-time gap. Figure 4.2 highlights the problem.

Figure 4.1 Forecast error and planning horizons

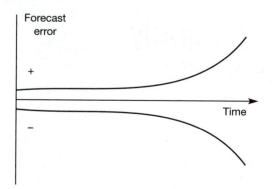

Figure 4.2 The lead-time gap

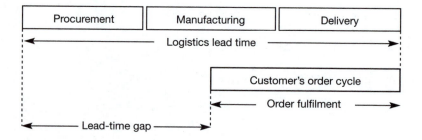

The customer's order cycle refers to the length of time that the customer is prepared to wait, from when the order is placed through to when the goods are received. This is the maximum period available for order fulfilment. In some cases this may be measured in months but in others it is measured in hours.

Clearly the competitive conditions of the market as well as the nature of the product will influence the customer's willingness to wait. Thus a customer may be willing to wait a few weeks for the delivery of a car with particular options but only a day for a new set of tyres.

In the conventional organisation the only way to bridge the gap between the logistics lead time (i.e. the time taken to complete the process from goods inwards to delivered product) and the customer's order cycle (i.e. the period they are prepared to wait for delivery) is by carrying inventory. This normally implies a forecast. Hence, the way most companies address this problem is by seeking to forecast the market's requirements and then to build inventory ahead of demand. Unfortunately all our experience suggests that no matter how sophisticated the forecast, its accuracy is always less than perfect. It has been suggested that all mistakes in forecasting end up as an inventory problem – whether too much or too little!

Whilst improving forecast accuracy will always be a desirable goal it may be that the answer to the problem lies not in investing ever greater sums of money and energy in improving forecasting techniques, but rather in reducing the lead-time gap.

The company that achieves a perfect match between the logistics lead time and the customer's required order cycle has no need of forecasts and no need for inventory.

The challenge for logistics management is to search for the means whereby the gap between the two lead times can be reduced if not closed (see Figure 4.3).

Figure 4.3  **Closing the lead-time gap**

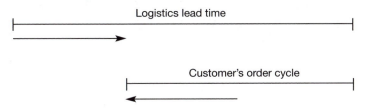

Reducing the gap can be achieved by shortening the logistics lead time (end-to-end pipeline time) whilst simultaneously trying to move the customer's order cycle closer by gaining earlier warning of requirements through improved visibility of demand.

Improving the visibility of demand

In many cases companies have an inadequate 'visibility' of real demand. By 'real' demand we mean the demand in the final marketplace, not the 'derived' demand that is filtered upstream through any intermediary organisations that may lie between the company and the final user. The challenge is to find a way to receive earlier warning of the customers' requirements. What we frequently find is that, firstly, the *demand penetration point* is too far down the pipeline and, secondly, real demand is hidden from view and all we tend to see are orders. Both these points need further explanation; we will deal with the concept of the demand penetration point first.

The simplest definition of the demand penetration point is that it occurs at that point in the logistics chain where real demand meets the plan. Upstream from this point everything is driven by a forecast and/or a plan. Downstream we can respond to customer demand. Clearly in an ideal world we would like everything to be demand-driven so that nothing is purchased, manufactured or shipped unless there is a known requirement. The demand penetration point is often referred to as the *decoupling point* and is ideally the point in the supply chain where strategic inventory is held.

A key concern of logistics management should be to seek to identify ways in which the demand penetration point can be pushed as far as possible upstream. This might be achieved by the use of information so that manufacturing and purchasing get to hear of what is happening in the marketplace faster than they currently do. Figure 4.4 illustrates a range of possible demand penetration points in different industrial and market contexts. The inverted triangles represent the strategic inventory that is held at that point, preferably in as 'generic' a form as possible.

Figure 4.4 Demand penetration points and strategic inventory

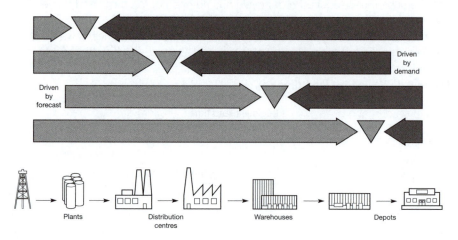

Perhaps the greatest opportunity for extending the customer's order cycle is by gaining earlier notice of their requirements. In so many cases the supplying company receives no indication of the customer's actual usage until an order arrives. For example, the customer may be using 10 items a day but because he/she orders only intermittently the supplier sometimes receives an order for 100, sometimes for 150 and sometimes for 200. If the supplier could receive 'feed-forward' on what was being consumed he would anticipate the customer's requirement and better schedule his own logistics activities.

In a sense, the information we receive, if we only have the order to rely on, is like the tip of an iceberg. Only a small proportion of the total iceberg is visible above the surface. Likewise the order cycle time (i.e. the required response time from order to delivery) may only be the visible tip of the 'information iceberg' (see Figure 4.5).

Figure 4.5 The information iceberg

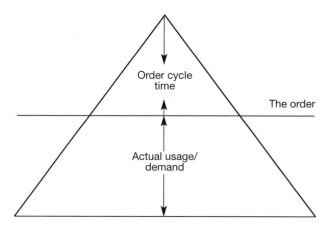

The area below the surface of the iceberg represents the on-going consumption, demand or usage of the product which is hidden from the view of the supplier. It is only when an order is issued that any visibility of demand becomes transparent.

There are now signs that buyers and suppliers are recognising the opportunities for mutual advantage if information on requirements can be shared on a continuing basis. If the supplier can see right to the end of the pipeline then the logistics system can become much more responsive to actual demand. Thus, whilst the customer will still require ever swifter delivery, if an on-going feed-forward of information on demand or usage can be established there is a greater chance that the service to the customer will be enhanced and the supplier's costs reduced.

This twin-pronged approach of simultaneously seeking to reduce the logistics lead time whilst extending the customer's order cycle may never completely close the lead-time gap. However, the experience of a growing number of companies is that substantial improvements can be made both in responsiveness and in the early capture of information on demand – the end result of which is better customer service at lower cost.

The supply chain fulcrum

As we have previously noted, the purpose of the supply chain is to balance supply and demand. Traditionally, this has been achieved through forecasting ahead of demand and creating inventory against that forecast. Alternatively additional capacity might be maintained to cope if demand turned out to be greater than forecast. In this context 'capacity' refers to the ability to access supply not currently held as inventory. Either way demand is balanced with supply. Figure 4.6(a) below illustrates a balance with the box marked 'D' representing demand and the boxes 'I' and 'C' representing inventory and capacity respectively. In other words there must be enough capacity and/or inventory to meet anticipated demand.

Figure 4.6(a)

Now imagine that the fulcrum is moved closer to the box marked 'D' as in Figure 4.6(b) below. Obviously the same amount of demand can be balanced with less inventory and/or less capacity.

Figure 4.6(b)

What does the fulcrum represent in a supply chain? The fulcrum is the point at which we commit to source/produce/ship the product in its final form and where decisions on volume and mix are made. The idea being that if that point of commitment can be delayed as long as possible then the closer we are to make-to-order, with all the benefits that brings.

The problem for many companies is that the fulcrum in their supply chains is more like that shown in Figure 4.6(c) below.

Figure 4.6(c)

Here the fulcrum is a long way from demand, i.e. the forecasting horizon is long, necessitating more inventory and capacity to balance against demand.

How in reality do we move the fulcrum closer to demand? The answer in effect is to improve the *visibility* of demand along with enhancing the *velocity* of the supply chain. In other words if we can have a clearer view of real demand in the final marketplace, rather than the distorted picture that more typically is the case, and if we can respond more rapidly, then a more effective matching of supply and demand can be achieved.

Thus it can be argued that visibility and velocity are the foundations for a responsive supply chain.

Figure 4.7 indicates some of the key drivers of velocity and visibility in a supply chain and these will be discussed in later chapters.

Figure 4.7 Velocity and visibility drive responsiveness

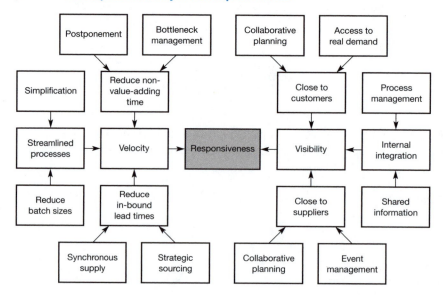

Forecast for capacity, execute against demand

We have already made the point that in today's volatile business environment it is much harder to achieve high levels of forecast accuracy for individual items. Whilst managers will always be seeking better forecasts, the fact is that as uncertainty increases it gets harder to run a business on the basis of forecast demand at the stock keeping unit (SKU) level. Instead the focus has to be on how the company can move from a forecast-driven to a demand-driven mentality. Basically what this means is that ways have to be found to make it possible to react to demand within the customer's order cycle. Thus if the customer's expectation is for a five-day lead time from order to delivery, the goal is to be able to respond within that lead time.

Whilst forecasts will always be required, the argument is that what we should be forecasting is not at the individual item level but rather for aggregate volume to enable the company to plan for the capacity and the resources that will be required to produce that volume.

To enable this goal to be achieved will require a radical re-think of conventional ways of balancing supply and demand. In particular it highlights the importance of the 'de-coupling point' idea introduced earlier in this chapter. If it is possible to add 'generic' inventory at that point (which we might term 'strategic inventory'), this will facilitate the late configuration or even manufacture of the product against a customer's specific requirements. Thus at Zara, for example, the generic strategic inventory is the un-dyed fabric. When the market requirement is known, that is when the final garment is manufactured – making use of Zara's flexible sewing capacity provided by their network of small, independent workshops. So at Zara the forecast is for the resources and the materials, not for the final garment. In many ways Zara is an exemplar of the concept of 'forecast for capacity, execute against demand'.

Demand management and planning

In the past 'demand' was often seen as a given and the business must react to it as best it could with only a less-than-accurate sales forecast to help it do so. Today the best run companies are taking a more proactive stance. They recognise that not only do the actions of the business impact demand (e.g. new product launches, sales promotions, advertising campaigns, etc.), but also that even market volatility can be coped with if the appropriate supply chain planning processes are in place. *Demand management* is the term that has come to be used to describe the various tools and procedures that enable a more effective balancing of supply and demand to be achieved through a deeper understanding of the causes of demand volatility. *Demand planning* is the translation of our understanding of what the real requirement of the market is into a fulfilment programme, i.e. making sure that products can be made available at the right times and place. Many companies today have put in place a formalised approach to demand management and planning that is often referred to as *sales and operations planning* (S&OP).

S&OP seeks to ensure that the organisation is able to anticipate the real requirement of the market and to react in the most cost-effective way. The aim is to ensure the highest level of customer satisfaction through on-time, in-full deliveries with minimum inventory.

There are a number of pre-requisites for successful S&OP and these are summarised in Figure 4.8.

Figure 4.8 The sales and operations planning process

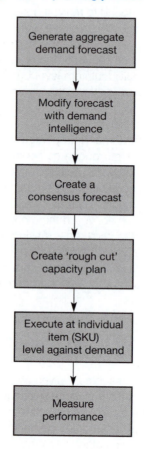

1 Generate aggregate demand forecast

Part of the reason that so many forecasts have so little accuracy is that they try to achieve the impossible, i.e. to forecast at the individual item level (SKU) too far ahead. Clearly every business needs to plan ahead in order to ensure that they have access to enough capacity and materials. However, wherever possible these plans should be made on the basis of high-level aggregate *volume* forecasts at the product family level. As we get closer to the point of demand fulfilment then we can start to think about product *mix* requirements.

Because it is generally easier to forecast at the aggregate level, statistical forecasting tools should enable a reasonable level of accuracy to be achieved. Thus a company manufacturing a product that will be sold in many markets around the world will find it easy to forecast and plan on the basis of projected global demand rather than have to forecast for individual customers in individual countries – that will come later.

2 Modify the forecast with demand intelligence

Because the stage 1 forecast was based upon a statistical projection using past data, it may be necessary to modify it utilising specific intelligence on current market conditions and events. Thus, for example, there may be information about a planned competitive product launch that could affect our sales, or there is a change planned for the price of the product which could impact sales and so on.

Ideally, this stage of the S&OP process should involve key customers or accounts. Later we will discuss the benefits of moving towards a collaborative approach to forecasting and supply chain planning. The benefit of a joint supplier/customer process to create a forecast is that a wider array of intelligence can be taken into account.

3 Create a consensus forecast

At the heart of the S&OP process is the use of a cross-functional approach to achieving a balance between supply and demand. Whilst the process may be different from one company to the next, essentially the principle is that marketing and sales people will meet at regular intervals with operations and supply chain people. The former will present their modified sales forecast from stage 2 and the latter will detail any constraints that might curtail the achievement of that forecast, e.g. capacity issues, supply shortages, etc.

These meetings will also provide the opportunity to look ahead, to recognise the future impact of current trends and to plan for promotion and new product introductions.

Figure 4.9 highlights the integrative nature of S&OP processes. Whereas in conventional businesses there is little integration between the demand creation side of the business (i.e. sales and marketing) with the demand fulfilment activity (i.e. logistics and operations), with the S&OP philosophy there is a seamless alignment between the two.

4 Create a 'rough cut' capacity plan

To ensure that there is enough capacity and resources available to achieve the consensus forecast it is necessary to produce a 'rough cut' capacity plan – otherwise known as a resource plan. Essentially the logic behind the rough cut capacity plan is to look at the aggregate product family forecast for the planning period and to translate that into the capacity and resources needed, e.g. how much machine time, how much time in an assembly process, how much transport capacity and so on.

Figure 4.9 The focus of demand management and planning

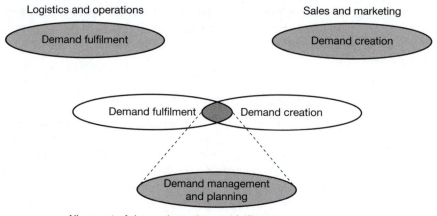

Alignment of demand creation and fulfilment processes across
functional and organisational boundaries

A similar approach should be used to calculate the requirements for materials and supplies to enable arrangements with vendors to be put in place.

If the result of this rough cut planning activity is that there is not enough capacity, resources or material to achieve the aggregate forecast then either demand has to be 'managed', e.g. delivery lead times re-negotiated, prices adjusted to reduce demand, etc, or additional capacity has to be found – possibly by using external providers.

Since this is still an aggregate, probably medium-term, exercise there is room for adjustment as we get closer to real demand.

5 Execute at SKU levels against demand

As we get closer to real demand then clearly the plan has become much more detailed. Ideally nothing is finally assembled, configured or packaged until we know what the customer's order specifies. To achieve this ideal state clearly requires a high level of agility – a challenge that will be addressed in Chapter 5. Even if the customer's required delivery lead time is less than the time we need to make/source and deliver and we have to make inventory ahead of time, at least the forecast will be more accurate since the forecast horizon is closer.

A further enabler of more accurate forecasts is visibility of real demand. We have earlier commented on the difficulty that many companies have in seeing what is happening in the final marketplace (real demand) – particularly the further upstream in the supply chain they are. The prizes to be gained through a greater degree of information sharing in the supply chain are significant, which perhaps make it all the more surprising that only slow progress is being made in this direction.

6 Measure performance

The real test of how well a demand management/planning process is working should be how high the percentage of perfect order achievement is compared to the number of days of inventory and the amount of capacity needed to achieve that level.

The accuracy of short term statistical forecasts can be easily measured but since the goal of the S&OP system is to reduce the dependency on the forecast we should also measure the lead-time gap at the individual item level. The aim should be to progressively reduce this gap by a concerted focus on time compression and improved visibility.

One of the exemplars of world class demand management and planning is Dell Inc., the computer company. Their ability to offer high levels of product availability with minimal inventory has given then a leadership position in many markets (see box below).

Demand management and planning at Dell

The computer company Dell has long been seen as one of the most agile businesses in the industry. The success of Dell is in large part due to its highly responsive supply chain, which is capable of building and delivering customised products in a matter of days with minimal inventory.

Dell's ability to operate a build-to-order strategy is based partly on the modular design of many of their products but more particularly on a very high level of synchronisation with their suppliers. There is a high level of visibility across the Dell supply chain with suppliers receiving information on Dell's order book every two hours. Ahead of this information, suppliers are provided with capacity forecasts from Dell to enable them to produce at a rate that is planned to match actual demand.

Each of Dell's factories is served from a 'vendor hub', operated by third-party logistics service providers, the purpose of which is to keep a buffer of inventory from which Dell can draw as required. Suppliers are required to keep a defined level of inventory at these hubs and Dell only takes ownership of the inventory when it reaches their factories.

Dell adopts a very proactive approach to demand management by using the price mechanism to regulate demand for specific products or features. If a product is in short supply the price will rise and/or the price of an alternative substitute product will fall. This facility to actively manage demand enables a very close matching of supply and demand.

Collaborative planning, forecasting and replenishment

Over the last 25 years or so, a number of breakthroughs have occurred in collaborative working in supply chains. Many of these initiatives have originated in the retail sector but the ideas have universal application. The underpinning logic of all these collaborative initiatives has been the idea that through sharing information and by working together to create joint plans and forecasts, both the supply side and the demand side of the supply chain can benefit.

Collaborative planning, forecasting and replenishment (CPFR) is the name given to a partnership-based approach to managing the buyer/supplier interfaces across the supply chain. The idea is a development of vendor managed inventory (VMI). VMI is a process through which the supplier rather than the customer manages the flow of product into the customer's operations. This flow is driven by frequent exchanges of information about the actual off-take or usage of the product by the customer. With this information the supplier is able to take account of current inventories at each level in the chain, as well as goods in transit, when determining what quantity to ship and when to ship it. The supplier is in effect managing the customer's inventory on the customer's behalf. In a VMI environment there are no customer orders; instead the supplier makes decisions on shipping quantities based upon the information it receives direct from the point-of-use or the point-of-sale, or more usually from off-take data at the customer's distribution centre. The supplier can use this information to forecast future requirements and hence to utilise their own production and logistics capacity better.

Under conventional replenishment systems both sides need to carry safety stock as a buffer against the uncertainty that is inevitable when there is no visibility or exchange of information. With VMI the need to carry safety stock is greatly reduced as a result of 'substituting information for inventory'.

CPFR is in effect an extension of VMI in that it takes the idea of collaboration amongst supply chain partners a step further. Underpinning CPFR is the creation of an agreed framework for how information will be shared between partners and how decisions on replenishment will be taken. A key element of CPFR is the generation of a joint forecast which is agreed and signed off by both the supplier and the customer.

Figure 4.10 presents a nine-step model for the implementation of CPFR programmes developed by the US-based organisation VICS (Voluntary Inter-Industry Commerce Standards).

Whilst many of the early CPFR pilot implementation exercises were in retail environments, there is no doubt that these principles can be applied successfully in most industries. A study by Accenture[1] highlights a number of significant benefits that can flow from successful CPFR (see box below).

Figure 4.10 VICS-ECR nine-step CPFR model

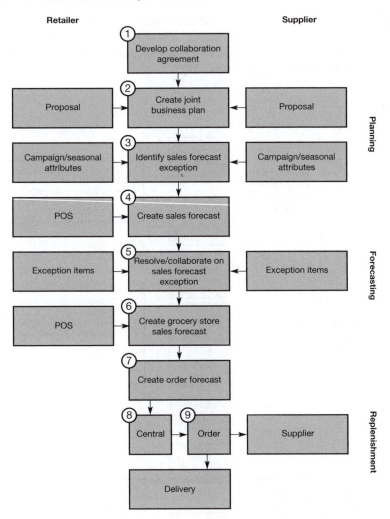

Source: ECR Europe/Accenture, *European CPFR Insights*, 2002

Benefits of CPFR Until now, most CPFR initiatives focused on reducing variable costs, such as decreasing inventory levels. However, there are further benefits to be gained for companies that integrate CPFR into their standard operational procedure and scale to critical mass (see Figure 4.11).

Figure 4.11

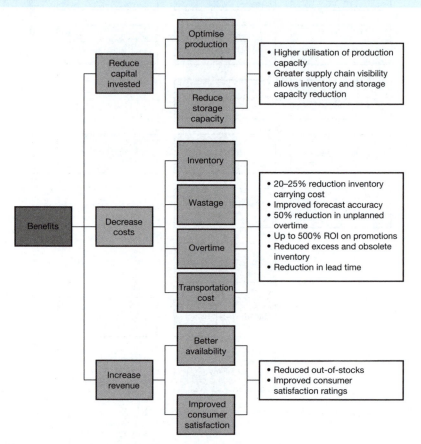

- *Reduce capital investment*
  Companies reaching critical mass with their CPFR initiatives may also harvest additional benefits from a reduction in capital investment. Reducing warehousing capacity is possible for the collaboration partners in the long term through the increased supply chain visibility and a reduction in uncertainty. Increased forecast accuracy alongside collaborative long-term planning reduces the need to build up inventories or production capacity to cover unexpected changes in demand.

- *Decrease cost of goods sold*
  The results from the pilots have shown that CPFR can significantly impact the cost of goods sold. In particular, reductions in inventory, product obsoletes, changeover times and transportation costs can be achieved. Based on an improved forecast accuracy and long-term planning, trading partners are able to reduce inventory levels along the supply chain, stabilise production runs, improve truck fill rates and reduce obsoletes after promotions.

- *Increase sales revenue*
  Reducing the incidence of out-of-stocks at the point of sale (increase in on-shelf availability) improves the service to the consumer and reduces lost sales. Furthermore, the continued availability of the products increases consumer satisfaction and therefore benefits store loyalty for the retailer and the product loyalty for the manufacturer.

SOURCE: ACCENTURE ECR EUROPE

Reference

1. Accenture/ECR Europe, *European CPFR Insight*, ECR Europe, Brussels, 2000.

Creating the responsive supply chain

5

- Product 'push' versus demand 'pull'

- The Japanese philosophy

- The foundations of agility

- A routemap to responsiveness

One of the biggest challenges facing organisations today is the need to respond to ever increasing levels of volatility in demand. For a variety of reasons product and technology life cycles are shortening, competitive pressures force more frequent product changes and consumers demand greater variety than ever before.

To meet this challenge the organisation needs to focus its efforts upon achieving greater agility such that it can respond in shorter time-frames both in terms of volume change and variety change. In other words it needs to be able to adjust output quickly to match market demand and to switch rapidly from one variant to another. To a truly agile business volatility of demand is not a problem; its processes and organisational structure as well as its supply chain relationships enable it to cope with whatever demands are placed upon it.

Agility in the sense of the ability to match supply with demand is not necessarily synonymous with 'leanness'. Much has been written about lean manufacturing – often with reference to the automobile industry.[1] The lean approach to manufacturing seeks to minimise inventory of components and work-in-progress and to move towards a 'just-in-time' environment wherever possible. However, while 'leanness' may be an element of 'agility' in certain circumstances, by itself it will not enable the organisation to meet the precise needs of the customer more rapidly. Indeed it could be argued that, at least until recently, the automobile industry, for all its leanness, is one of the least agile industries around. *Webster's Dictionary* makes the distinction clearly when it defines lean as 'containing little fat', whereas agile is defined as 'nimble'.

Agility has many dimensions and the concept applies as much to networks as it does to individual companies. Indeed a key to agile response is the presence of agile partners upstream and downstream of the focal firm. Whilst organisations may have internal processes that are capable of rapid response, their agility will still be constrained if they face long replenishment lead times from suppliers, for example.

Agility, as we have said, is not synonymous with 'leanness' but it can build upon it. Leanness in a sense is about doing more with less. It owes its origins to the Toyota Production System (TPS) and its pre-occupation with the reduction or elimination of waste (*muda*).[2] Lean manufacturing is characterised by 'level schedules', i.e. a forward plan to ensure that the use of resources is optimised.

The backdrop against which lean thinking originated was the Japanese automobile industry of the 1970s. This was an industrial context typified by the volume manufacture of relatively standard products (i.e. low levels of variety) and a focus on achieving efficiencies in the use of resources and in maximising economies of scale. In this type of situation, i.e. standard products and relatively predictable demand, experience has shown that lean practices work well.

However, in market environments where demand is uncertain, the levels of variety are high and consequently volume per stock keeping unit (SKU) is low, then a different response is required. Whilst efficiency is always desirable, in the context of unpredictable demand it may have to take second place to 'effectiveness' as the main priority for supply chain management. By effectiveness in this context is meant the ability to respond rapidly to meet the precise needs of an often fragmented marketplace. In other words, rather than the emphasis being on producing standard products for mass markets ahead of demand, the requirement becomes one of producing multiple product variants (often customised) for much smaller market segments in response to known demand.

Figure 5.1 reflects the different contexts in which the 'lean' and 'agile' paradigms might work best.

Figure 5.1 Agile or lean?

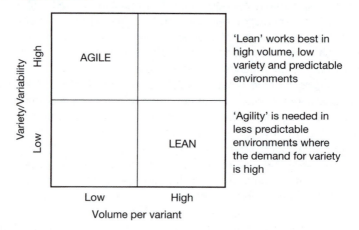

In reality, within the same business it is likely that there will exist the need for both lean and agile supply chain solutions since some products will have predictable demand whilst for others demand will be far more volatile. In fact it can be argued that rather than the conventional 'one size fits all' strategy for supply chain design, the need today is for multiple supply chain solutions. One way to identify what types of supply chain strategies might be appropriate in different circumstances is to position the products in an organisation's portfolio according to their supply and demand characteristics.

By 'supply characteristic' is meant the lead time of replenishment. This could be replenishment of the product itself if it is bought in (e.g. a retailer) or of components in the case of a manufacturer. Clearly, if replenishment lead times are short then a different supply chain strategy can be employed than when lead times are long.

Demand conditions may be characterised by the predictability of demand. One measure of demand predictability is the variability of demand; by definition demand that does not vary much from one period to another is easier to predict.

Figure 5.2 suggests four broad generic supply chains strategies dependent upon the combination of supply/demand conditions for each product.

Figure 5.2 Generic supply chain strategies

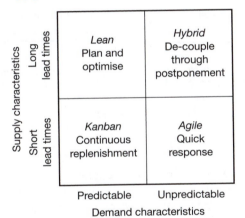

In those cases where demand is predictable and replenishment lead times are short, then a 'Kanban' type of solution is indicated. This is a philosophy of continuous replenishment where, at its extreme, as each product is sold or used it is replaced.

In the top left-hand box where lead times are long but demand is predictable then a 'lean' type approach will be appropriate. Materials, components or products can be ordered ahead of demand and manufacturing and transportation facilities can be optimised in terms of cost and asset utilisation. Conversely the bottom right-hand corner is the real domain of the agile supply chain. Here demand is unpredictable but lead times are short, enabling 'quick response' type solutions – the extreme case being make-to-order (but in very short time-frames).

The top right-hand corner presents an interesting situation: lead times are long and demand is unpredictable. In situations such as this, the first priority should be to seek to reduce lead times since the variability of demand is almost certainly outside the organisation's control. Lead-time reduction would enable the application of agile solutions. However, if lead times cannot be reduced the next option is to seek to create a hybrid lean/agile solution. These hybrid solutions require the supply chain to be 'de-coupled' through holding strategic inventory in some generic or unfinished form, with final configuration being completed rapidly once real demand is known. This is the classic 'postponement' strategy. An alternative form of postponement where the final physical configuration cannot be delayed is to postpone the actual distribution of the product by holding it in fewer (or even only one) locations and using express transportation to move it to the final market or point-of-use once actual demand is known.

The goal of a hybrid (or 'leagile' as it is sometimes termed) strategy should be to build an agile response upon a lean platform by seeking to follow lean principles up to the de-coupling point and agile practices after that point.[3] Figure 5.3 illustrates this idea.

Figure 5.3 The de-coupling point

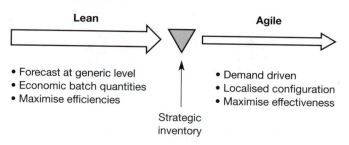

• Forecast at generic level
• Economic batch quantities
• Maximise efficiencies

Strategic inventory

• Demand driven
• Localised configuration
• Maximise effectiveness

A good example of a de-coupling point enabling a lean/agile hybrid strategy is provided by the paint industry. Today, consumers can be offered customised solutions in terms of the colour of paint through the use of paint mixing machines located in retail outlets. The retailers only need to stock a relatively small number of base colours to provide an almost infinite number of final colours. Thus the paint manufacturer can utilise lean processes in producing base colours in volume but can provide an agile and timely response to end users. This example also illustrates the principle of seeking to reduce *complexity* whilst providing the requisite level of *variety* that the market demands.

To be truly agile a supply chain must possess a number of distinguishing characteristics, as Figure 5.4 suggests.

Firstly, the agile supply chain is *market-sensitive*. By market-sensitive is meant that the supply chain is capable of reading and responding to real demand. Most organisations are forecast-driven rather than demand-driven. In other words, because they have little direct feed-forward from the marketplace by way of data on actual customer requirements, they are forced to make forecasts based upon past sales or shipments and convert these forecasts into inventory. The break-throughs of the last decade in the use of information technology to capture data on demand direct from the point-of-sale or point-of-use are now transforming the organisation's ability to hear the voice of the market and to respond directly to it.

Figure 5.4 The agile supply chain

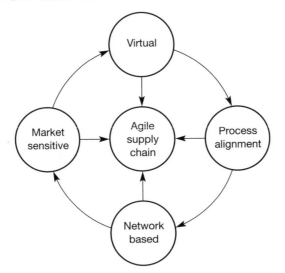

Source: Adapted from Harrison, A., Christopher, M. and van Hoek, R., *Creating the Agile Supply Chain*, Chartered Institute of Logistics and Transport, 1999

The use of information technology to share data between buyers and suppliers is, in effect, creating a *virtual* supply chain. Virtual supply chains are information based rather than inventory based.

Conventional logistics systems are based upon a paradigm that seeks to identify the optimal quantities and the spatial location of inventory. Complex for-mulae and algorithms exist to support this inventory-based business model. Paradoxically, what we are now learning is that once we have visibility of demand through shared information, the premise upon which these formulae are based no longer holds. Electronic Data Interchange (EDI) and now the Internet have enabled partners in the supply chain to act upon the same data, i.e. real demand, rather than be dependent upon the distorted and noisy picture that emerges when orders are transmitted from one step to another in an extended chain.

Supply chain partners can only make full use of shared information through *process alignment*, i.e. collaborative working between buyers and suppliers, joint product development, common systems and shared information. This form of co-operation in the supply chain is becoming ever more prevalent as companies focus on managing their core competencies and outsource all other activities. In this new world a greater reliance on suppliers and alliance partners becomes inevitable and, hence, a new style of relationship is essential. In the 'extended enterprise', as it is often called, there can be no boundaries and an ethos of trust and commitment must prevail. Along with process integration comes joint strategy determination, buyer/supplier teams, transparency of information and even open-book accounting.

This idea of the supply chain as a confederation of partners linked together as a *network* provides the fourth ingredient of agility. There is a growing recognition that individual businesses no longer compete as stand-alone entities but rather as supply chains. Managing networks calls for an entirely difference model than the conventional 'arm's-length' approach to managing customer and supplier relation-ships. Clearly a much higher level of collaboration and synchronisation is required if the network is to be truly agile. It can be argued that, in today's challenging global markets, the route to sustainable advantage lies in being able to make best use of the respective strengths and competencies of network partners to achieve greater responsiveness to market needs.

Product 'push' versus demand 'pull'

There have been many new ideas and concepts in business management over the last 30 or so years, some of which have endured and others soon discarded. However, perhaps one of the most significant principles to become widely adopted and practised is that of just-in-time. Just-in-time, or JIT, is a philosophy as much as it is a technique. It is based upon the simple idea that wherever possible no activity should take place in a system until there is a need for it.

Thus no products should be made, no components ordered, until there is a downstream requirement. Essentially JIT is a 'pull' concept, where demand at the end of the pipeline pulls products towards the market and behind those products the flow of components is also determined by that same demand. This contrasts with the traditional 'push' system where products are manufactured or assembled in batches in anticipation of demand and are positioned in the supply chain as 'buffers' between the various functions and entities (see Figure 5.5).

The conventional approach to meeting customer requirements is based upon some form of statistical inventory control which typically might rely upon reordering when inventory levels fall to a certain predetermined point – the so-called reorder point (ROP).

Under this approach a reorder point or reorder level is predetermined based upon the expected length of the replenishment lead time (see Figure 5.6). The amount to be ordered may be based upon the economic order quantity (EOQ) for-mulation which balances the cost of holding inventory against the costs of placing replenishment orders.

Alternative methods include the regular review of stock levels with fixed intervals between orders when the amount to be ordered is determined with reference to a predetermined replenishment level, as in Figure 5.7.

Figure 5.5 'Push' versus 'pull' in the logistics chain

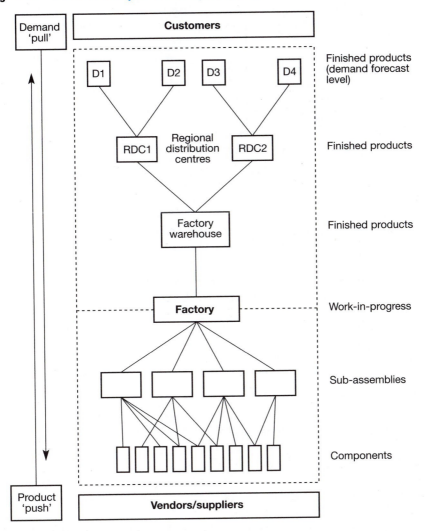

There are numerous variations on these themes and the techniques have been well documented and practised for many years. However, they all tend to share one weakness, that is they frequently lead to stock levels being higher or lower than necessary, particularly in those cases where the rate of demand may change or occurs in discrete 'lumps'. This latter situation frequently occurs when demand for an item is 'dependent' upon demand for another item, e.g. demand for a TV component is dependent upon the demand for TV sets; or where demand is 'derived', e.g. the demand for TV sets at the factory is determined by demand from the retailer, which is derived from ultimate demand in the marketplace.

Figure 5.6 The reorder point method of stock control

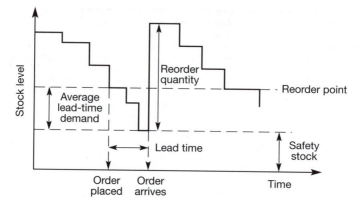

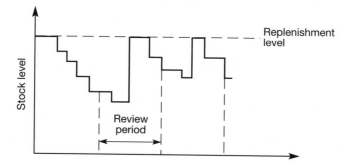

Figure 5.7 The review period method of stock control

The implications of dependent demand are illustrated in the example given in Figure 5.8, which shows how a regular off-take at the retail level can be converted into a much more 'lumpy' demand situation at the plant by the use of reorder points.

A similar situation can occur in a multi-level distribution system where the combined demand from each level is aggregated at the next level in the system. Figure 5.9 demonstrates such an occurrence.

The common feature of these examples is that demand at each level in the logistics system is dependent upon the demand at the next level in the system. Demand is termed 'dependent' when it is directly related to, or derives from, the demand for another inventory item or product. Conversely, the demand for a given item is termed 'independent' when such demand is unrelated to demand for other items – when it is not a function of demand for other items. This distinction is crucial because whilst independent demand may be forecast using traditional methods, dependent demand must be calculated, based upon the demand at the next level in the logistics chain.

Figure 5.8 Order point and dependent demand

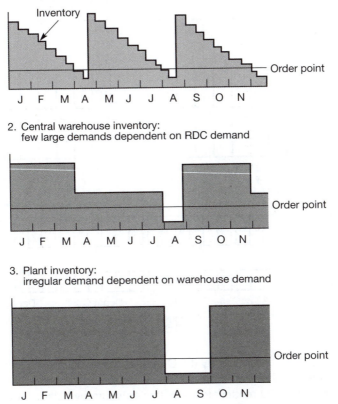

1. Regional distribution centre (RDC) inventory:
   many small independent demands from customers

   Inventory

   Order point

   J F M A M J J A S O N

2. Central warehouse inventory:
   few large demands dependent on RDC demand

   Order point

   J F M A M J J A S O N

3. Plant inventory:
   irregular demand dependent on warehouse demand

   Order point

   J F M A M J J A S O N

> Whilst independent demand may be forecast using traditional methods, dependent demand must be calculated, based upon the demand at the next level in the logistics chain.

Using the example in Figure 5.9 it would clearly be inappropriate to attempt to forecast demand at the factory using data based upon the pattern of combined demand from the regional centres. Rather it has to be calculated from the identified requirements at each of the preceding levels. It is only at the point of final demand, in this case at the depots, where forecasts can sensibly be made – in fact in most cases demand at the depot would itself be dependent upon retailers' or other intermediaries' demand, but since this is obviously outside the supplier's direct control it is necessary to produce a forecasted estimate of demand.

Figure 5.9 Causes of uneven demand at the plant

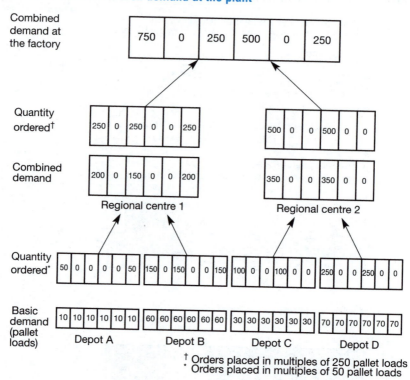

The classic economic order quantity (EOQ) model has tended to channel our thinking towards the idea that there is some 'optimum' amount to order (and hence to hold in stock). The EOQ model arrives at this optimum by balancing the holding cost of inventory against the cost of issuing replenishment orders and/or the costs of production set-ups (see Figure 5.10).

Figure 5.10 Determining the economic order quantity

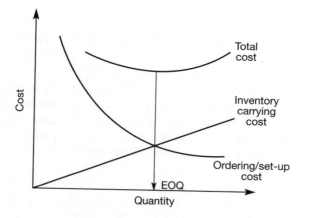

The EOQ can be easily determined by the formula:

$$EOQ = \sqrt{\frac{2AS}{i}}$$

where,

A = annual usage

S = ordering cost/set-up cost

i = inventory carrying cost

So, for example, if we use 1,000 units of product X a year, each costing £40, and each order/set-up costs £100 and the carrying cost of inventory is 25 per cent then:

$$EOQ = \sqrt{\frac{2 \times 1000 \times 100}{40 \times 0.25}} = 141$$

The problem is that this reorder quantity means that we will be carrying more inventory than is actually required per day over the complete order cycle (except on the last day). For example, if the EOQ were 100 units and daily usage was 10 units then on the first day of the cycle we will be overstocked by 90 units, on the second day by 80 units and so on.

To compound the problem we have additional inventory in the form of 'safety' stock, which is carried in order to provide a safeguard against demand during the replenishment lead time being greater than expected and/or variation in the lead time itself.

The result is that we end up with a lot of unproductive inventory, which represents a continuing drain on working capital.

The Japanese philosophy

It has often been said that the scarcity of space in industrialised Japan has made the nation conscious of the need to make the most productive use of all physical resources, including inventory – whether this is true is of academic interest only – what is the case is that it is the widely held view in Japan that inventory is waste.

An analogy that is frequently drawn in Japan is that an organisation's investment in inventory is like a large, deep lake (see Figure 5.11). Well below the surface of this lake are numerous jagged rocks, but because of the depth of the water, the captain of the ship need have no fear of striking one of them.

The comparison with business is simple: the depth of the water in the lake represents inventory and the rocks represent problems. These problems might include such things as inaccurate forecasts, unreliable suppliers, quality problems, bottlenecks, industrial relations problems and so on. The Japanese philosophy is that inventory merely hides the problems. Their view is that the level of water in the lake should be reduced (say to level 'B' in Figure 5.11). Now the captain of the ship is forced to confront the problems – they cannot be avoided. In the same way if inventory is reduced then management must grasp the various nettles of forecast inaccuracy, unreliable suppliers and so on.

Figure 5.11 Inventory hides the problems

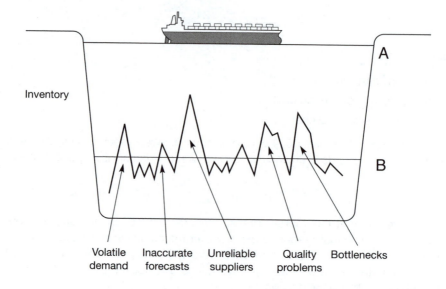

The Japanese developed the so-called Kanban concept as a way of lowering the water in the lake. Kanban originated in assembly-type operations but the principles can be extended across the supply chain and to all types of operations. The name Kanban comes from the Japanese for a type of card that was used in early systems to signal to the upstream supply point that a certain quantity of material could be released.

Kanban is a 'pull' system that is driven by the demand at the lowest point in the chain. In a production operation the aim would be to produce only that quantity needed for immediate demand. When parts are needed on the assembly line they are fed from the next stage up the chain in just the quantity needed at the time they are needed. Likewise this movement now triggers demand at the next work station in the chain and so on.

By progressively reducing the Kanban quantity (i.e. the amount demanded from the supplying work station) bottlenecks will become apparent. Management will then focus attention on the bottleneck to remove it by the most cost-effective means possible. Again the Kanban quantity will be reduced until a further bottleneck is revealed. Hence the Kanban philosophy essentially seeks to achieve a balanced supply chain with minimal inventory at every stage and where the process and transit quantities of materials and stock are reduced to the lowest possible amount. The ultimate aim, say the Japanese, should be the 'economic batch quantity of 1'!

In fact this logic does not necessarily conflict with the traditional view of how the economic batch (or order) quantity is determined. All that is different is that the Japanese are seeking to minimise the batch quantity by shifting the curve that represents the cost of ordering or the cost of set-ups to the left (see Figure 5.12). In other words, they focus on finding ways to reduce set-up costs and ordering costs.

Figure 5.12 **Reducing set-up costs/ordering costs**

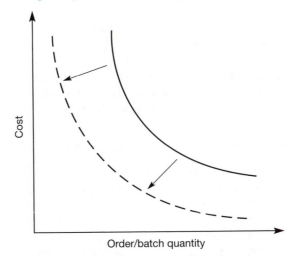

The effect of moving the curve to the left on the economic batch/order quantity is seen in Figure 5.13.

Figure 5.13 **Reducing the economic batch/order quantity**

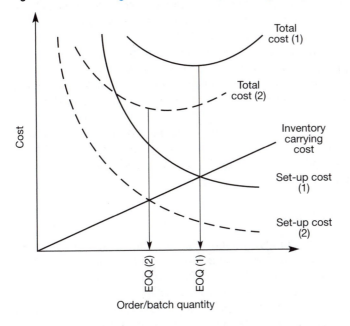

The foundations of agility

It will be apparent that agility is not a single company concept but rather it extends from one end of the supply chain to the other. The concept of agility has significant implications for how organisations within the supply/demand network relate to each other and how they can best work together on the basis of shared information.

To bring these ideas together, a number of basic principles can be identified as the starting point for the creation of the agile supply chain.

1 Synchronise activities through shared information

Synchronisation implies that all parties in the supply chain are 'marching to the same drumbeat'. In other words, through shared information and process alignment there is in effect one set of numbers and a single schedule for the entire supply chain. This somewhat Utopian vision is increasingly becoming reality as web-based technology enables different entities in a network to share information on real demand, inventory and capacity in a collaborative context.

In the fast moving consumer goods (fmcg) sector there is a growing number of examples of supply chain synchronisation made possible by the retailers' increasing willingness to share point-of-sale data with manufacturers. One such instance is the web-based system established by the UK's biggest retailer, Tesco. The Tesco Information Exchange (TIE) is an extranet that enables Tesco's suppliers to access their own sales data, item by item. This data is updated several times a day and potentially can provide manufacturers with the means to link their production schedules to Tesco's replenishment requirements.

In the automobile industry most of the volume car manufacturers have established 'seamless' processes with their first tier suppliers based upon providing immediate access to production plans and schedules. This enables just-in-time deliveries to be achieved without the need for major buffers of inventory at the first tier level.

In the US the 'quick response' initiative in the apparel industry has linked retailers to garment manufacturers and also to the fabric producers through shared information. The impact of this collaboration has been a significant improvement in the competitiveness of that industry.

2 Work smarter, not harder

Detailed examination of the processes that together constitute a supply chain inevitably highlights the fact that a large proportion of the end-to-end time is 'non-value-adding'. In other words, time is being spent on activities that typically create cost but do not create a benefit for the customer. Time spent in inventory is a classic example of non-value-adding time. Supply chain mapping can reveal where this idle time occurs; to attack it then requires a review of the processes that precede or follow that idle time. Process time is directly correlated with inventory, e.g. if it takes three weeks from raising a purchase order to receiving the goods, at least three weeks of inventory will be required to buffer ourselves during that lead time.

Business process re-engineering (BPR) is the term frequently applied to the activity of simplifying and reshaping the organisational processes with the goal of achieving the desired outcomes in shorter time-frames at less cost. Many processes in the supply chain are lengthy because the constituent activities are performed in 'series', i.e. in a linear, 'one after the other' way. It is often possible to re-engineer the process so that those same activities can be performed 'in parallel', i.e. simultaneously.

Time compression in a supply chain can be achieved not necessarily by speeding up activities, but rather by doing fewer things – i.e. eliminating where possible non-value-adding activities. Many existing practices in business are performed for historical reasons; there was once a justification for those practices but, with changed conditions, that justification may no longer exist.

Supply chains can be transformed in terms of their agility by the rigorous application of process re-engineering principles.

3 Partner with suppliers to reduce in-bound lead times

Conventionally, firms have maintained an arm's-length relationship with suppliers. Suppliers have often been chosen on the basis of price rather than their responsiveness. A major opportunity exists for reducing in-bound lead times through close working with key suppliers. Because in the past there was often a view that suppliers should be held at 'arms length', many opportunities for improving responsiveness have been missed. Since supplier agility is one of the main requirements in the creation of a more responsive supply chain it is perhaps surprising that some businesses even now have few collaborative programmes with suppliers in place.

Using joint supplier/customer teams to explore opportunities for re-aligning and re-engineering processes, on both sides of the interface, which impact overall responsiveness can produce significant dividends. Because conventionally companies have designed processes in a vacuum, it is not surprising to find that those processes do not align easily with their supply chain partners' processes. Many companies have gained real benefits, for instance, by allowing their suppliers to access their own information and planning systems, e.g. providing access to enterprise planning systems such as SAP.

Often suppliers may well be able to transfer knowledge and best practice from their operation to their customers' – and vice versa. In either case, the opportunities to reduce in-bound lead times by closer partnership across the supply chain are considerable.

4 Seek to reduce complexity

Complexity comes in many guises in supply chains. Complexity may be generated by multiple variants of the same product, e.g. different pack sizes, or by each product in a family having greatly different Bills of Material, or by frequent product changes, and so on. Complexity can also be generated through cumbersome processes that involve many different stages and hand-offs. Simplification is an obvious remedy for complexity but one which may not always be available.

However, there will often be opportunities to reduce complexity by questioning the reasons why things are the way they are.

For example, is the level of product variety greater than the customer actually requires? Often product proliferation is driven by sales or marketing departments and may not actually achieve additional sales but spread the same total demand over a greater number of stock keeping units (SKUs). The greater the fragmentation of demand the harder it becomes to manage availability in that the variability of demand at the individual item level will tend to be higher.

Simplification can sometimes be achieved through seeking greater commonality of components or sub-assembly across a family of products. For example, in automobile design these days it is increasingly the case that several different models of car are built on the same platform and 'under the skin' share common components and sub-assemblies.

The point about complexity is that it provides a barrier to agility as well as generating cost. Complexity in the supply chain is addressed in more detail in Chapter 8.

5 Postpone the final configuration/assembly/distribution of products

Postponement refers to the process by which the commitment of a product to its final form or location is delayed for as long as possible. When decisions on the final configuration or pack have to be made ahead of demand there is the inevitable risk that the products that are available are not the ones the customer wants. For example, the customer may want a blue four-door car with air-conditioning but the dealer has a red, two-door with a sunroof. Or, again, there may be a blue four-door available but it is at a different dealer at the other end of the country.

The philosophy of postponement ideally would begin on the drawing board so that products are designed with late configuration in mind. The longer that products can remain as generic 'work in progress' then the more flexibility there will be to ensure the 'right product in the right place at the right time'.

An example of late configuration is provided by Hewlett Packard and its DeskJet printers. These products are designed so that they can be manufactured as generic, but incomplete, units. They are then localised at regional centres where the appropriate power pack, plug and cable, local packaging, etc., are added. In this way inventory is minimised but availability is enhanced.

Postponement may not always be feasible in terms of late configuration but there may be scope for spatial postponement through holding inventory in just a few locations with the ability to ship the product rapidly to the location required when an order is received.

6 Manage processes not just functions

For centuries organisations have followed an organisational logic based upon the 'division of labour' whereby activities take place within functions or departments. Whilst this functionally based organisational concept may ensure the efficient use of resources it is actually inwardly focused and tends to lead to a 'silo' type mentality. It also seems to be the case that these functionally based organisations are slow to respond to changes in the market or business environment. Because there are often multiple 'hand-offs' as things get passed from one function to another there is an inevitable lengthening in the time to respond. In functionally based businesses the new product development activity, for example, is often lengthy as it moves from R&D to product engineering to market research and eventually into production.

On the other hand, those companies that are able to respond rapidly to changing customer requirements tend to focus more upon managing 'processes'. Processes are the horizontal, market-facing sequences of activities that create value for customers. They are cross-functional by definition and are usually best managed through the means of interdisciplinary teams. The critical business processes that cut across the organisation would include innovation, customer relationship management and supplier relationship management.

The way businesses are organised can have a significant impact upon their agility; those companies with cumbersome, multi-level decision-making processes tend to be far slower to respond to market changes than their competitors who give autonomy to self-managed process teams.

A further reason why process management is critical to agility across the wider supply chain is that process alignment between entities in that chain is clearly facilitated if organisational structures are horizontal rather than vertical.

7 Utilise appropriate performance metrics

It is a truism that performance measurement shapes behaviour. This is particularly the case in business organisations where formal measurement systems drive the business. In functionally based organisations these measurements often are based upon departmental budgets and are underpinned by objectives such as cost minimisation, asset utilisation and efficiency, and productivity improvement. Whilst on the face of it these objectives may appear to be desirable, they will not necessarily encourage agile practices within the organisation. If, for example, a manufacturing facility is measured on, say, unit cost of production then the incentive will be to go for big batch sizes to take advantage of economies of scale. However, such actions will probably lead to a loss of flexibility and the creation of additional inventory. If, on the other hand, time-based metrics were to be employed then the focus could be on cycle-time reduction, set-up time reduction and other measures that encourage agile practices.

A further incentive to agility can be created by linking processes to customer-based metrics. One such widely used measure is 'perfect order achievement'. A perfect order is one where the customer gets exactly what they want at the time and place they want it. It will also usually be the case that different customers may well have different requirements and expectations, so the definition of what constitutes a perfect order will have to be specific to each segment, channel or even individual key accounts.

A fundamental tenet of agility is customer responsiveness, hence the need to ensure that the primary measures of business performance reflect this imperative.

'Time to market' and 'time to volume' are powerful metrics employed by companies such as Sony and Canon where short life cycles dictate a focus on rapid response to fast-changing technologies and volatile customer demand.

In the past, the focus of many companies was primarily on *efficiency*, i.e. a continuing search for lower costs, better use of capacity, reduced inventories and so on. These are still worthy goals today but the priority has shifted. Now the emphasis must be on *effectiveness*. In other words the challenge is to create strategies and procedures that will enable organisations to become the supplier of choice and to sustain that position through higher levels of customer responsiveness. This is the logic that underpins the concept of the agile supply chain.

A routemap to responsiveness

The shift in the balance of power in the distribution channel has highlighted the need for the business to be driven by the market rather than by its own internal goals. However, for organisations to become truly market-driven, there has to be a sustained focus on responsiveness across the business and its wider supply chain. There are many prerequisites for responsiveness and Figure 5.14 summarises the key elements.

The responsive business will have agile suppliers and will work very closely with them to align processes across the extended enterprise. It will also be very close to its customers, capturing information on real demand and sharing that information with its partners across the network. Internally the business will also be focused on agility through the way it organises – breaking through functional silos to create process teams. In terms of its manufacturing and sourcing strategy, the responsive business will seek to marry the lean and agile paradigm through de-coupling its upstream and downstream processes, utilising the principles of postponement wherever possible.

Those companies that can follow this routemap will be more likely to be the leaders in their field. More often than not, when we look at the successful companies in any market, they tend to be the ones that have demonstrated their ability to respond more rapidly to the changing needs of their customers. The case study that concludes this chapter underlines the challenges that organisations must confront as they seek to become more responsive to customer needs.

Figure 5.14 Routemap to the responsive business

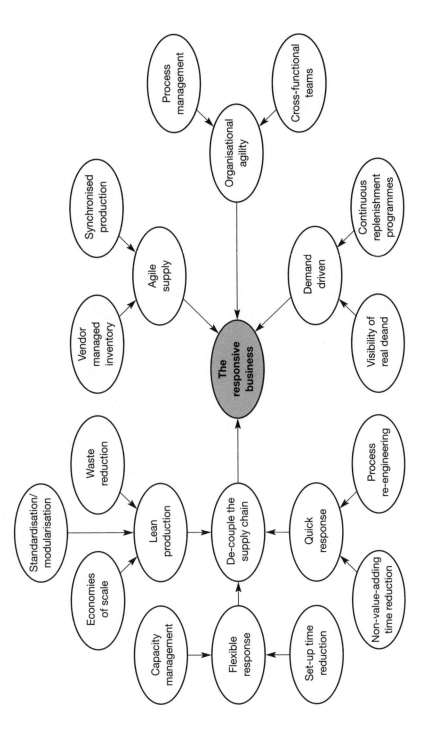

World Duty Free

World Duty Free (WDF) is the UK's biggest airport duty free goods retailer, accounting for 90 per cent of all UK airport duty free sales. WDF is wholly owned by the Italian group Autogrill in which Benetton have a 40 per cent stake.

Even though WDF has experienced significant growth in recent years (partly organic and partly through merger – in particularly the merger in 2009 with Spanish duty free retailer, Alpha), it has been faced with an increasing degree of market turbulence and volatility of late. At the macro level the world recession has had a big impact on passenger numbers generally, particularly at regional airports which have a higher proportion of leisure passengers. Sources of volatility at the micro level include the security arrangements at airports, where the length of time taken to process passengers will vary according to daily changes in procedures (e.g. requesting passengers to remove their shoes), which itself directly impacts the amount of time individual passengers will have available for duty free shopping.

Further sources of volatility at the micro level can be airlines changing their departure times – for example, passengers leaving the UK for non-EU destinations can generally buy goods at a lower price and if the time of the flight changes or the plane is delayed there can be a significant change in demand patterns. A further impact on sales is created when airlines either withdraw a service or change airports – Ryanair moving some of its services from one airport to another because of lower landing charges is a case in point.

Against this background of uncertainty and increasingly unpredictable demand, WDF is seeking to make the transition from a forecast-driven to a demand-driven business.

One of the strategies that it has adopted is to focus on its single distribution centre (based near London Heathrow Airport) to find ways in which its existing capacity can be used more flexibly. Using what are in effect six sigma methodologies, WDF has been able to improve the utilisation of capacity and to improve flow-through so that it can cope better with the peaks and troughs in demand. So successful has this strategy been that WDF was able to cope with the opening of Terminal 5 without additional warehousing capacity. A further degree of flexibility in the Heathrow distribution centre is through the use of agency staff.

Becoming demand-driven requires a 'just-in-time' delivery philosophy based upon more frequent deliveries to their air-side outlets based on more frequent demand signals, i.e. point-of-sale data polls. The intention is, wherever possible, to move to a 'continuous replenishment' philosophy where products are rapidly replenished after they are sold.

WDF has recognised that demand-driven supply chains require suppliers to be highly responsive. The company is actively examining ways in which suppliers' inbound lead times can be reduced – particularly through a greater level of shared information and the introduction of vendor managed inventory (VMI) arrangements.

With a product range of approximately 15,000 SKUs there is inevitably a 'long-tail' on the sales pareto curve – for example 88 per cent of WDF's SKUs sell less than 1 unit per day per store. One response to this issue has been a focus on range rationalisation. Keeping control of variety is a continuing challenge with new product launches and promotions increasing every year. There are more and more niche segments, e.g. vodka with different flavours, different price points and positioning strategies. About half WDF's SKUs change each year, making it difficult to use traditional methods of sales forecasting.

One realisation has been that WDF will need to move away from the traditional 'one size fits all' approach to a multiple supply chain strategy that seeks to manage the different volume and variability profiles of individual products in different ways. Equally for certain products – particularly in more fashion-oriented categories such as sunglasses – the company has to plan ahead for specific seasons and because of long lead times need to order these products well in advance. Here the strategy is one of 'when its gone, its gone', which requires a completely different logistics capability to the 'continuous replenishment' type of products.

References

1. Womack, J.P., Jones, D.T. and Roos, D., *The Machine that Changed the World*, Macmillan, 1990.
2. Monden, Y., *The Toyota Production System*, Productivity Press, 1983.
3. Christopher, M. and Towill, D., 'An integrated model for the design of agile supply chains', *International Journal of Physical Distribution and Logistics Management*, Vol. 31, No. 4, 2001.

Strategic lead-time management

6

- Time-based competition

- Lead-time concepts

- Logistics pipeline management

'Time is money' is perhaps an over-worked cliché in common parlance, but in logistics management it goes to the heart of the matter. Not only does time represent cost to the logistics manager but extended lead times also imply a customer service penalty. As far as cost is concerned there is a direct relationship between the length of the logistics pipeline and the inventory that is locked up in it; every day that the product is in the pipeline it incurs an inventory holding cost. Secondly, long lead times mean a slower response to customer requirements, and, given the increased importance of delivery speed in today's internationally competitive environment, this combination of high costs and lack of responsiveness provides a recipe for decline and decay.

Time-based competition

Customers in all markets, industrial or consumer, are increasingly time-sensitive.[1] In other words they value time and this is reflected in their purchasing behaviour. Thus, for example, in industrial markets buyers tend to source from suppliers with the shortest lead times who can meet their quality specification. In consumer markets customers make their choice from amongst the brands available at the time; hence if the preferred brand is out of stock it is quite likely that a substitute brand will be purchased instead.

> Customers in all markets, industrial or consumer, are increasingly time-sensitive.

In the past it was often the case that price was paramount as an influence on the purchase decision. Now, whilst price is still important, a major determinant of choice of supplier or brand is the 'cost of time'. The cost of time is simply the additional costs that a customer must bear whilst waiting for delivery or whilst seeking out alternatives.

There are many pressures leading to the growth of time-sensitive markets, but perhaps the most significant are:

1 Shortening life cycles

2 Customers' drive for reduced inventories

3 Volatile markets making reliance on forecasts dangerous

1 Shortening life cycles

The concept of the product life cycle is well established. It suggests that for many products there is a recognisable pattern of sales from launch through to final decline (see Figure 6.1).

Figure 6.1 The product life cycle

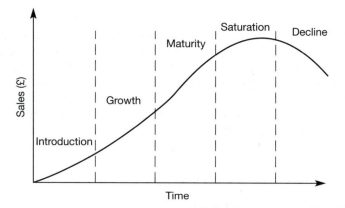

A feature of the last few decades has been the shortening of these life cycles. Take as an example the case of the typewriter. The early mechanical typewriter had a life cycle of about 30 years – meaning that an individual model would be little changed during that period. These mechanical typewriters were replaced by the electro-mechanical typewriter, which had a life cycle of approximately ten years. The electro-mechanical typewriter gave way to the electronic typewriter with a four-year life cycle. Now personal computers have taken over with a life cycle of one year or less!

In situations like this the time available to develop new products, to launch them and to meet marketplace demand is clearly greatly reduced. Hence the ability to 'fast track' product development, manufacturing and logistics becomes a key element of competitive strategy. Figure 6.2 shows the effect of being late into the market and slow to meet demand.

Figure 6.2  Shorter life cycles make timing crucial

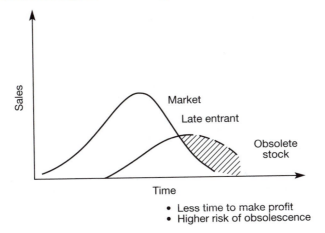

- Less time to make profit
- Higher risk of obsolescence

However, it is not just time-to-market that is important. Once a product is on the market the ability to respond quickly to demand is equally important. Here the lead time to re-supply a market determines the organisation's ability to exploit demand during the life cycle. It is apparent that those companies that can achieve reductions in the order-to-delivery cycle will have a strong advantage over their slower competitors.

2 Customers' drive for reduced inventories

One of the most pronounced phenomena of recent years has been the almost universal move by companies to reduce their inventories. Whether the inventory is in the form of raw materials, components, work-in-progress or finished products, the pressure has been to release the capital locked up in stock and hence simultaneously to reduce the holding cost of that stock. The same companies that have reduced their inventories in this way have also recognised the advantage that they gain in terms of improved flexibility and responsiveness to their customers.

The knock-on effect of this development upstream to suppliers has been considerable. It is now imperative that suppliers can provide a just-in-time delivery service. Timeliness of delivery – meaning delivery of the complete order at the time required by the customer – becomes the number one order-winning criterion.

Many companies still think that the only way to service customers who require just-in-time deliveries is for them, the supplier, to carry the inventory instead of the customer. Whilst the requirements of such customers could always be met by the supplier carrying inventory close to the customer(s), this is simply shifting the cost burden from one part of the supply chain to another – indeed the cost may even be higher. Instead what is needed is for the supplier to substitute responsiveness for inventory whenever possible.

As we discussed in Chapter 5, responsiveness essentially is achieved through agility in the supply chain. Not only can customers be serviced more rapidly but the degree of flexibility offered can be greater and yet the cost should be less because the pipeline is shorter. Figure 6.3 suggests that agility can enable companies to break free of the classic trade-off between service and cost. Instead of having to choose between either higher service levels or lower costs it is possible to have the best of both worlds.

Figure 6.3 Breaking free of the classic service/cost trade-off

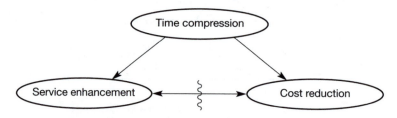

3 Volatile markets make reliance on forecasts dangerous

A continuing problem for most organisations is the inaccuracy of forecasts. It seems that no matter how sophisticated the forecasting techniques employed, the volatility of markets ensures that the forecast will be wrong! Whilst many forecasting errors are the result of inappropriate forecasting methodology, the root cause of these problems is that forecast error increases as lead time increases.

The evidence from most markets is that demand volatility is tending to increase, often due to competitive activity, sometimes due to unexpected responses to promotions or price changes and as a result of intermediaries' reordering policies. In situations such as these there are very few forecasting methods that will be able to predict short-term changes in demand with any accuracy.

The conventional response to such a problem has been to increase the safety stock to provide protection against such forecast errors. However, it is surely preferable to reduce lead times in order to reduce forecast error and hence reduce the need for inventory.

Many businesses have invested heavily in automation in the factory with the aim of reducing throughput times. In some cases processes that used to take days to complete now only take hours and activities that took hours now only take minutes. However, it is paradoxical that many of those same businesses that have spent millions of pounds on automation to speed up the time it takes to manufacture a product are then content to let it sit in a distribution centre or warehouse for weeks waiting to be sold! The requirement is to look across the different stages in the supply chain to see how time as a whole can be reduced through re-engineering the way the chain is structured.

One of the basic fallacies of management is that long lead times provide security and cover against uncertainty. In fact the reverse is true! Imagine a utopian situation where a company had reduced its procurement, manufacturing and delivery lead time to zero. In other words, as soon as a customer ordered an item – any item – that product was made and delivered instantaneously. In such a situation there would be no need for a forecast and no need for inventory and at the same time a greater variety could be offered to the customer.

Whilst clearly zero lead times are hardly likely to exist in the real world, the target for any organisation should be to reduce lead times, at every stage in the logistics pipeline, to as close to zero as possible. In so many cases it is possible to find considerable opportunity for total lead-time reduction, often through some very simple changes in procedure.

Lead-time concepts

From the customer's viewpoint there is only one lead time: the elapsed time from order to delivery. Clearly this is a crucial competitive variable as more and more markets become increasingly time competitive. Nevertheless it represents only a partial view of lead time. Just as important, from the supplier's perspective, is the time it takes to convert an order into cash and, indeed, the total time that working capital is committed from when materials are first procured through to when the customer's payment is received.

Let us examine both of these lead-time concepts in turn.

1 The order-to-delivery cycle

From a marketing point of view the time taken from receipt of a customer's order through to delivery (sometimes referred to as order cycle time (OCT)) is critical. In today's just-in-time environment short lead times are a major source of competitive advantage. Equally important, however, is the reliability or consistency of that lead time. It can actually be argued that reliability of delivery is more important than the length of the order cycle – at least up to a point – because the impact of a failure to deliver on time is more severe than the need to order further in advance. However, because, as we have seen, long lead times require longer-term forecasts, then the pressure from the customer will continue to be for deliveries to be made in ever shorter time-frames.

What are the components of order cycle time? Figure 6.4 highlights the major elements.

Figure 6.4 The order cycle

Customer places order	Order entry	Order processing	Order assembly	Transport	Order received

Each of these steps in the chain will consume time. Because of bottlenecks, inefficient processes and fluctuations in the volume of orders handled there will often be considerable variation in the time taken for these activities to be completed.

The overall effect can lead to a substantial reduction in the reliability of delivery. As an example, Figure 6.5 shows the cumulative effect of variations in an order cycle which results in a range of possible cycle times from 5 days to 25 days.

Figure 6.5 Total order cycle with variability

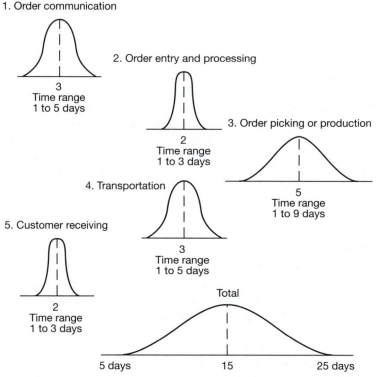

Source: Stock, J.R. and Lambert, D.M., *Strategic Logistics Management*, 2nd edition, Irwin, 1987

In those situations where orders are not met from stock but may have to be manu-factured, assembled or sourced from external vendors, then clearly lead times will be even further extended, with the possibility of still greater variations in total order-to-delivery time. Figure 6.6 highlights typical activities in such extended lead times.

2 The cash-to-cash cycle

As we have already observed, a basic concern of any organisation is: how long does it take to convert an order into cash? In reality the issue is not just how long it takes to process orders, raise invoices and receive payment, but also how long is the pipeline from the sourcing of raw material through to the finished product because throughout the pipeline resources are being consumed and working capital needs to be financed.

Figure 6.6 Lead-time components

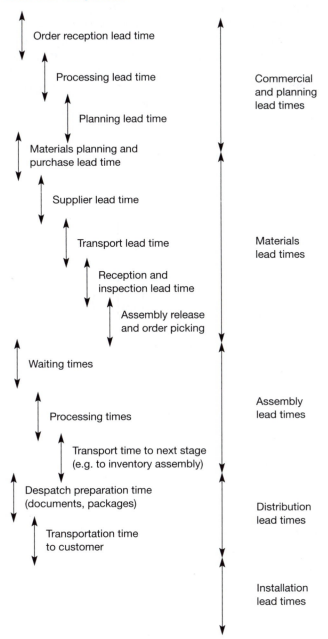

From the moment when decisions are taken on the sourcing and procurement of materials and components, through the manufacturing and assembly process to final distribution, time is being consumed. That time is represented by the number of days of inventory in the pipeline, whether as raw materials, work-in-progress, goods in transit, or time taken to process orders, issue replenishment orders, as well as time spent in manufacturing, time in queues or bottlenecks and so on. The control of this total pipeline is the true scope of logistics lead-time management. Figure 6.7 illustrates the way in which cumulative lead time builds up from procurement through to payment.

Figure 6.7  Strategic lead-time management

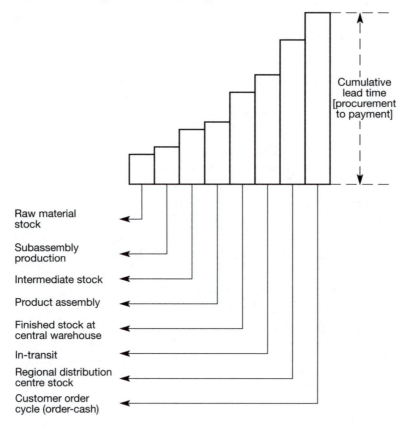

As we shall see later in this chapter, the longer the pipeline from source of materials to the final user the less responsive to changes in demand the system will be. It is also the case that longer pipelines obscure the 'visibility' of end demand so that it is difficult to link manufacturing and procurement decisions to marketplace requirements. Thus we find an inevitable build-up of inventory as a buffer at each step along the supply chain. An approximate rule of thumb suggests that the amount of safety stock in a pipeline varies with the square root of the pipeline length.

> The longer the pipeline from source of materials to the final user the less responsive to changes in demand the system will be.

Overcoming these problems and ensuring timely response to volatile demand requires a new and fundamentally different approach to the management of lead times.

Logistics pipeline management

The key to the successful control of logistics lead times is pipeline management. Pipeline management is the process whereby manufacturing and procurement lead times are linked to the needs of the marketplace. At the same time, pipeline management seeks to meet the competitive challenge of increasing the speed of response to those market needs.

The goals of logistics pipeline management are:

- Lower costs
- Higher quality
- More flexibility
- Faster response times

The achievement of these goals is dependent upon managing the supply chain as an entity and seeking to reduce the pipeline length and/or to speed up the flow through that pipeline. In examining the efficiency of supply chains it is often found that many of the activities that take place add more cost than value. For example, moving a pallet into a warehouse, repositioning it, storing it and then moving it out in all likelihood has added no value but has added considerably to the total cost.

Very simply, value-adding time is time spent doing something that creates a benefit for which the customer is prepared to pay. Thus we could classify manufacturing as a value-added activity as well as the physical movement of the product and the means of creating the exchange. The old adage 'the right product in the right place at the right time' summarises the idea of customer value-adding activities. Thus any activity that contributes to the achievement of that goal could be classified as value adding.

On the other hand, non-value-adding time is time spent on an activity whose elimination would lead to no reduction of benefit to the customer. Some non-value-adding activities are necessary because of the current design of our processes but they still represent a cost and should be minimised.

The difference between value-adding time and non-value-adding time is crucial to an understanding of how logistics processes can be improved. Flowcharting supply chain processes is the first step towards understanding the opportunities that exist for improvements in productivity through re-engineering those processes.

Once processes have been flowcharted, the first step is to bring together the managers involved in those processes to debate and agree exactly which elements of the process can truly be described as value adding. Agreement may not easily be achieved as no one likes to admit that the activity they are responsible for does not actually add any value for customers.

> The difference between value-adding time and non-value-adding time is crucial to an understanding of how logistics processes can be improved.

The next step is to do a rough-cut graph highlighting visually how much time is consumed in both non-value-adding and value-adding activities. Figure 6.8 shows a generic example of such a graph.

Figure 6.8 Which activities add cost and which add value?

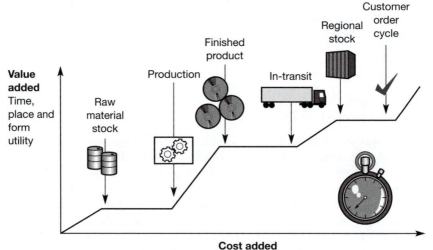

Production, storage and transport costs and the time cost of money

Figure 6.9 shows an actual analysis for a pharmaceutical product where the total process time was 40 weeks and yet value was only being added for 6.2 per cent of that time.

It will be noted from this example that most of the value is added early in the process and hence the product is more expensive to hold as inventory. Furthermore, much of the flexibility is probably lost as the product is configured and/or packaged in specific forms early in that process. Figure 6.10 shows that this product started as a combination of three active ingredients but very rapidly became 25 stock keeping units because it was packaged in different sizes, formats, etc., and was then held in inventory for the rest of the time in the company's pipeline.

Figure 6.9 Value added through time

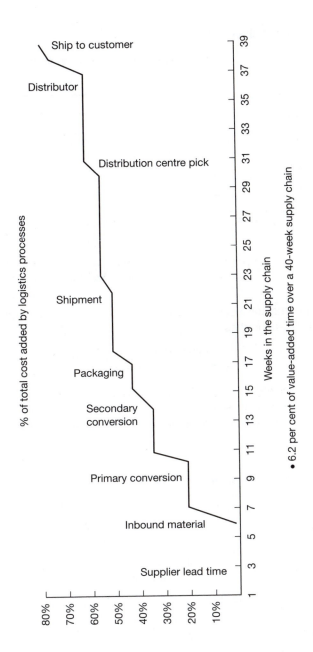

- 6.2 per cent of value-added time over a 40-week supply chain

Figure 6.10 Variety through time

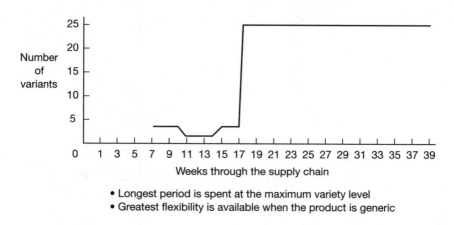

Plot of variety through the supply chain

Number of variants (y-axis: 5, 10, 15, 20, 25)

Weeks through the supply chain (x-axis: 0, 1, 3, 5, 7, 9, 11, 13, 15, 17, 19, 21, 23, 25, 27, 29, 31, 33, 35, 37, 39)

- Longest period is spent at the maximum variety level
- Greatest flexibility is available when the product is generic

An indicator of the efficiency of a supply chain is given by its throughput efficiency, which can be measured as:

$$\frac{\text{Value-added time}}{\text{End-to-end pipeline time}} \times 100$$

Throughput efficiency can be as low as 10 per cent, meaning that most time spent in a supply chain is non-value-adding time.

Figure 6.11 shows how cost-adding activities can easily outstrip value-adding activities.

Figure 6.11 Cost-added versus value-added time

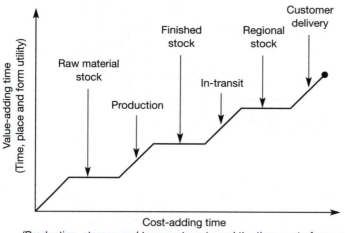

Value-adding time (Time, place and form utility)

Raw material stock

Production

Finished stock

In-transit

Regional stock

Customer delivery

Cost-adding time
(Production, storage and transport costs and the time cost of money)

The challenge to pipeline management is to find ways in which the ratio of value-added to cost-added time in the pipeline can be improved. Figure 6.12 graphically shows the goal of strategic lead-time management: to compress the chain in terms of time consumption so that cost-added time is reduced. Focusing on those parts of the graph that are depicted horizontally (i.e. representing periods of time when no value is being added), enables opportunities for improvement to be identified.

Figure 6.12 Reducing non-value-adding time improves service and reduces cost

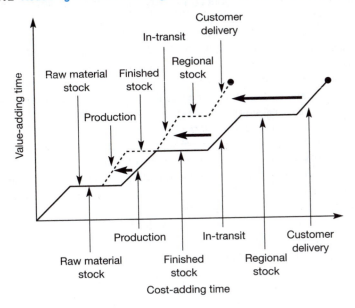

Pipeline management is concerned with removing the blockages and the fractures that occur in the pipeline and which lead to inventory build-ups and lengthened response times. The sources of these blockages and fractures are such things as extended set-up and change-over times, bottlenecks, excessive inventory, sequential order processing and inadequate pipeline visibility.

To achieve improvement in the logistics process requires a focus upon the lead time as a whole, rather than the individual components of that lead time. In particular the interfaces between the components must be examined in detail. These interfaces provide fertile ground for logistics process re-engineering.

Reducing logistics lead time

Because companies have typically not managed well the total flow of materials and information that link the source of supply with the ultimate customer, what we find is that there is an incredibly rich opportunity for improving the efficiency of that process.

In those companies that do not recognise the importance of managing the supply chain as an integrated system it is usually the case that considerable periods of time are consumed at the interfaces between adjacent stages in the total process and in inefficiently performed procedures.

Because no one department or individual manager has complete visibility of the total logistics process, it is often the case that major opportunities for time reduction across the pipeline as a whole are not recognised. One electronics company in Europe did not realise for many years that, although it had reduced its throughput time in the factory from days down to hours, finished inventory was still sitting in the warehouse for three weeks! The reason was that finished inventory was the responsibility of the distribution function, which was outside the concern of production management.

To enable the identification of opportunities for reducing end-to-end pipeline time an essential starting point is the construction of a supply chain map.

A supply chain map is essentially a time-based representation of the processes and activities that are involved as the materials or products move through the chain. At the same time the map highlights the time that is consumed when those materials or products are simply standing still, i.e. as inventory.

In these maps, it is usual to distinguish between 'horizontal' time and 'vertical' time. Horizontal time is time spent in process. It could be in-transit time, manufacturing or assembly time, time spent in production planning or processing, and so on. It may not necessarily be time when customer value is being created but at least something is going on. The other type of time is vertical time, which is time when nothing is happening and hence the material or product is standing still as inventory. No value is being added during vertical time, only cost.

The labels 'horizontal' and 'vertical' refer to the maps themselves where the two axes reflect process time and time spent as static inventory respectively. Figure 6.13 depicts such a map for the manufacture and distribution of men's underwear.

From this map it can be seen that horizontal time is 60 days. In other words, the various processes of gathering materials, spinning, knitting, dyeing, finishing, sewing and so on take 60 days to complete from start to finish. This is important because horizontal time determines the time that it would take for the system to respond to an increase in demand. Hence, if there were to be a sustained increase in demand, it would take that long to 'ramp up' output to the new level. Conversely, if there was a downturn in demand then the critical measure is pipeline volume, i.e. the sum of both horizontal and vertical time. In other words it would take 175 days to 'drain' the system of inventory. So in volatile fashion markets, for instance, pipeline volume is a critical determinant of business risk.

Pipeline maps can also provide a useful internal benchmark. Because each day of process time requires a day of inventory to 'cover' that day then, in an ideal world, the only inventory would be that needed to cover during the process lead time. So a 60-day total process time would result in 60 days' inventory. However, in the case highlighted here there are actually 175 days of inventory in the pipeline. Clearly, unless the individual processes are highly time variable or unless demand is very volatile, there is more inventory than can be justified.

It must be remembered that in multi-product businesses each product will have a different end-to-end pipeline time. Furthermore, where products comprise multiple components, packaging materials or sub-assemblies, total pipeline time will

Figure 6.13 Supply chain mapping – an example

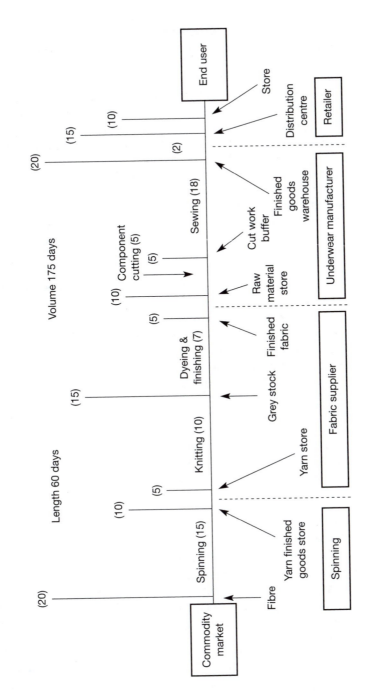

Source: Scott, C. and Westbrook, R., 'New strategic tools for supply chain management', *International Journal of Physical Distribution and Logistics Management*, Vol. 21, No. 1, 1991

be determined by the speed of the slowest moving item or element in that product. Hence in procuring materials for and manufacturing a household aerosol air freshener, it was found that the replenishment lead time for one of the fragrances used was such that weeks were added to the total pipeline.

Mapping pipelines in this way provides a powerful basis for logistics re-engineering projects. Because it makes the total process and its associated inventory transparent, the opportunities for reducing non-value-adding time become apparent. In many cases much of the non-value-adding time in a supply chain is there because it is self-inflicted through the 'rules' that are imposed or that have been inherited. Such rules include: economic batch quantities, economic order quantities, minimum order sizes, fixed inventory review periods, production planning cycles and forecasting review periods.

The importance of strategic lead-time management is that it forces us to challenge every process and every activity in the supply chain and to apply the acid test of 'does this activity add value for a customer or consumer or does it simply add cost?'

The basic principle to be noted is that every hour of time in the pipeline is directly reflected in the quantity of inventory in the pipeline and thus the time it takes to respond to marketplace requirements.

A simple analogy is with an oil pipeline. Imagine a pipeline from a refinery to a port that is 500 kilometres long. In normal conditions there will be 500 kilometres equivalent of oil in the pipeline. If there is a change in requirement at the end of the pipeline (say, for a different grade of oil) then 500 kilometres of the original grade has to be pumped through before the changed grade reaches the point of demand.

In the case of the logistics pipeline it is the case that time is consumed not just in slow-moving processes but also in unnecessary stock holding – whether it be raw materials, work-in-progress, waiting at a bottleneck or finished inventory. By focusing on improving key supply chain processes companies can dramatically improve their competitiveness, as the case of Johnstons of Elgin (see box below) illustrates.

Johnstons of Elgin

Johnstons of Elgin can trace its history back to 1797 when Alexander Johnston first took a lease on a woollen factory at Newmill in Aberdeenshire, Scotland. Over two hundred years later, the mill of Johnstons of Elgin is still on the same site and is the UK's last remaining vertically integrated woollen mill – the only mill still to carry out all the processes from the receipt of raw materials to finished product at a single location.

In the middle of the nineteenth century the company developed a successful business producing 'Estate Tweeds'. Estate Tweeds are a derivative of 'tartans'. Tartan is a distinctive plaid traditionally worn by Scottish highlanders to denote their clan. The patterns of Estate Tweeds were specific to an individual estate – an estate being a (usually) large house or castle with significant land attached. The people who worked on that estate would often wear clothes made from the custom designed and produced tweed. This proved to be a very successful line for Johnstons and they are still produced today to specific customers' orders.

At the same time the company had begun to import cashmere and slowly developed a range of fine woven clothes made from this fibre. Much later in 1973 Johnstons entered the cashmere knitting industry through a separate factory at Hawick in the Scottish borders.

The impact of low-cost competition

For many years cashmere-based products had tended to be highly priced and as a result bought only by a more affluent customer. However, with the increasing globalisation of markets, partly influenced by the reduction or removal of trade barriers, new sources of low-cost competition began to emerge as the twentieth century moved to a close. Products labelled as 'cashmere' were now selling in supermarkets in western countries for a fraction of the price that traditional manufacturers and retailers were charging. Admittedly many of these low-cost imports were not of the same quality and contained only enough cashmere wool to enable them legally to be labelled as cashmere; however, they very quickly had a severe impact on the sales of UK-produced cashmere products. For example, in 2008 a cashmere pashmina could be bought in Tesco for £29 compared to as much as £200 for one manufactured in the UK and bought at a store such as Harvey Nichols.

Many traditional manufacturers were not able to withstand this competition and the steady decline in the UK knitted garment industry – which had been evident for years – looked set to continue.

Johnstons of Elgin was not immune from this competition pressure and in 2006 it saw its profits fall from £2.2 million to £336,000.

A shift of focus

For many years Johnstons had been predominantly a menswear business with highly stable products with long life cycles (e.g. suiting fabrics), but over time the company has become predominantly a womenswear business with a higher fashion content and with much shorter life cycles. At the same time there was a transition from a business producing mainly standard products on a repetitive basis to a much more customised product base, often made as own-labels for major fashion houses such as Hermes.

As a result, design became a much more critical element in the product development process. It was also recognised that becoming a design-led company could provide a powerful platform for competing against low-cost country sources.

However, it was not sufficient to be innovative in design if new products could not be introduced rapidly and production adjusted quickly to match uncertain demand.

Time-based competition

As is common in the textile and apparel industry, generally the time from design to market was often lengthy at Johnstons. Partly this was caused by the inflexibility of the traditional production and finishing processes, but also a significant cause of delay was the need to produce samples of the finished fabric for clients and often to make frequent changes to the design of the product at the request of those clients.

Not only did these delays add significantly to the cost (the cost of a sample might be in the region of £80 per metre) but also it meant that the time-to-market was extended. As Johnston's traditional markets became much more fashion-oriented with shorter life cycles, timing becomes critical and hence there was a growing recognition in the business that there was a pressing need to reduce lead times.

As competition increased and as many of the product categories (e.g. a plain cashmere scarf) had become, in effect, commodities, it was recognised that design was an increasingly important source of differentiation.

There was an emerging view that the current design process might be an inhibitor to greater agility. Whilst a number of innovations had occurred in manufacturing, e.g. the introduction of late-dyeing of yarn and the purchase of new equipment that can produce in smaller batches, design still tended to follow a fixed cycle.

For their own range of products (as distinct from those manufactured for other customers) their design process followed a regular cycle: work on new designs and colour ideas begins in February, June is the deadline for the first review of new product ideas with a sign-off at the end of August. These products would appear in the shops the following April/May. For those products which Johnstons manufactured for other customers, e.g. fashion houses or retailers, the design cycle had to be shorter and more flexible. These customers, who were of growing importance to Johnstons, were highly demanding in their requirements – often making late changes to product designs and specification.

Many of their retail customers, such as Burberry, increased the number of seasons for their range changes, e.g. from two to four a year. They also required the introduction of new colours in mid-season with the need for pre-production samples.

Agile or lean?

The textile industry in Scotland in 2007 was significantly smaller than it had been even ten years previously. Estimates suggested that there were only about 17,000 people working in the industry compared to probably twice that number a decade before. Similarly, the number of firms involved in the industry was under 500 compared to over 1,000 in the 1980s. However, the fall in the level of activity has been compensated for to some extent by the increase in the value of the output of the remaining industry. It is estimated that the industry in 2007 was creating a turnover of over £1 billion including export sales of £390 million.

James Sugden, the managing director of Johnstons and also the chairman of the Scottish Textiles Manufacturing Association, was quoted as saying:

There is no future in bulk manufacturing (in this industry), but there remains considerable mileage in the value of the 'made in Scotland' brand which can drive forward luxury sales worldwide if the quality of the products can be maintained to back it up. The brand is one that commands a lot of respect because of the history of design and innovation, not just in textiles.

SOURCE: THE SCOTSMAN, 14 FEBRUARY 2007

However, Sugden recognised that this opportunity also brought with it a major challenge. As a result of the reduction in the total capacity of the industry and the disappearance of many of the specialist process providers (e.g. finishing) there was a lack of capability to cope with large increases in demand. The problem was particularly acute when dealing with large international brands such as Chanel – an order from such a company, whilst welcome, could place great strains on the capacity of a single business such as Johnstons.

Whereas in the past the focus had been on reducing capacity to take costs out of the business now there was a need either to find better ways to use existing capacity or possibly to access capacity elsewhere.

The problem with capacity was not so much the number of machine hours available but rather the availability of skilled people. As the workforce was gradually ageing the pool of experienced workers was diminishing – this was particularly the case with those tasks involving hand-sewing.

To overcome these problems Johnstons instituted a major review of all their critical supply chain processes. Using process mapping they were quickly able to identify the opportunities for reducing non-value-adding time and removing bottlenecks. They also recognised that in their new, more fashion-oriented marketplace they needed to introduce more cross-functional approaches to decision making. Significant improvements were made in reducing the time from receipt of order to final delivery – partly through the installation of an enterprise planning system but also through a continuing focus on process improvement. As a result the company has managed to improve profitability even against a backdrop of challenging market conditions.

SOURCE: EUROPEAN CASE CLEARING HOUSE, 2010

Bottleneck management

All the logistics processes can be viewed as a network of interlinked activities that can only be optimised as a whole by focusing on total throughput time. Any attempt to manage by optimising individual elements or activities in the process will lead to a less-than-optimal result overall. A significant contribution to the way we view logistics processes has been made by Goldratt,[2] who developed the theory of constraints more usually known as optimised production technology (OPT).

The essence of OPT is that all activities in a logistics chain can be categorised as either 'bottlenecks' or 'non-bottlenecks'. A bottleneck is the slowest activity in a chain and whilst it may often be a machine, it could also be a part of the information flow such as order processing. The throughput time of the entire system is determined by bottleneck activities. It follows therefore that to speed up total system throughput time it is important to focus on the bottlenecks, to add capacity where possible and to reduce set-ups and set-up times if applicable.

Equally important, however, is the realisation that non-bottlenecks should not be treated in the same way. It is unnecessary to improve throughput at non-bottlenecks as this will only lead to the build-up of unwanted inventory at the bottleneck.

Consequently, the output of non-bottlenecks that feed bottlenecks must be governed by the requirements of the bottlenecks they serve.

These ideas have profound implications for the re-engineering of logistics systems where the objective is to improve throughput time overall, whilst simultaneously reducing total inventory in the system. The aim is to manage the bottlenecks for throughput efficiency, which implies larger batch quantities and fewer set-ups at those crucial points, whereas non-bottlenecks should minimise batch quantities even though more set-ups will be involved. This has the effect of speeding up the flow of work-in-progress and these 'transfer batches' merge into larger 'process batches' at the bottlenecks, enabling a faster flow through the bottleneck. It follows that idle time at a non-bottleneck need not be a concern, indeed it should be welcomed if the effect is to reduce the amount of work-in-progress waiting at a bottleneck.

Emerging from the theory of constraints is the idea of 'drum-buffer-rope'. The drum is beating the pace at which the system as a whole should work. The buffer is placed before the bottleneck to ensure that this limiting factor in the system is always working to its full capacity. The rope is drawn from an analogy with a column of marching soldiers where the slowest man sets the pace. The rope attaches the leader of the column to the slowest man – in a supply chain the rope is the means by which replenishment quantities of materials, components, etc., are communicated to suppliers.

References

1. Stalk, G. and Hout, T.M., *Competing Against Time*, The Free Press, 1990.
2. Goldratt, E.M., *Theory of Constraints*, North River Press, 1990.

The synchronous supply chain

7

- The extended enterprise and the virtual supply chain

- The role of information in the virtual supply chain

- Laying the foundations for synchronisation

- 'Quick response' logistics

- Production strategies for quick response

- Logistics systems dynamics

In conventional supply chains each stage in the chain tends to be disconnected from the others. Even within the same company the tendency is for separate functions to seek to optimise their own performance. As a result the interfaces between organisations and between functions within those organisations need to be buffered with inventory and/or time lags. The effect of this is that end-to-end pipeline times are long, responsiveness is low and total costs are high.

To overcome these problems it is clear that the supply chain needs to act as a synchronised network – not as a series of separate islands. Synchronisation implies that each stage in the chain is connected to the other and that they all 'march to the same drumbeat'. The way in which entities in a supply chain become connected is through shared information.

The information to be shared between supply chain partners includes demand data and forecasts, production schedules, new product launch details and bill of material changes.

To enable this degree of visibility and transparency, synchronisation requires a high level of *process alignment*, which itself demands a higher level of collaborative working. These are issues to which we shall return. The box below indicates some of the key processes that need to be linked, upstream and downstream, to provide the foundation for supply chain synchronisation.

- **Planning and scheduling**: Material positioning/visibility, advanced planning, scheduling, forecasting, capacity management.

- **Design**: Mechanical design, electrical design, design for supply chain, component selection.

- **New product introduction**: Bill of materials management, prototyping, design validation, testing, production validation, transfer to volume.

- **Product content management**: Change generation, change impact assessment, product change release, change cut-in/phase-out.

- **Order management**: Order capture/configuration, available to promise, order tracking, exception management.

- **Sourcing and procurement**: Approved vendor management, strategic sourcing, supplier selection, component selection.

Source: Cookson, C. 'Linking supply chains to support collaborative manufacturing', *Ascet*, Vol. 3, 2001, www.ascet.com

Figure 7.1 depicts the difference between the conventional supply chain with limited transfer of information and the synchronous supply chain with network-wide visibility and transparency.

The extended enterprise and the virtual supply chain

The nature of business enterprise is changing. Today's business is increasingly 'boundaryless', meaning that internal functional barriers are being eroded in favour of horizontal process management and externally the separation between vendors, distributors, customers and the firm is gradually lessening. This is the idea of the *extended enterprise*, which is transforming our thinking on how organisations compete and how value chains might be reformulated.

Underpinning the concept of the extended enterprise is a common information 'highway'. It is the use of shared information that enables cross-functional, horizontal management to become a reality. Even more importantly it is information shared between partners in the supply chain that makes possible the responsive flow of product from one end of the pipeline to another. What has now come to be termed the virtual enterprise or supply chain is in effect a series of relationships between partners that is based upon the *value-added exchange of information*. Figure 7.2 illustrates the concept.

The notion that partnership arrangements and a mentality of co-operation are more effective than the traditional arm's-length and often adversarial basis of relationships is now gaining ground. Thus the supply chain is becoming a confederation of organisations that agree common goals and who bring specific

Figure 7.1 Achieving synchronisation through shared information: (a) before synchronisation; (b) after sychronisation

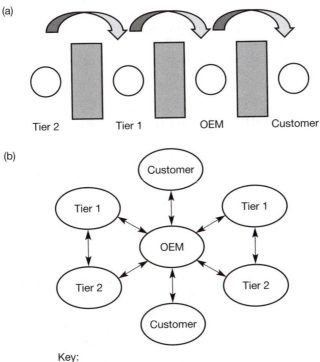

Key:
OEM = Original equipment manufacturer
Tier 1 and 2 = Supplier echelons

Figure 7.2 The extended enterprise and the virtual supply chain

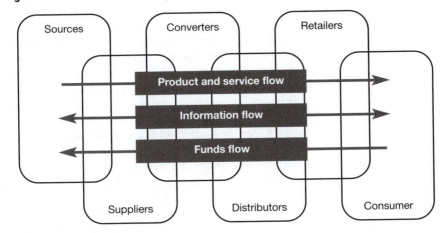

Source: A.T. Kearney

strengths to the overall value creation and value delivery system. This process is being accelerated as the trend towards outsourcing continues. Outsourcing should not be confused with 'subcontracting' where a task or an activity is simply handed over to a specialist. In a way it would be better to use the term 'in-sourcing' or 're-sourcing', when we refer to the quite different concept of partnering that the virtual supply chain depends upon. These partnerships may not be for all time – quite possibly they exist only to exploit a specific market opportunity – but they will be 'seamless' and truly synergetic.

The role of information in the virtual supply chain

Leading organisations have long recognised that the key to success in supply chain management is the information system. However, what we are now learning is that there is a dimension to information that enables supply and demand to be matched in multiple markets, often with tailored products, in ever-shorter time-frames.

This extension of the information system beyond the classical dimensions of simple planning and control enables time and space to be collapsed through the ability to link the customer directly to the supplier and for the supplier to react, sometimes in real time, to changes in the market. Rayport and Sviokla[1] have coined the term 'marketspace' to describe the new world of electronic commerce, internets and virtual supply chains. In the marketspace, customer demand can be identified as it occurs and, through CAD/CAM and flexible manufacturing, products created in minimal batch sizes. Equally, networks of specialist suppliers can be joined together to create innovative yet cost-effective solutions for complex design and manufacturing problems. The way that Airbus now designs and assembles its advanced aeroplanes, for example, would not be possible without the use of global information networks that link one end of the value chain to the other.

The Internet has in many ways transformed the ways in which supply chain members can connect with each other.[2] It provides a perfect vehicle for the establishment of the virtual supply chain. Not only does it enable vast global markets to be accessed at minimal cost and allow customers to shorten dramatically search time and reduce transaction costs, but it also enables different organisations in a supply chain to share information with each other in a highly cost-effective way. *Extranets* as they have come to be termed are revolutionising supply chain management. Organisations with quite different internal information systems can now access data from customers on sales or product usage and can use that information to manage replenishment and to alert their suppliers of forthcoming requirements.

One of Britain's major retailers, Tesco, is using an extranet to link with its suppliers to share point-of-sale data. At the same time the company is successfully running a home shopping and delivery system for consumers over the Internet. Within the business, *intranets* are in place that enable information to be shared between stores and to facilitate communication across the business. We are probably even now only scraping the surface in terms of how the Internet and its associated technologies can be used to further exploit the virtual supply chain. Figure 7.3 highlights some of the current applications of Internet-based concepts to supply chain management.

Figure 7.3 Internet applications and the supply chain

Customer service
- Information and support products and services
- Electronic help desk
- Mass customisation and order processing

Marketing channel
- Public relations and advertising
- Market research and test
- Electronic mails and catalogues

Information retrieval
- Online news
- Statistics, reports and databases
- Data mining
- Competitive analysis

Supplier relationships
- Logistics
- Product search
- Electronic data interchange
- Ordering and payment
- Supply chain integration

Financial transactions
- Selling and payment
- Managing accounts
- Credit card payments

Building strategic alliances
- Newsletters, bulletin boards, discussion databases
- Sharing knowledge and experience

Electronic distribution
- Product, data, information

Internal communications
- Complete internal, external, vertical and horizontal communications
- Groupware
- E-mail
- Collaboration
- Knowledge transfer
- Telecommuting

Human resources and employee relations
- Job opening posting
- Expert search
- Employee training and support
- Distance learning

Sales force automation
- On-site configuration and order processing
- Sales process transformation

Internet
Intranet
Extranet

Source: A.T. Kearney

The IT solutions now exist to enable supply chain partners to share information easily and at relatively low cost. A major benefit that flows from this greater transparency is that the internal operations of the business can become much more efficient as a result. For example, by capturing customer demand data sooner, better utilisation of production and transport capacity can be achieved through better planning or scheduling. Figure 7.4 indicates some of the uses to which improved logistics information can be put.

Figure 7.4 Functions of a logistics information system

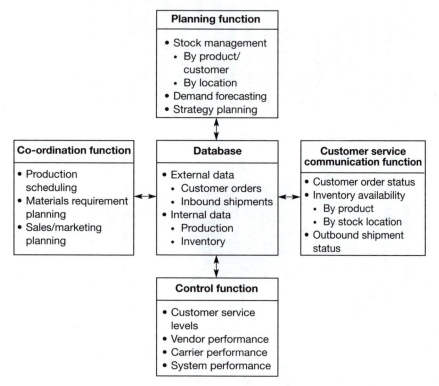

Increasingly, it seems that successful companies have one thing in common – their use of information and information technology to improve customer responsiveness. Information systems are reshaping the organisation and also the nature of the linkages between organisations. Information has always been central to the efficient management of logistics but now, enabled by technology, it is providing the driving force for competitive logistics strategy.

We are now starting to see the emergence of integrated logistics systems that link the operations of the business, such as production and distribution, with the supplier's operations on the one hand and the customer on the other.[3] Already it is the case that companies can literally link the replenishment of product in the marketplace with their upstream operations and those of their suppliers through the use of shared information. The use of these systems has the potential to convert supply chains into demand chains in the sense that the system can now respond to known demand rather than having to anticipate that demand through a forecast. Figure 7.5 describes the architecture of such a system.

One company that has recognised the importance of improving supply chain visibility through shared information is Cisco Systems, a market leader in telecommunications and network equipment (see below).

Cisco Systems: creating a virtual supply chain through shared information

Cisco Systems, one of the world's leading players in the networking and telecommunications markets, has created a virtual supply chain in which almost all manufacturing and physical logistics are outsourced to specialist contract manufacturers and third-party logistics companies. Only a very small proportion of their 20,000 different stock keeping units are actually 'touched' by Cisco.

Following a sudden collapse in sales as the Internet bubble of the closing years of the twentieth century finally burst, Cisco was forced to write off over $2 billion of obsolete inventory. Subsequent investigations highlighted the reason for this spectacular fall from grace: inadequate visibility of real demand across the entire supply chain leading to significant over-ordering of components.

Determined not to see a repeat of this catastrophic event – the size of the inventory write-off created a new world record and led to a major financial setback for the company – Cisco set out to build a state of the art communications network to enable information to be shared across the 'extended enterprise' of their major tier 1 suppliers and logistics service providers. This has been achieved through the creation of an 'e-hub'. The purpose of the e-hub is to act as the nerve centre and to ensure real-time visibility of demand, inventory levels and production schedules. Through its event management capability it can provide early warning of supply chain problems.

As a result of its investment in creating supply chain wide visibility through shared information, Cisco has enabled a highly synchronised network of global partners to act as if they were a single business.

Laying the foundations for synchronisation

In the same way that the conventional wisdom in production and manufacturing is to seek economies of scale through larger batch quantities, similar thinking can often be found in the rest of the supply chain. Thus companies might seek to ship by the container or truck load, customers are discouraged from ordering in smaller quantities by price penalties and delivery schedules are typically based on optimising the efficiency of routes and the consolidation of deliveries. Clearly such an

Figure 7.5 An integrated logistics information system

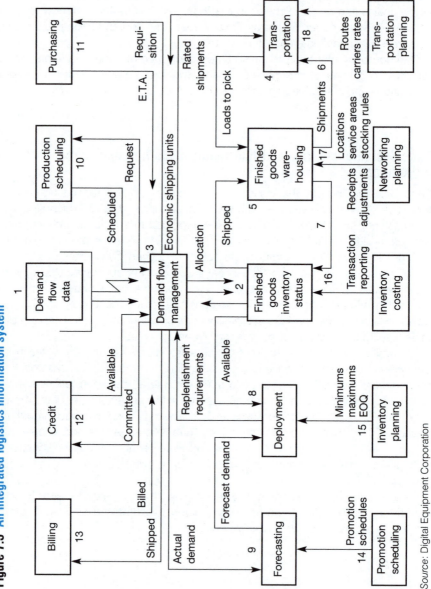

Source: Digital Equipment Corporation

approach runs counter to the requirements of a synchronous supply chain. Under the synchronisation philosophy the requirement is for small shipments to be made more frequently and to meet the precise time requirements of the customer.

The challenge to logistics management is to find ways in which these changed requirements can be achieved without an uneconomic escalation of costs. There may have to be trade-offs but the goal must be to improve total supply chain cost effectiveness.

The basic principle of synchronisation is to ensure that all elements of the chain act as one, and hence there must be early identification of shipping and replenishment requirements and, most importantly of all, there must be the highest level of planning discipline.

In a synchronous supply chain the management of in-bound materials flow becomes a crucial issue. In particular the search for consolidation opportunities has to be a priority. Thus, for example, rather than one supplier making a series of deliveries in small quantities to a customer, the orders from a number of suppliers are combined into a single delivery. It is perhaps not surprising that the emergence of synchronous supply chains as a management philosophy has coincided with the growth of third-party distribution and logistics companies specialising in providing an in-bound consolidation service.

These logistics service companies can manage the pick-up of materials and components from suppliers on a 'milk round' basis, using a central 'hub' or transhipment centre for re-sorting and consolidating for in-bound delivery. They may also perform certain value-adding activities such as quality control, kitting, sequencing or final finishing. In complex assembly operations such as motor manufacture the prior sequencing of parts and components prior to assembly is a crucial activity (see the example below of seat delivery to Nissan's assembly line in north-east England).

Synchronised delivery: how Nissan Motors UK receives vehicle seats
Elapsed hours

0   Painted body passes to trim line in Nissan
    Precise vehicle specifications of next 12 vehicles transmitted by computer from Nissan to seat suppliers
    Supplier transfers information to picking lists
    Seat covers selected from range

1   Covers prepared for assembly (in reverse order)
    Seat assembly from synchronised manufacture of sub-assemblies (frames, foams, finishers, plastic parts)

2   Quality audit and load
    Delivery of seats to stock holding point by special purpose vehicle
    Stock to lineside

3   Rear seats fitted followed by front seats (waiting stillages returned to empty wagon)
    Delivery frequency now every 15–20 minutes

Similar developments have enabled the transformation of retail logistics. The idea of 'stockless distribution centres' or 'cross-docking' enables a more frequent and efficient replenishment of product from manufacture to individual stores. Cross-docking, often facilitated by a logistics service provider, is a simple, but powerful, concept. Point-of-sale data from individual stores is transmitted to the retailer's head office to enable them to determine replenishment requirements. This information is then transmitted directly to the suppliers who assemble orders for specific stores and the pallets or cases are then bar-coded (or increasingly electronically tagged). On a pre-planned basis these store orders are then collected by the logistics service provider and are taken to a transhipment centre (the 'cross-dock' facility) – possibly operated by the logistics service provider – where they are sorted for store delivery along with other suppliers' orders. In effect, a just-in-time delivery is achieved, which enables minimum stock to be carried in the retail stores, and yet transport costs are contained through the principles of consolidation (see Figures 7.6 and 7.7).

Figure 7.6 Daily sales data drives the replenishment order system

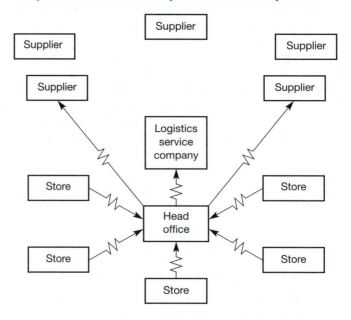

'Quick response' logistics

An outgrowth of the synchronisation philosophy has emerged in recent years under the banner of 'quick response' logistics.[4] The basic idea behind quick response (QR) is that in order to reap the advantages of time-based competition it is necessary to develop systems that are responsive and fast. Hence QR is the umbrella term for the information systems and the logistics systems that combine to provide 'the right product in the right place at the right time'.

Figure 7.7 Acting on this information a consolidated pick-up and store delivery sequence is activated

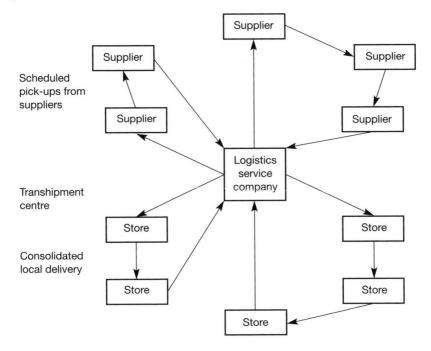

Scheduled pick-ups from suppliers

Transhipment centre

Consolidated local delivery

> The basic idea behind quick response (QR) is that in order to reap the advantages of time-based competition it is necessary to develop systems that are responsive and fast.

What has made QR possible is the development of information technology and in particular the rise of Internet-enabled data exchange, bar coding, the use of electronic point-of-sale (EPOS) systems with laser scanners and so on.

Essentially the logic behind QR is that demand is captured in as close to real-time as possible and as close to the final consumer as possible. The logistics response is then made directly as a result of that information. An example of such an approach is provided in the United States by Procter & Gamble which receives sales data directly from the check-out counters of North America's largest retailer, Wal-Mart. Making use of this information P&G can plan production and schedule delivery to Wal-Mart on a replenishment basis. The result is that Wal-Mart carries less inventory yet has fewer stock-outs and P&G benefits from better economies in production and logistics as a result of the early warning and – most importantly – greatly increased sales to Wal-Mart. Whilst the investment in the information system is considerable, so too is the payback.

A further feature in favour of QR systems is that by speeding up processing time in the system, cumulative lead times are reduced. This can then result in lower inventory (see Figure 7.8) and thus further reduce response times. In effect a 'virtuous circle'!

Figure 7.8 Quick response system can trigger a 'virtuous circle' in logistics

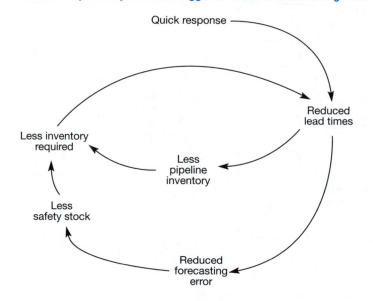

Quick response systems have begun to emerge in the fashion and apparel industry where the costs of traditional inventory-based systems based upon buyers' prior purchase decisions (in effect a 'push' system) can be considerable. In the United States it is estimated that the annual costs to the US textile and apparel industry of conventional logistics systems is $25 billion. This comprises the following elements:

Forced markdowns	$14.08bn
Stock-outs	$6.08bn
Inventory carrying costs	$5.08bn
Total:	**$25.24bn**

There could be massive advantages to be gained by all parties in the supply chain if the concept of QR was adopted throughout the chain. Thus in the case of fashion garments the aim should be to link retail sales with the apparel manufacturers, who in turn are linked to the textile producers who themselves are linked to the suppliers of fibres. One such reported case is the linkage through shared information of the US textile company Milliken with the Seminole Manufacturing Company (a manufacturer of men's slacks) and the retailer Wal-Mart. Information on end-user demand was captured at the point-of-sale and rapidly fed back up the supply chain, enabling dramatic reductions in lead times to be achieved and hence substantial reductions in inventory.

Another case from the US is provided by the chain of retail fashion stores, The Limited. Each of the several thousand stores in the chain tracks consumer preferences daily using their point-of-sale data. Based upon this, orders are sent by satellite links to the suppliers around the world. Using Hong Kong as a consolidation centre, goods are flown back to The Limited's distribution centre in Columbus, Ohio. At the distribution centre the goods are price-marked and re-sorted for immediate onward shipment by truck and plane to the retail stores. The whole cycle from reorder to in-store display can be achieved in six weeks. Conventional systems take more like six months.

Production strategies for quick response

As the demand by all partners in the supply chain for a quick response increases, the greater will be the pressure placed upon manufacturing to meet the customer's needs for variety in shorter and shorter time-frames.

The answer has to lie in flexibility. As we have already observed, if it were possible to reduce manufacturing and logistics lead times to zero then total flexibility could be achieved. In other words the organisation could respond to any request that was technologically feasible in any quantity. Whilst zero lead times are obviously not achievable, the new focus on flexible manufacturing systems (FMS) has highlighted the possibility of substantial progress in this direction.

The key to flexibility in manufacturing is not just new technology, e.g. robotics, although this can contribute dramatically to its achievement. The main barrier to flexibility is the time taken to change; to change from one level of volume to another and to change from making one variant to another. Typically we call this 'set-up time'. It will be apparent that if set-up times can be driven as close as possible to zero then flexible response to customer requirements presents no problem.

The Japanese, not surprisingly, have led the way in developing techniques for set-up time reduction. 'Single minute exchange of die', or SMED, is the goal in many Japanese plants. In other words continuous attention by management and the workforce is focused upon the ways in which set-up times can be reduced. Sometimes it will involve new technology, but more often than not it is achieved through taking a totally different look at the process itself. In many cases set-up times have been reduced from hours down to minutes, simply by questioning the conventional wisdom.

What in effect we are seeing is a fundamental shift away from the economies of scale model, which is volume based and hence implies long production runs with few change-overs, to the economies of scope model, which is based upon producing small quantities of a wider range, hence requiring more change-overs.

It has been suggested that under the economies of scope model:

... a single plant can produce a variety of output at the same cost as (if not lower than) a separate plant, dedicated to producing only one type of product at a given level. In other words an economic order quantity (EOQ) of one unit, and specific production designs, engender no additional costs. Economies of scope change the materials-driven, batch-system technology into a multi-functional, flow system configuration.

SOURCE: D. LEI AND J.D. GOLDHARS[5]

The marketing advantages that such flexibility brings are considerable. It means that in effect the company can cater for the precise needs of multiple customers, and they can offer even higher levels of customisation. In today's marketplace where customers seek individuality and where segments or 'niches' are getting ever smaller, a major source of competitive advantage can be gained by linking production flexibility to customers' needs for variety.

A classic example is provided by Benetton, the Italian fashion goods manufacturer and distributor, which has created a worldwide business based upon responsiveness to fashion changes – with a particular emphasis upon colour. By developing an innovative process whereby entire knitted garments can be dyed in small batches, they reduced the need to carry inventory of multiple colours, and because of the small batch sizes for dying they greatly enhanced their flexibility. Benetton's speed of response is also assisted by the investment that they have made in high-speed distribution systems, which are themselves aided by rapid feedback of sales information from the marketplace.

Many companies are now seeking to construct supply chains to enable them to support a marketing strategy of *mass customisation*. The idea behind this is that today's customers in many markets are increasingly demanding tailored solutions for their specific requirements. The challenge is to find ways of achieving this marketing goal without increasing finished goods inventory and without incurring the higher costs of production normally associated with make-to-order.

Often this can be achieved by postponing the final configuration or assembly of the product until the actual customer requirement is known – a strategy pursued by Dell and Hewlett Packard, for example.

In other cases high technology in the form of computer-aided design/computer-aided manufacturing (CAD/CAM) can provide the means for this mass customisation.

Logistics systems dynamics

One of the major advantages of moving to QR and synchronous supply chain strategies is that, by reducing lot quantities and increasing the rate of throughput in the logistics system, modulations in the level of activity in the pipeline can be reduced.

Logistics systems are prone to what has been called the 'Bullwhip' or 'Forrester Effect', after Jay Forrester, who developed a set of techniques known as Industrial Dynamics.Forrester defined industrial dynamics as:

The study of the information feedback characteristics of industrial activity to show how organizational structure, amplification (in policies) and time delays (in decisions and returns) interact to influence the success of the enterprise. It treats the interactions between the flows of information, money, orders, materials, personnel, and capital equipment in a company, an industry or a national economy.[6]

Using a specially developed computer simulation language, DYNAMO, Forrester built a model of a production/distribution system involving three levels in the distribution channel: a retailer's inventory, a distributor's inventory and a factory inventory. Each level was interconnected through information flows and flows of goods. The model used real-world relationships and data and included parameters such as order transmission times, order processing times, factory lead times and shipment delivery times. Management could then examine the effects on the total system of, say, a change in retail sales or the impact of changing production levels or any other policy change or combination of changes.

What becomes apparent from this modelling of complex systems is that small disturbances in one part of the system can very quickly become magnified as the effect spreads through the pipeline.

For example, many consumer product companies that are heavy spenders on trade promotions (e.g. special discounts, incentives, etc.) do not realise what the true costs of such activities are. In the first instance there is the loss of profit through the discount itself, and then there is the hidden cost of the disturbance to the logistics system. Consider first the loss of profit. When a discount is offered for a limited period then that discount obviously will apply to all sales – not just any incremental sales. So if sales during the promotional period are, say, 1,100 cases but without the promotion they would have been 1,000, then whilst the incremental revenue comes only from the additional 100 cases, the discount applies to all 1,100. Additionally the retailer may decide to take advantage of the discount and 'forward order'; in other words buy ahead of requirement to sell at a later time at the regular price. One study[7] found that for these reasons only 16 per cent of promotions were profitable, the rest only 'bought sales' at a loss.

The second impact of promotional activity on profit is the potential it provides for triggering the 'acceleration effect' and hence creating a Forrester-type surge throughout the logistics pipeline. This is because in most logistics systems there will be 'leads and lags', in other words the response to an input or a change in the system may be delayed. For example, the presence of a warehouse or a stock holding intermediary in the distribution channel can cause a substantial distortion in demand at the factory. This is due to the 'acceleration effect', which can cause self-generated fluctuations in the operating characteristics of a system.

As an example, imagine a retailer with an inventory management reordering strategy based on starting each week with the equivalent of three weeks' demand in stock. So if weekly demand were 100 units for a particular item the target starting inventory would be 300 (i.e. 100 × 3). Now let us assume that as a result of a promotion demand increases by 10 per cent to 110. This means that the system would place an order to bring the next week's starting inventory up to 330 (i.e. 110 × 3). So the reorder quantity would have to be 140 (i.e. the 110 units sold to consumers plus the extra 30 required to meet the new starting level).

In this particular case an increase in consumer demand of 10 per cent leads to a one-off increase in demand on the supplier of 40 per cent!

If in the next period consumer demand were to fall back to its old level then the same effect would happen in reverse.

It is not unusual for companies undertaking frequent promotional activity to experience considerable upswings and downswings in factory shipments on a continuing basis. Figure 7.9 illustrates the lagged and magnified effect of such promotional activity upon the factory. It can be imagined that such unpredictable changes in production requirements add considerably to the unit costs of production.

Figure 7.9 **The impact of promotional activity upon production requirement**

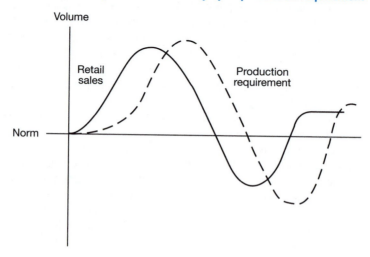

In the grocery industry, where much of this promotional activity is found, there is a growing recognition of the need to achieve a closer linkage between the ordering policies of the retail trade and the manufacturing schedules of the supplier. In the United States it was estimated that the time from the end of the production line to purchase by the consumer in a retail store was 84 days for a typical dry grocery product (see Figures 7.10 and 7.11).

This means that the 'tidal wave' effect of changes in demand can be considerably magnified as they pass through all the intermediate stock holding and reorder points. One of the benefits of a quick response system is that by linking the retail check-out desk to the point of production through electronic data transfer, the surge effect can be dramatically reduced. This fact alone could more than justify the initial investment in linked buyer/supplier logistics information systems.

Figure 7.10 Grocery industry delivery system order cycle

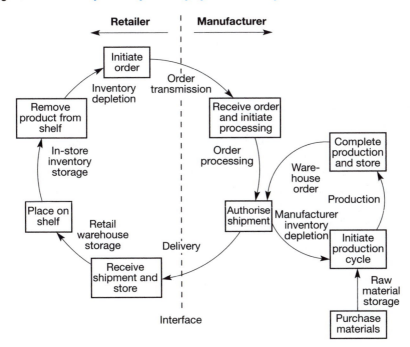

Source: Grocery Manufacturers Association of America

Figure 7.11 Grocery industry product flow

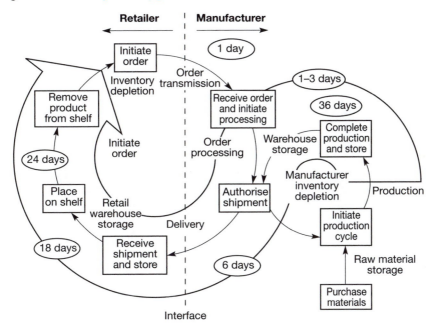

Source: Grocery Manufacturers Association of America

References

1. Rayport, J.F. and Sviokla, J.J., 'Managing in the marketspace', *Harvard Business Review*, November–December 1994.
2. Chandrashekar, A. and Schary, P., 'The virtual web-based supply chain', in Franke, U. (ed.), *Managing Virtual Web Organizations in the 21st Century*, Idea Group Publishing, 2002.
3. Heinrich, C., *Adapt or Die: Transforming your Supply Chain into an Adaptive Business Network*, John Wiley & Sons, 2003.
4. Lowson, R., King, R. and Hunter, A., *Quick Response: Managing the Supply Chain to Meet Consumer Demand*, John Wiley & Sons, 1999.
5. Lei, D. and Goldhars, J.D., 'Computer-Integrated manufacturing: redefining the manufacturing firm into a global service business', *International Journal of Operations & Production Management*, Vol. 11, No. 10, 1991.
6. Forrester, J., *Industrial Dynamics*, MIT Press, 1961.
7. Abraham, M.M. and Lodish, L.M., 'Getting the most out of advertising and promotion', *Harvard Business Review*, May–June 1990.

Complexity and the supply chain

8

- The sources of supply chain complexity

- The cost of complexity

- Product design and supply chain complexity

- Mastering complexity

We have several times in previous chapters suggested that rather than refer to supply *chains* we should talk instead about *networks*. The idea of a chain suggests a series of linear one-to-one relationships whereas the reality is that the focal firm lies at the centre of a complex web of interconnected and interrelated yet independent entities.

Partly as a result of outsourcing activities that previously were performed in-house combined with the trend to offshore manufacturing, many companies have found that they have added to the complexity of their operations because the degree of *interdependency* across the network has increased. Thus an event or action taking place in one part of the network will often have unforeseen impacts somewhere else in the network. The unpredictability of these events is heightened by the growing volatility that characterises today's business environment.

The well-known 'butterfly' effect seems to typify much of today's supply chain turbulence. The idea is that a butterfly, flapping its wings somewhere over the Amazon basin, can cause a hurricane thousands of miles away! Whilst this example of what is sometimes described as 'chaotic' effects may be a little far-fetched, it provides a useful reminder of how the 'law of unintended consequences' applies to today's highly interconnected supply chains.

In April 2010 a previously dormant volcano in Iceland erupted, sending a plume of ash into the upper atmosphere. A cloud of ash and debris from the eruption began to drift across the skies of Northern Europe. Because of a concern for aircraft safety most airports in the region were closed for the best part of a week. Whilst there was a considerable impact on individuals' travel plans – many thousands of people were stranded away from home – there was also a less visible, but significant, impact on a number of supply chains. Many time-critical components are sent by air freight or air express and as major hubs in the UK and continental Europe were forced to close, the 'butterfly effect' was felt around the world. The extract from The *Times* below illustrates some of the problems caused by a volcano a long way from the factories that were affected, and thus highlights the increasing interconnectedness of global supply chains.

Parts shortage starts to choke production

The impact of the ash cloud has been felt on the economy for the first time, with manufacturing companies warning that they will have to shut down production because of a shortage of components.

Airbus, the aircraft manufacturer, said yesterday that its wing assembly facility in North Wales would have to slow or shut production within days if the airspace did not reopen.

The company, which employs 11,000 people in Britain, has been unable to get parts into the country. It has also been unable to fly completed wings to Airbus's other factories in Hamburg and Toulouse, which could result in the final assembly of aircraft grinding to a halt.

The impact on the globalised nature of industry has affected Nissan. Two factories in Japan will stop production of cars from today after running out of a key component sourced from the Irish Republic.

The closure of airspace is estimated to be costing the European economy about £400 million a day in lost productivity.

SOURCE: ROBERTSON, D. AND DEROUX, M., 'PARTS SHORTAGE STARTS TO CHOKE PRODUCTION', *THE TIMES*, 21 APRIL 2010

In its strictest sense, complexity does not mean complicated (although complex systems often are complicated) but rather it describes a condition of interconnectedness and interdependency across a network. A good example of a complex system is the weather. Many different influences combine to create a specific weather condition; each of those influences are themselves the result of interactions and hence a small change in one element can fundamentally affect the final outcome. Hence the difficulties faced by weather forecasters trying to predict even tomorrow's weather.

Therefore the outcome of complexity in a supply chain, as with the weather, is uncertainty and with that uncertainty comes an increased likelihood that forecast error will increase in line with complexity. This growing uncertainty brings with it a serious challenge to the classic practice of running the business on the basis of forecasts. It will be apparent that in conditions of stability – and hence lower uncertainty – forecast accuracy should generally be high. Equally, the converse will be true, i.e. as uncertainty increases so too will forecast accuracy reduce. Hence the argument that if uncertainty is to be the norm – at least for the foreseeable future – then a new approach will be required. Indeed, the challenge that organisations now face is how to reduce their dependence on forecasts and to become increasingly demand- and event-driven.

The sources of supply chain complexity

Complexity in a supply chain can arise from a number of sources and some of the most common causes are detailed below.

1 Network complexity

The more nodes and links that exist in a network then clearly the more complex it becomes. As a result of outsourcing non-core activities many companies are today much more reliant on external suppliers of goods and services. Those external suppliers also are dependent upon a web of second tier suppliers, and so on. There is a strong likelihood that the focal firm at the centre of the network will not even be aware of many of the second or third tier suppliers that feed their upstream supply chain. The potential for unexpected disruptions to the supply chain is clearly heightened by these extended networks as evidenced by the following example.

Following the shut-down of Dell's American assembly line within days of the September 1999 earthquake in Taiwan the company set out to understand why this had happened.

To do this Dell studied where their tier-one suppliers did their shopping and this in turn soon yielded the first important answer – the Taiwan Semiconductor Manufacturing Corporation (TSMC). Dell's executives realised that they were in fact buying hundreds of millions of dollars of chips each year from TSMC indirectly.

Source: Abridged from Lynn, B.C., *The End of the Line*, Doubleday, 2005

---

2 Process complexity

Underpinning every supply chain are innumerable processes – processes internal to the firm as well as those processes managed by upstream and downstream partners. Often these processes have been developed in a haphazard way and have been added to and modified to reflect current requirements and as a result have become more complex. This complexity is manifested in processes with multiple steps, often performed in series rather than in parallel.

Lengthy processes containing many different activities will not only create extended lead times but are also more prone to variability in performance.

The more steps in a process and the more 'hand-offs' that exist, the greater the likelihood that there will be frequent discrepancies between planned and actual outcomes.

There is a need for a constant review of process structure and a consequent re-engineering if this pervasive source of supply chain complexity is to be kept to a minimum.

When end-to-end supply chains are examined in detail it usually transpires that the majority of time is non-value-adding time. More often than not this non-value-adding time is idle time – in other words time spent as inventory. This non-value-adding time is itself generated by the processes that underpin the supply chain.

3 Range complexity

Most business organisations find that the range of products and/or services that they offer to the market has a tendency to grow rather than reduce. The rate of introduction of new products or services, new pack sizes or variants and brand extensions seems to outpace the rate at which existing products or services are eliminated. The general effect of this mushrooming of the product/service portfolio is to extend the 'long tail' of the Pareto distribution.

Typically as more variants are added to a range the demand per variant will reduce, with a subsequent impact on forecast accuracy. Consider the difference between the Ford Motor Company at the time of Henry Ford I producing a single model – the Model T, with the reputed offer of 'any colour you like as long as it's black' – with the company today.

Ford, even in today's troubled markets, offers a vast range of models with extensive options. In theory there are possibly millions of different variants! This multiplication of the product range means that, inevitably, the average demand per variant is very low. Hence the difficulty of forecasting at the individual variant level and thus the typically large inventories that build up as a result of forecast error.

4 Product complexity

The design of products can have a significant impact on supply chain complexity. It can be argued that the supply chain begins on the drawing board in that decisions on the choice of materials and components can directly or indirectly impact total life cycle costs as well as agility and responsiveness.

Product complexity can arise because the number of components or sub-assemblies is high, or because there is little commonality across the Bills of Materials for different products. The less the commonality at the Bill of Materials level the less the flexibility to vary product mix or volume.

A further unforeseen impact of product design decisions is that if components or materials are specified which happen to have lengthy replenishment lead times then the ability to respond rapidly to changes in demand for the product will be impeded.

By involving logistics and supply chain planners early in the design process much of the subsequent complexity can be avoided. For example, at Motorola all new product ideas are screened for complexity[1] before they can be considered for commercialisation.

In the past at Motorola there was often little commonality of parts across the range. For a single mobile phone there could be over 100 possible configurations, i.e. four different colours and 30 software choices. Furthermore, these product variations were made ahead of demand to a forecast that was only accurate 3 per cent of the time! To tackle this problem Motorola devised a 'Complexity Index' for each product, which included the number of components, the degree of commonality, lead time of supply and so on. Ideas for new products with high scores on the Complexity Index tend not to be proceeded with.

5 Customer complexity

Customer complexity arises as a result of too many non-standard service options or customised solutions. The costs of serving different customers can vary significantly. Each customer will exhibit different characteristics in terms of their ordering patterns, e.g. frequency of orders, size of orders, delivery requirements and so on. These differences will be increased further as a result of the availability of different service options or packages and/or customisation possibilities.

Gottfredson and Aspinall give an example of how too extensive a service offer can add complexity to the sales process:

> One telecommunications company, for example, has used the power of information technology to slice and dice its service set into ever more finely differentiated options. The firm hoped it would boost revenues by more precisely fulfilling the needs of every imaginable buyer. But offering so many options has had the opposite effect. The company's customer service reps are now forced to sort through more than a thousand promotion codes whilst they're talking to a potential customer. Most of the promotions offer distinct levels of discounts and product benefits. Making sense of them all is an overwhelming task.[2]

Even though from a sales and marketing perspective there may be advantages to be gained from offering a range of options to customers, these decisions must be tempered by a detailed knowledge of their cost and agility implications. Ultimately the only complexity that can be justified is that complexity which delivers real value for which customers are prepared to pay.

A problem that is faced by many businesses is that they have a limited understanding of the true costs of servicing individual customers. It is quite possible that because some customers generate a high cost-to-serve and order products with relatively low margins they could actually lose money for the company. Using tools such as activity-based costing can help identify those customers whose cost-to-serve is high relative to the revenue that they generate. Using this information, alternative service options might be devised that could improve the profitability of those customers.

6 Supplier complexity

The size of the supplier base can add to supply chain complexity by increasing the number of relationships that must be managed as well as increasing total transaction costs. Because one of the pre-requisites for agility is a high level of collaborative working with key suppliers, this implies a high level of active supplier management and supplier involvement in process integration. It is unlikely that this degree of closeness can be achieved across a diverse supplier base and hence the need for rationalisation. The implications of such a supply base rationalisation are profound. Clearly careful regard must be paid to the effect of a smaller number of suppliers on the resulting supply chain risk profile. Too high a level of dependence on just a few critical suppliers can be dangerous. Instead a better option, if available, is to have a lead supplier across a category of products who takes responsibility for the management of that category across a number of suppliers, for example in the same way a logistics service company such as UPS might co-ordinate a number of logistics and transport providers for a client company.

With a smaller supplier base, a company can more proactively manage supplier relationships through 'supplier development' programmes. Typically such programmes involve the company working closely with individual suppliers to identify opportunities to improve not just product quality, but also process quality and to work jointly on cost-reduction initiatives.

5 Organisational complexity

Most businesses have traditionally organised around functions and departments and their organisation charts have many levels and tend to be hierarchical in their structure. Such 'vertical' organisational arrangements are no doubt administratively convenient in that there can be a 'division of labour' between functions as well as effective budgetary control. However, they tend to inhibit agility because they are, of necessity, inwardly looking with a focus on efficiency rather than customer facing with a focus on effectiveness. A further problem is that over time the functions have a tendency to become 'silos' with their own agendas and they can lose sight of the fundamental purpose of the business, i.e. to win and keep profitable customers.

The challenge is to find a way to break through these silos and to re-shape the organisation around the key value-creating and value-delivery processes. Such process-oriented businesses are 'horizontal' rather than 'vertical' in their orientation. They are cross-functional and hence there is a stronger emphasis on teams and on process improvement in terms of speed and reliability.

As organisations grow, either organically or through merger and acquisition, the likelihood is that they will become more cumbersome and less able to respond rapidly to change. Consequently there is a constant need to re-engineer existing processes and to root out the complexity that will inevitably arise if things are left to themselves. Organisational complexity can also be exacerbated by having to work across time zones and cultures as a result of the globalisation of business. Frequently this added complexity is an unintended consequence of low-cost country sourcing and/or cross-border mergers.

8 Information complexity

Today's supply chains are underpinned by the exchange of information between all the entities and levels that comprise the complete end-to-end network. The volume of data that flows in all directions is immense and not always accurate and can be prone to misinterpretation. Visibility of actual demand and supply conditions can be obscured through the way that information is filtered and modified as it passes from one entity or level to another. The so-called 'bullwhip' effect is a manifestation of the way that demand signals can be considerably distorted as a result of multiple steps in the chain. As a result of this distortion, the data that is used as input to planning and forecasting activities can be flawed and hence forecast accuracy is reduced and more costs are incurred.

In a sense, information complexity in a supply chain is directly or indirectly influenced by the preceding seven sources of complexity. Network and process complexity will impact the number of stages, steps and levels through which the information must pass; range and product complexity add variety and lead to multiple Bills of Materials and hence more data; customer and supplier complexity means that the exchange of data increases significantly and organisational complexity implies more levels through which information must pass as well as more hand-offs from one function to another.

The antidote to information complexity is firstly a reduction in the other seven sources of complexity as well as greater visibility. A key to that visibility has to be a greater level of collaborative working across the supply chain where information transparency is seen as a vital pre-requisite for a more efficient and effective value delivery system.

The cost of complexity

It can be argued that an increasing proportion of total end-to-end costs in the supply chain are driven by complexity in one form or another. Often these costs may not be readily transparent as they are hidden in general overheads or the costs of carrying inventory, which as we observed in Chapter 3 are not always properly accounted for.

Underlying much of the cost of complexity in the supply chain is the Pareto Law (the so-called 80:20 rule). Vilfredo Pareto (1848–1923) was an Italian industrialist, sociologist, economist and philosopher. In 1909 he identified that 80 per cent of the total wealth of Italy was held by just 20 per cent of the population. Thus was born the 80:20 rule that has been found to hold across many aspects of social and economic life. In Chapter 2 it was suggested that an 80:20 relationship exists with regard to customers and products, i.e. typically 80 per cent of the profit derives from 20 per cent of the customer and likewise 80 per cent of the profit comes from just 20 per cent of the products. Generally this 80:20 relationship applies across most elements of the supply chain and is a key contributor to complexity and hence cost.

Most businesses will find if they perform an 80:20 analysis that they have a 'long-tail' of customers who, whilst significant in numbers, actually contribute very little to overall profitability – indeed some may actually make a loss. Likewise, the same conclusions would probably emerge from an 80:20 analysis of products.

Sometimes when performing the 80:20 analysis across the product range, it is tempting to suggest that where a 'long tail' exists it should be removed through product rationalisation. However, there may be strategic reasons for maintaining a high level of variety or indeed there may be opportunities to use alternative strategies to manage the slow movers to make them profitable. For example, it has been suggested that if an Internet distribution channel is available then the 'long tail' can become a source of profitable business.[3] Because the 'long tail' represents such a large number of products, even though individual item sales levels are low, if inventory and distribution costs can be reduced by creating a single, virtual inventory through working with partners across multiple channels, the economics may be transformed. To a certain extent this is the approach that Amazon has taken, enabling it to offer a vast range of book titles (and other products) but with minimal inventory.

However, for most companies it is likely that a selective rationalisation of slow-moving lines will have a positive impact on overall profitability.

Product design and supply chain complexity

It is important to recognise that often a significant source of supply chain complexity is the actual design of the product itself. It has long been known that a large part of total through-life costs are determined at the drawing board stage – sometimes as much as 80 per cent.[4] There are a number of ways in which product design decisions can impact subsequent supply chain complexity and hence costs. These are some of the ways that product design decisions can affect supply chain complexity:

- *Time-to-market and time-to-volume*

  Decisions on the functionality of products can increase manufacturing complexity and reduce flexibility and responsiveness

- *Added complexity through lack of commonality*

  Decisions on product design impact the Bill of Materials. Low levels of component commonality will add complexity.

- *Increased replenishment lead times*

  Some design decisions will determine the choice of supplier and therefore could impact replenishment lead time, e.g. where the supply source is offshore.

- *Supply chain vulnerability*

  Again, if the design decision involves unreliable supply sources this could potentially increase the chance of supply chain disruption.

- *After sales support*

  For those products requiring after sales support, e.g. service parts, the design of the product will have implications for inventory levels.

● *Late stage customisation*

The ability to postpone the final configuration or the packaging of a product will be enhanced or constrained by product design decisions.

Mastering complexity

Because supply chain complexity is such a major source of total end-to-end pipeline cost as well as being a significant inhibitor of responsiveness, it is essential that complexity reduction becomes a priority. It can be argued that today's supply chain managers need to be 'complexity masters', such is the importance of containing and removing this impediment to enhanced profitability. Figure 8.1 suggests a five-stage process for bringing the supply chain under control.

Figure 8.1 Complexity management

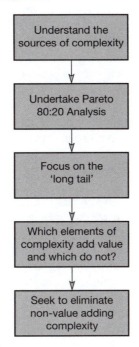

The first step in managing supply chain complexity is to understand where it is coming from. A good starting point to identifying the source of complexity is to review the eight categories previously identified, i.e. network, process, range, product, customer, supplier, organisational and information complexity.

Network and process complexity can be identified through the use of mapping procedures such as those described in Chapter 7. Because networks and processes are not often managed holistically, i.e. they tend to be managed by individual activity rather than as a whole, the likelihood is that they will contain the potential for unnecessary complexity, e.g. too many echelons, poorly managed interfaces and too many activities that do not add value. Network simplification and process re-engineering should be on-going in every supply chain that seeks to become less complex.

Range, customer and supplier complexity can be identified through Pareto analysis. In other words what proportion of total revenue, spend or inventory is accounted for by what proportion of customers, suppliers or SKUs? By focusing on the 'long tail' previously discussed, it should be possible to identify opportunities for rationalisation. Again, it should be stressed that such rationalisation needs to be addressed cautiously with regard to the wider business strategy and financial consequences.

Product complexity will be revealed through a detailed analysis of the Bills of Materials of each product in the range. The goal is to both minimise the number of components in each product and to maximise the commonality of components, sub-assemblies and platforms across the range.

Organisational complexity is partly driven by the number of levels in the business and by the decision-making structure. Typically organisations with many levels and with many functional 'silos' tend to be slow to respond to changed conditions and slow in new product development and introduction. One effective way to reduce this source of complexity is by a greater emphasis on working across functions, particularly by creating process teams – an idea to which we shall return in Chapter 12.

It should however, be recognised that not all complexity is bad. In some respects it is through complexity that organisations differentiate themselves from their competitors. For example, customers often seek product variety, they are not prepared to settle for the previously quoted Henry Ford I offer of 'any colour you like as long as it's black'!

The challenge for supply chain managers is to understand the value that customers seek and to find ways to deliver that value with least complexity.

Also it can be argued, perhaps paradoxically, that a focus on complexity reduction could increase supply chain risk. For example, an over-ambitious programme of supplier rationalisation could leave the company vulnerable to disruption if, for whatever reason, a critical supply source were to fail.

Complexity management in the supply chain has to be a careful balance between over-simplification on the one hand and a focus on cost and efficiency on the other. The aim should be to reduce or eliminate any complexity that does not add value to the customer or that does not protect against supply chain risk. The impact that complexity can have on supply chain risk is well illustrated by the case of the Boeing 787 described below.

The Boeing 787 Dreamliner: an outsourcing nightmare

On 15 December 2009, over two years later than originally planned, the Boeing 787 – the so-called 'Dreamliner' – made its maiden test flight. The 787 was a radically new concept embodying highly innovative technology and design features. The market positioning of the aircraft had proved to be highly successful with pre-launch sales options from airlines around the world in the region of 850 planes. With a passenger capacity of up to 330 and with a range of 8,500 nautical miles the 787 would use less fuel and operate at a cost per seat mile approximately 10 per cent less than other comparable aircraft. These savings were enabled primarily by the lower weight of the 787, which was achieved through the use of novel composite materials, and new engine technology.

Even though most industry commentators expected that in the long term the 787 would be a great success, there was no doubt that the delay in the launch had impacted negatively on Boeing's financial performance.

Clearly, a design as innovative as the 787 brought with it many challenges as much of the technology was untried and untested. Beyond this, however, there were a number of risks that were systemic, i.e. risks that arose as a result of decisions taken by the company on the precise form of the chosen supply chain architecture.

Traditionally Boeing has built most of its aircraft in its own facilities in Washington State, USA. In the case of the 787 the only part manufactured in the Washington factory is the tail fin (and even this manufacturing is shared with another facility outside Washington). The other parts of the aircraft are manufactured as sub-assemblies by a myriad of external suppliers around the world. For example, the forward fuselage and nose are made by Spirit AeroSystems in Witchita, Kansas, whereas parts of the midsection are manufactured by Alenia in Italy and the wings and a further fuselage section are built by companies in Japan. The final assembly of the aircraft takes place in Boeing's facilities in Everett, Washington and Charleston, South Carolina.

Not only has the manufacture of most of the sub-assemblies been outsourced but those same suppliers were also involved in much of the detailed design of the sections/systems they were responsible for. Perhaps not surprisingly a number of problems were encountered.

Many of the suppliers found that the innovation involved challenged both their design and their engineering capabilities. Boeing had to send its own staff to help the suppliers sort out these problems. Often sub-assemblies would arrive at Everett incomplete or wrongly manufactured, requiring disassembly and rebuilding. Months were lost in the process of putting things right. These delays had financial consequences and the cost of additional design, rework and penalty payments ran into billions of dollars.

The paradox is that the business model adopted by Boeing, i.e. outsourcing the design and manufacture of sub-assemblies to supply chain partners, was motivated by the aim of speeding up time-to-market. The original view at Boeing was that using external specialists would enable a more flexible supply chain, capable

▶

of responding more rapidly to customer demand. In the event the outcome was a significant delay in time-to-market and a major cost over-run.

Undoubtedly a product as innovative as the 787, embracing as it does entirely new materials and technology, would always face significant challenges. However, beyond this, Boeing's experience highlights the fact that whilst companies might outsource the execution of an activity they should never outsource its control.

SOURCES: 'DREAMLINER MAKES HISTORY WITH PLASTIC, OUTSOURCING, DESIGN – AND DELAYS', *THE SEATTLE TIMES*, 12 DECEMBER 2009

'JET BLUES: BOEING SCRAMBLES TO REPAIR PROBLEMS WITH NEW PLANE', *THE WALL STREET JOURNAL*, 7 DECEMBER 2007

References

1. Whyte, C., 'Motorola's battle with supply and demand complexity', *Supply and Demand Chain Executive*, 12 August 2004.
2. Gottfredson, M. and Aspinal, K., 'Innovation vs complexity: what is too much of a good thing?', *Harvard Business Review*, November 2005.
3. Anderson, C., *The Long Tail : Why the Future of Business is Selling Less of More*, Hyperion, 2006.
4. Appelqvist, P., Lehtonen, J.M. and Kokkonene, J., 'Modelling in product and supply chain design: literature survey and case study', *Journal of Manufacturing Technology Management*, Vol. 15, No. 7, 2004.

Managing the
global pipeline

9

- The trend towards globalisation in the supply chain

- Gaining visibility in the global pipeline

- Organising for global logistics

- Thinking global, acting local

- The future of global sourcing

Global brands and companies now dominate most markets. Over the last two decades there has been a steady trend towards the worldwide marketing of products under a common brand umbrella – whether it be Coca-Cola or Marlborough, IBM or Toyota. At the same time the global company has revised its previously localised focus, manufacturing and marketing its products in individual countries, and now instead will typically source on a worldwide basis for global production and distribution.

The logic of the global company is clear: it seeks to grow its business by extending its markets whilst at the same time seeking cost reduction through scale economies in purchasing and production and through focused manufacturing and/or assembly operations.

However, whilst the logic of globalisation is strong, we must recognise that it also presents certain challenges. Firstly, world markets are not homogeneous, there is still a requirement for local variation in many product categories. Secondly, unless there is a high level of co-ordination the complex logistics of managing global supply chains may result in higher costs and extended lead times.

These two challenges are related: on the one hand, how to offer local markets the variety they seek whilst still gaining the advantage of standardised global production and, on the other, how to manage the links in the global chain from sources of supply through to end user. There is a danger that some global companies in their search for cost advantage may take too narrow a view of cost and only see the purchasing or manufacturing cost reduction that may be achieved through using low-cost supply sources. In reality it is a total cost trade-off where the costs of longer supply pipelines may outweigh the production cost saving. Figure 9.1 illustrates some of the potential cost trade-offs to be considered in establishing the extent to which a global strategy for logistics will be cost-justified. Clearly a key component of the decision to go global must be the service needs of the marketplace. There is a danger that companies might run the risk of sacrificing service on the altar of cost reduction through a failure to fully understand the service needs of individual markets.

Figure 9.1 Trade-offs in global logistics

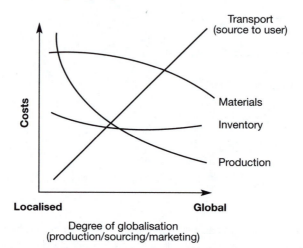

The trend towards global organisation of both manufacturing and marketing is highlighting the critical importance of logistics and supply chain management as the keys to profitability. The complexity of the logistics task appears to be increasing exponentially, influenced by such factors as the increasing range of products, shorter product life cycles, marketplace growth and the number of supply/market channels.

> The trend towards global organisation of both manufacturing and marketing is highlighting the critical importance of logistics and supply chain management as the keys to profitability.

There is no doubting that the globalisation of industrial activity has become a major issue in business. Articles in the business press, seminars and academic symposia have all focused upon the emerging global trend. The competitive pressures and challenges that have led to this upsurge of interest have been well documented. What are less well understood are the implications of globalisation for operations management in general and specifically for logistics management.

At the outset it is important that we define the global business and recognise its distinctiveness from an international or a multinational business. A global business is one that does more than simply export. The global business will typically source its materials and components in more than one country. Similarly it will often have multiple assembly or manufacturing locations geographically dispersed. It will subsequently market its products worldwide. A classic example is provided by Nike – the US-based sportswear company. The company outsources virtually 100 per cent of its shoe production, for example, only retaining in-house manufacturing in the US of a few key components of its patented Nike Air System. Nike's basketball shoe, for example, is designed in the USA but manufactured in South Korea and Indonesia from over 70 components supplied by companies in Japan, South Korea, Taiwan, Indonesia and the United States. The finished products are sold around the world.

The trend towards globalisation and offshore sourcing has been growing rapidly for several decades. There has been a transformation from a world where most markets used to be served from local sources to one where there is a growing worldwide interdependence of suppliers, manufacturers and customers in what has truly become a 'global village'.

Early commentators like Levitt[1] saw the growth of global brands and talked in terms of the growing convergence of customer preferences that would enable standardised products to be marketed in similar fashion around the world. However, the reality of global marketing is often different, with quite substantial differences in local requirements still very much in evidence. Thus, whilst the brand may be global, the product may need certain customisation to meet specific country needs, whether it be left- or right-hand-drive cars or different TV transmission standards or local tastes. A good example is Nescafé, the instant coffee made by Nestlé, which has over 200 slightly different formulations to cater for preferences in taste country by country.

The trend towards globalisation in the supply chain

Over the last 50 years or so the growth in world trade has tended to outstrip growth in global gross domestic product. In part this trend is driven by expanding demand in new markets, but the liberalisation of international trade through World Trade Organization (WTO) accords has also had a significant effect.

Once, companies established factories in overseas countries to manufacture products to meet local demand. Now, with the reduction of trade barriers and the development of a global transportation infrastructure, fewer factories can produce in larger quantities to meet global, rather than local, demand.

Paradoxically, as the barriers to global movement have come down so the sources of global competition have increased. Newly emerging economies are building their own industries with global capabilities. At the same time technological change and production efficiencies mean that most companies in most industries are capable of producing in greater quantity at less cost. The result of all of this is that there is now overcapacity in virtually every industry, meaning that competitive pressure is greater than ever before.

To remain competitive in this new global environment, companies will have to continually seek ways in which costs can be lowered and service enhanced, meaning that supply chain efficiency and effectiveness will become ever more critical.

In developing a global logistics strategy a number of issues arise which may require careful consideration. In particular, what degree of centralisation is appropriate in terms of management, manufacturing and distribution, and how can the needs of local markets be met at the same time as the achievement of economies of scale through standardisation?

Three of the ways in which businesses have sought to implement their global logistics strategies have been through focused factories, centralised inventories and postponement.

1 Focused factories

The idea behind the focused factory is simple: by limiting the range and mix of products manufactured in a single location the company can achieve considerable economies of scale. Typically the nationally oriented business will have 'local-for-local' production, meaning that each country's factory will produce the full range of products for sale in that country. On the other hand the global business will treat the world market as one market and will rationalise its production so that the remaining factories produce fewer products in volumes capable of satisfying perhaps the entire market.

One company that has moved in this direction is Mars. Their policy has been to simultaneously rationalise production capacity by seeking to manage demand as a whole on at least a regional level and to concentrate production by category, factory by factory. Hence M&Ms for sale in Moscow are likely to have been produced in the United States. In a similar fashion, Heinz produces tomato ketchup for all of Europe from just three plants and will switch production depending upon how local costs and demand conditions vary against exchange rate fluctuations. A further example is provided by Procter & Gamble which manufactures its successful product Pringles in just two plants to meet worldwide demand.

Such strategies have become widespread as 'global thinking' becomes the dominant mindset.

However, a number of crucial logistics trade-offs may be overlooked in what might possibly be a too-hasty search for low-cost producer status through greater economies of scale. The most obvious trade-off is the effect on transport costs and delivery lead times. The costs of shipping products, often of relatively low value, across greater distances may erode some or all of the production cost saving. Similarly the longer lead times involved may need to be countered by local stock holding, again possibly offsetting the production cost advantage.

Further problems of focused production may be encountered where the need for local packs exist, e.g. with labelling in different languages or even different brand names and packages for the same product. This problem might be overcome by 'postponing' the final packaging until closer to the point-of-sale.

Another issue is that created by customers ordering a variety of products from the same company on a single order but which are now produced in a number of focused factories in different locations. The solution here may be some type of transhipment or cross-dock operation where flows of goods from diverse localities and origins are merged for onward delivery to the customer.

Finally, what will be the impact on production flexibility of the trend towards focused factories where volume and economies of scale rule the day? Whilst these goals are not necessarily mutually incompatible it may be that organisations that put low-cost production at the top of their list of priorities may be at risk in markets where responsiveness and the ability to provide 'variety' are key success factors.

In response to these issues a number of companies are questioning decisions that previously were thought sound. For example, Sony used to manufacture digital cameras and camcorders in China, attracted by the lower labour costs. However, they came to recognise that because life cycles were so short for these products, it was better to bring the assembly back to Japan where the product design took place and, indeed, where most of the components originated. Other high-tech companies are also looking again at their offshore production and sourcing strategies for this same reason. Typically less than 10 per cent of a high-tech company's costs are direct labour. Hence the decision to source offshore, simply to save on labour costs, makes little sense if penalties are incurred elsewhere in the supply chain.

All in all it would appear that the total logistics impact of focused production will be complex and significant. To ensure that decisions are taken which are not sub-optimal it will become even more important to undertake detailed analysis based upon total system modelling and simulation prior to making commitments that may later be regretted.

Centralised logistics at Lever Europe

Lever, part of the global corporation Unilever, manufacture and market a wide range of soaps, detergents and cleaners. As part of a drive to implement a European strategy for manufacturing and the supply chain they created a centralised manufacturing and supply chain management structure – Lever Europe. A key part of this strategy involved a rationalisation of other production facilities from a total of 16 across western Europe to 11. The remaining facilities became 'focused factories', each one concentrating on certain product families. So, for example, most bar soaps for Europe are now made at Port Sunlight in England; Mannheim in Germany makes all the Dove soap products, not just for Europe but for much of the rest of the world; France focuses on machine dishwasher products and so on.

Because national markets are now supplied from many different European sources they have retained distribution facilities in each country to act as a local consolidation centre for final delivery to customers.

Whilst some significant production cost savings have been achieved, a certain amount of flexibility has been lost. There is still a high level of variation in requirement by individual market. Many countries sell the same product but under different brand names; the languages are different hence the need for local packs; sometimes too the formulations differ.

A further problem is that as retailers become more demanding in the delivery service they require and as the trend towards just-in-time delivery continues, the loss of flexibility becomes a problem. Even though manufacturing economies of scale are welcome, it has to be recognised that the achievement of these cost benefits may be offset by the loss of flexibility and responsiveness in the supply chain as a whole.

2 Centralisation of inventories

In the same way that the advent of globalisation has encouraged companies to rationalise production into fewer locations, so too has it led to a trend towards the centralisation of inventories. Making use of the well-known statistical fact that consolidating inventory into fewer locations can substantially reduce total inventory requirement, organisations have been steadily closing national warehouses and amalgamating them into regional distribution centres (RDCs) serving a much wider geographical area.

For example, Philips has reduced its consumer electronics products warehouses in western Europe from 22 to just four. Likewise Apple Computers replaced their 13 national warehouses with two European RDCs. Similar examples can be found in just about every industry.

Whilst the logic of centralisation is sound, it is becoming increasingly recognised that there may be even greater gains to be had by not physically centralising the inventory but rather by locating it strategically near the customer or the point of production but managing and controlling it centrally. This is the idea of 'virtual' or 'electronic' inventory. The idea is that by the use of information the organisation can achieve the same stock reduction that it would achieve through centralisation whilst retaining a greater flexibility by localising inventory. At the same time the penalties of centralising physical stock holding are reduced, i.e. double handling, higher transport charges and possibly longer total pipelines.

One of the arguments for centralised inventory is that advantage can be taken of the 'square root rule'.[2] Whilst an approximation, this rule of thumb provides an indication of the opportunity for inventory reduction that is possible through holding inventory in fewer locations. The rule states that the reduction in total safety stock that can be expected through reducing the number of stock locations is proportional to the square root of the number of stock locations before and after rationalisation. Thus if previously there were 25 stock locations and now there are only four then the overall reduction in inventory would be in the ratio of $\sqrt{25}$ to $\sqrt{4}$, or 5:2, i.e. a 60 per cent reduction.

Many organisations are now recognising the advantage of managing worldwide inventories on a centralised basis. To do so successfully, however, requires an information system that can provide complete visibility of demand from one end of the pipeline to another in as close to real time as possible. Equally such central-ised systems will typically lead to higher transport costs in that products inevitably have to move greater distances and often high-cost air express will be necessary to ensure short lead times for delivery to the customer.

Xerox, in its management of its European spares business, has demonstrated how great benefits can be derived by centralising the control of inventory and by using information systems and, in so doing, enabling a much higher service to its engineers to be provided but with only half the total inventory. SKF is another com-pany that for many years has been driving down its European inventory of bearings whilst still improving service to its customers. Again, the means to this remarkable achievement has been through a centralised information system.

3 Postponement and localisation

Although the trend to global brands and products continues, it should be recog-nised that there are still significant local differences in customer and consumer requirements. Even within a relatively compact market like western Europe there are major differences in consumer tastes and, of course, languages. Hence there are a large number of markets where standard, global products would not be suc-cessful. Take, for example, the differences in preference for domestic appliances such as refrigerators and washing machines. Northern Europeans prefer larger refrigerators because they shop once a week rather than daily, whilst southern Europeans, shopping more frequently, prefer smaller ones. Similarly, Britons con-sume more frozen foods than most other European countries and thus require more freezer space.

> Although the trend to global brands and products continues, it should be recognised that there are still significant local differences in customer and consumer requirements.

In the case of washing machines, there are differences in preference for top-load-ing versus front-loading machines – in the UK almost all the machines purchased are front loaders whilst in France the reverse is true.

How is it possible to reconcile the need to meet local requirements whilst seek-ing to organise logistics on a global basis? Ideally organisations would like to achieve the benefits of standardisation in terms of cost reduction whilst maximising their marketing success through localisation.

One strategy that is increasingly being adopted is the idea of *postponement* discussed earlier in this book. Postponement, or delayed configuration, is based on the principle of seeking to design products using common platforms, compo-nents or modules but where the final assembly or customisation does not take place until the final market destination and/or customer requirement is known.

The advantages of the strategy of postponement are several. Firstly, inventory can be held at a generic level so that there will be fewer stock keeping variants and hence less inventory in total. Secondly, because the inventory is generic, its flexibility is greater, meaning that the same components, modules or platforms can be embodied in a variety of end products. Thirdly, forecasting is easier at the generic level than at the level of the finished item. This last point is particularly relevant in global markets where local forecasts will be less accurate than a forecast for worldwide volume. Furthermore the ability to customise products locally means that a higher level of variety may be offered at lower total cost – this is the principle of 'mass customisation'.

To take full advantage of the possibilities offered by postponement often requires a 'design for localisation' philosophy. Products and processes must be designed and engineered in such a way that semi-finished product can be assembled, configured and finished to provide the highest level of variety to customers based upon the smallest number of standard modules or components. In many cases the final finishing will take place in the local market, perhaps at a distribution centre, and, increasingly, the physical activity outsourced to a third-party logistics service provider.

Gaining visibility in the global pipeline

One of the features of global pipelines is that there is often a higher level of *uncertainty* about the status of a shipment whilst in transit. This uncertainty is made worse by the many stages in a typical global pipeline as a product flows from factory to port, from the port to its country of destination, through customs clearance and so on until it finally reaches the point where it is required. Not surprisingly there is a high degree of *variation* in these extended pipelines.

Shipping, consolidation and customs clearance all contribute to delays and variability in the end-to-end lead time of global supply chains. This is highlighted in the example shown in Table 9.1. This can be a major issue for companies as they increasingly go global. It has the consequence that local managers tend to compensate for this unreliability by over-ordering and by building inventory buffers.

Table 9.1 End-to-end lead-time variability (days)

	From point of origin to port	Freight forwarding/ consolidation	Arrive in country of destination	Customs clearance	Transit to point of use	Total elapsed time
Maximum	5	7	15	5	5	37
Average	4	3	14	2	4	32
Minimum	1	1	12	1	2	17

One emerging tool that could greatly improve the visibility across complex global supply chains is supply chain event management.

Supply chain event management (SCEM) is the term given to the process of monitoring the planned sequence of activities along a supply chain and the subsequent reporting of any divergence from that plan. Ideally SCEM will also enable a proactive, even automatic, response to deviations from the plan.

'The SCEM system should act like an intensive care monitor in a hospital. To use an intensive care monitor, the doctor places probes at strategic points on the patient's body; each measures a discrete and different function – temperature, respiration rate, blood pressure. The monitor is programmed with separate upper and lower control limits for each probe and for each patient. If any of the watched bodily functions go above or below the defined tolerance, the monitor sets off an alarm to the doctor for immediate follow-up and corrective action. The SCEM application should act in the same manner.

'The company determines its unique measurement points along its supply chain and installs probes. The company then programmes the SCEM application to monitor the plan-to-actual supply chain progress, and establishes upper and lower control limits. If any of the control limits are exceeded, or if anomalies occur, the application publishes alerts or alarms so that the functional manager can take appropriate corrective action.'

Source: Styles, Peter, 'Determining supply chain event management', in *Achieving Supply Chain Excellence Through Technology*, Montgomery Research, San Francisco, 2002

The Internet can provide the means whereby SCEM reporting systems can link together even widely dispersed partners in global supply chains. The use of XML communications across the web means that even organisations with different information systems can be linked together. The key requirement though is not technological, it is the willingness of the different entities in a supply chain to work in a collaborative mode and to agree to share information.

Supply chain event management enables organisations to gain visibility upstream and downstream of their own operations and to assume an *active* rather than a *passive* approach to supply chain risk. Figure 9.2 shows the progression from the traditional, limited scope of supply chain visibility to the intended goal of an 'intelligent' supply chain information system.

Event management software is now becoming available from a number of providers. The principles underpinning event management are that 'intelligent agents' are created within the software that are instructed to respond within pre-determined decision rules, e.g. upper and lower limits for inventory levels at different stages in a supply chain. These agents monitor the critical stage in a process and issue alerts when deviations from required performance occurs. The agents can also be instructed to take corrective action where necessary, and they can identify

Figure 9.2 The progression to supply chain event management

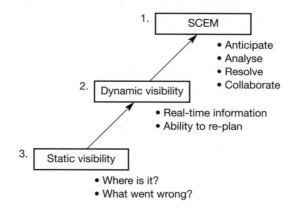

trends and anomalies and report back to supply chain managers on emerging situations that might require pre-emptive attention.

Whilst event management is primarily a tool for managing processes, its advantage is that it can look across networks, thus enabling connected processes to be monitored and, if necessary, modified.

Clearly the complexity of most supply networks is such that in reality event management needs to be restricted to the critical paths in that network. Critical paths might be typified by such features as: long lead times to react to unplanned events, reliance on single-source suppliers, bottlenecks, etc.

Event management is rooted in the concept of workflow and milestones, and Figure 9.3 uses nodes and links to illustrate the idea of workflow across the supply chain. Once a chain has been described in terms of the nodes that are in place and the links that have been established, the controls that have been defined respond to events across the chain. An event is a conversion of material at a node in the chain or a movement of material between nodes in the chain.

When an event does not occur on time and/or in full, the system will automatically raise alerts and alarms through an escalation sequence to the managers controlling the chain requiring them to take action.

Organising for global logistics

As companies have extended their supply chains internationally they have been forced to confront the issue of how to structure their global logistics organisation. In their different ways these companies have moved towards the same conclusion: effectiveness in global logistics can only be achieved through a greater element of centralisation. This in many respects runs counter to much of the conventional wisdom, which tends to argue that decision-making responsibility should be devolved and decentralised at least to the strategic business unit level. This philosophy has manifested itself in many companies in the form of strong local management, often with autonomous decision making at the country level. Good

Figure 9.3 Event management across the supply chain

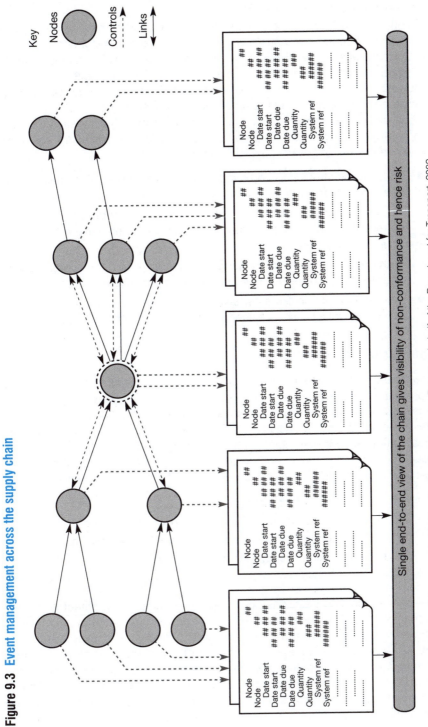

Key

Nodes

Controls

Links

Node
Node
Date start
Date start
Date due
Date due
Quantity
Quantity
System ref
System ref

Single end-to-end view of the chain gives visibility of non-conformance and hence risk

Source: Cranfield School of Management, *Creating Resilient Supply Chains*, Report on behalf of the Department for Transport, 2002

though this may be for encouraging local initiatives, it tends to be dysfunctional when integrated global strategies are required.

Clearly there will still be many areas where local decision making will be preferable – for example, sales strategy and, possibly, promotional and marketing communications strategy. Likewise the implementation of global strategy can still be adjusted to take account of national differences and requirements.

How then can the appropriate balance of global versus local decision making be achieved in formulating and implementing logistics strategy?

Because specific market environments and industry characteristics will differ from company to company it is dangerous to offer all-embracing solutions. However, a number of general principles are beginning to emerge:

- The strategic structuring and overall control of logistics flows must be centralised to achieve worldwide optimisation of costs.

- The control and management of customer service must be localised against the requirements of specific markets to ensure competitive advantage is gained and maintained.

- As the trend towards outsourcing everything except core competencies increases then so does the need for global co-ordination.

- A global logistics information system is the prerequisite for enabling the achievement of local service needs whilst seeking global cost optimisation.

1 Structure and control

If the potential trade-offs in rationalising sourcing, production and distribution across national boundaries are to be achieved then it is essential that a central decision-making structure for logistics is established. Many companies that are active on an international basis find that they are constrained in their search for global optimisation by strongly entrenched local systems and structures. Only through centralised planning and co-ordination of logistics can the organisation hope to achieve the twin goals of cost minimisation and service maximisation.

> If the potential trade-offs in rationalising sourcing, production and distribution across national boundaries are to be achieved then it is essential that a central decision-making structure for logistics is established.

For example, location decisions are a basic determinant of profitability in international logistics. The decision on where to manufacture, to assemble, to store, to transship and to consolidate can make the difference between profit and loss. Because of international differences in basic factor costs and because of exchange rate movements, location decisions are fundamental. Also these decisions tend to involve investment in fixed assets in the form of facilities and equipment. Decisions taken today can therefore have a continuing impact over time on the company's financial and competitive position.

As the trend towards global manufacturing continues, organisations will increasingly need to look at location decisions through total cost analysis. The requirement there is for improved access to activity-related costs such as manufacturing, transportation and handling. Accurate information on inventory holding costs and the cost/benefit of postponement also becomes a key variable in location decisions.

The opportunities for reducing costs and improving throughput efficiency by a reappraisal of the global logistics network, and in particular manufacturing and inventory locations, can be substantial. By their very nature, decisions on location in a global network can only be taken centrally.

2 Customer service management

Because local markets have their own specific characteristics and needs there is considerable advantage to be achieved by shaping marketing strategies locally – albeit within overall global guidelines. This is particularly true of customer service management where the opportunities for tailoring service against individual customer requirements are great. The management of customer service involves the monitoring of service needs as well as performance and extends to the management of the entire order fulfilment process – from order through to delivery. Whilst order fulfilment systems are increasingly global and centrally managed there will always remain the need to have strong local customer service management.

Key account management (KAM) has become a widely adopted approach for managing the interfaces between suppliers and their global customers. Because of the growing shift in the balance of power in many industries, it is now a critical pre-requisite for commercial success that suppliers tailor their service offerings to meet the requirements of individual customers. The purpose of key account management in a global business is to ensure that all the resources of the supplier are harnessed to deliver solutions that are specific to a particular customer. This contrasts with the 'one size fits all' approach to global customer service which typified many companies' policies in the past.

3 Outsourcing and partnerships

As we have previously noted, one of the greatest changes in the global business today is the trend towards outsourcing. Not just outsourcing the procurement of materials and components but also outsourcing of services that traditionally have been provided in-house. The logic of this trend is that the organisation will increasingly focus on those activities in the value chain where it has a distinctive advantage – the core competencies of the business – and everything else it will outsource. This movement has been particularly evident in logistics where the provision of transport, warehousing and inventory control is increasingly subcontracted to specialists or logistics partners.

To manage and control this network of partners and suppliers requires a blend of both central and local involvement. The argument once again is that the strategic decisions need to be taken centrally, with the monitoring and control of supplier performance and day-to-day liaison with logistics partners being best managed at a local level.

4 Logistics information

The management of global logistics is in reality the management of information flows. The information system is the mechanism whereby the complex flows of materials, parts, subassemblies and finished products can be co-ordinated to achieve cost-effective service. Any organisation with aspirations to global leadership is dependent upon the visibility it can gain of materials flows, inventories and demand throughout the pipeline. Without the ability to see down the pipeline into end-user markets, to read actual demand and subsequently to manage replenishment in virtual real time, the system is doomed to depend upon inventory. To 'substitute information for inventory' has become something of a cliché but it should be a prime objective nevertheless. Time lapses in information flows are directly translated into inventory. The great advances that are being made in introducing 'quick response' logistics systems are all based upon information flow from the point of actual demand directly into the supplier's logistics and replenishment systems. On a global scale we typically find that the presence of intervening inventories between the plant and the marketplace obscure the view of real demand. Hence the need for information systems that can read demand at every level in the pipeline and provide the driving power for a centrally controlled logistics system.

Thinking global, acting local

The implementation of global pipeline control is highly dependent upon the ability of the organisation to find the correct balance between central control and local management. It is unwise to be too prescriptive but the experience that global organisations are gaining every day suggests that certain tasks and functions lend themselves to central control and others to local management. Table 9.2 summarises some of the possibilities.

Table 9.2 Global co-ordination and local management

Global	Local
• Network structuring for production and transportation optimisation	• Customer service management
• Information systems development and control	• Gathering market intelligence
• Inventory positioning	• Warehouse management and local delivery
• Sourcing decisions	• Customer profitability analyses
• International transport mode and sourcing decisions	• Liaison with local sales and marketing management
• Trade-off analyses and supply chain cost control	• Human resource management

Much has been learned in the last 20 years or so about the opportunities for cost and service enhancement through better management of logistics at a national level. Now organisations are faced with applying those lessons on a much broader stage. As international competition becomes more intense and as national barriers to trade gradually reduce, the era of the global business has arrived. Increasingly the difference between success and failure in the global marketplace will be determined not by the sophistication of product technology or even of marketing communications, but rather by the way in which we manage and control the global logistics pipeline.

The future of global sourcing

One of the most pronounced trends of recent decades has been the move to off-shore sourcing, often motivated by the opportunity to make or buy products or materials at significantly lower prices than could be obtained locally. Companies such as the large British retailer Marks & Spencer, which once made it a point of policy to source the majority of their clothing products in the United Kingdom, moved most of their sourcing to low-cost countries, particularly in the Far East. Manufacturers, too, closed down western European or North American factories and sought out cheaper places to make things – often many thousands of miles away from their major markets.

At the time that many of these offshore sourcing and manufacturing decisions were being made, the cost differential between traditional sources and the new low-cost locations was significant. However, in recent years there has been a growing realisation that the true cost of global sourcing may be greater than originally thought.[3] Not only have the costs of transport increased in many cases, but exchange rate fluctuations and the need for higher levels of inventory because of longer and more variable lead times have affected total costs. In short life cycle markets there is the additional risk of obsolescence with consequent mark-downs or write-offs. Other costs that can arise may relate to quality problems and loss of intellectual property. With growing concern for environmental issues, there is also now the emerging issue of 'carbon footprints' (to be dealt with in more detail in Chapter 13).

All of these issues are now causing many companies and organisations to review their offshore sourcing/manufacturing decisions. Whilst there will always be a case for low-cost country sourcing for many products, it will not universally be the case as the following news item suggests.

Disenchanted companies begin moving production back to UK

Manufacturers increasingly are moving production back to Britain as shoddy quality and higher freight prices are undermining the cost advantage of producing goods overseas.

A report into the state of the manufacturing sector by the Engineering Employers' Federation (EEF) and BDO, the accountants, finds that one in seven companies surveyed had moved production back to the UK from abroad in the past two years

Many British manufacturers have outsourced production to countries with lower labour costs, in Eastern Europe or Asia, in the past decade, a trend that has accelerated as an increasing number of British companies have fallen into foreign ownership.

But higher freight, energy and commodity costs have increased the expense of production overseas, while the recession has put pressure on companies to re-evaluate decisions on location. According to the EEF, the manufacturers' organisation, 14 per cent of companies have moved production back to the UK because cost savings have not been as great as expected.

Other reasons were that the quality of goods was not up to standard and that the speed of getting products to market was not fast enough.

Two thirds of the 300 businesses surveyed for the report – which include makers of mechanical equipment, plastics manufacturers, food manufacturers and suppliers to the automotive industry – plan to re-evaluate their supply-chain strategies as a result of the global recession.

Tom Lawton, head of manufacturing at BDO, said: 'The recession has made companies look at their whole supply chain and their costs.

'It will not be a flood back [to the UK] but quite a few companies are saying that it is possibly better now for us to source locally.'

Mr Lawton said that while many companies would still find it attractive to consider moving production overseas, a significant minority had concerns over quality and reliability of low-cost suppliers.

Three in five companies have also expressed significant or moderate concerns about the health of their overseas suppliers, with insolvencies among overseas suppliers posing a significant threat of disruption to the supply chain.

'We are optimistic that those firms who have relocated production back to the UK will stay here,' Mr Lawton said.

SOURCE: JAMESON, A., 'DISENCHANTED COMPANIES BEGIN MOVING PRODUCTION BACK TO UK', *THE TIMES*, 30 DECEMBER 2009

References

1. Levitt, T., 'The globalization of markets', *Harvard Business Review*, Vol. 61, May–June 1983.
2. Sussams, J.E., 'Buffer stocks and the square root law', *Focus*, Institute of Logistics, UK, Vol. 5, No. 5, 1986.
3. Centre for Logistics & Supply Chain Management (2008), *The True Costs of Global Sourcing*, Cranfield School of Management, UK

Managing risk in the supply chain

10

- Why are supply chains more vulnerable?

- Understanding the supply chain risk profile

- Managing supply chain risk

- Achieving supply chain resilience

Today's marketplace is characterised by turbulence and uncertainty. Market turbulence has tended to increase in recent years for a number of reasons. Demand in almost every industrial sector seems to be more volatile than was the case in the past. Product and technology life cycles have shortened significantly and competitive product introductions make life-cycle demand difficult to predict. Considerable 'chaos' exists in our supply chains through the effects of such actions as sales promotions, quarterly sales incentives or decision rules such as reorder quantities.

At the same time the vulnerability of supply chains to disturbance or disruption has increased. It is not only the effect of external events such as natural disasters, strikes or terrorist attacks but also the impact of changes in business strategy. Many companies have experienced a change in their supply chain risk profile as a result of changes in their business models. For example, the adoption of 'lean' practices, the move to outsourcing and a general tendency to reduce the size of the supplier base potentially increase supply chain vulnerability.

As a result of this heightened risk, organisations will need to develop appropriate programmes to mitigate and manage that risk.

The impact of unplanned and unforeseen events in supply chains can have severe financial effects across the network as a whole. Research in North America[1] suggests that when companies experience disruptions to their supply chains the impact on their share price once the problem becomes public knowledge can be significant. The research suggests that companies experiencing these sorts of problems saw their average operating income drop 107 per cent, return on sales fall 114 per cent and return on assets decrease by 93 per cent. Figure 10.1 shows the impact on shareholder value of supply chain disruption.

Figure 10.1 The impact of supply chain disruptions on shareholder value

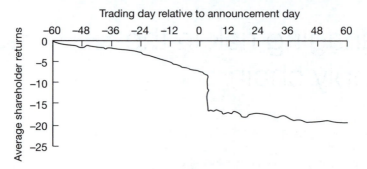

Source: Singhal, V.R. and Hendricks, K., *Supply Chain Management Review*, January/Fenruary 2002

A survey[2] of over 3,000 senior executives undertaken by the consultancy company McKinsey in 2006 reported that they believed their companies faced growing risk to disruptions to their supply chains. However, the same survey found that in many cases companies had inadequate processes in place for the management and mitigation of that risk. Whilst most organisations recognise the need to regularly assess their risk profile, that assessment has tended to be focused on broader regulatory and financial risk issues rather than supply chain vulnerability.

It can be argued that in today's volatile business environment the biggest risks to business continuity lie in the wider supply chain.

Clearly, there are risks that are *external* to the supply chain and those that are *internal*. External risks may arise from natural disasters, wars, terrorism and epidemics, or from government-imposed legal restrictions. Internal risks will be described in more detail later in this chapter but essentially they refer to the risks that arise as a result of how the supply chain is structured and managed. Whilst external risk cannot be influenced by managerial actions, internal risk can.

Why are supply chains more vulnerable?

A study conducted by Cranfield University[3] for the UK government defines supply chain vulnerability as:

an exposure to serious disturbance, arising from risks within the supply chain as well as risks external to the supply chain.

The same study identified a number of reasons why modern supply chains have become more vulnerable.

These factors are considered below in more depth.

A focus on efficiency rather than effectiveness

The prevailing business model of the closing decades of the twentieth century was very much based upon the search for greater levels of efficiency in the supply chain. Experience highlighted that there was an opportunity in many sectors of industry to take out significant cost by focusing on inventory reduction. Just-in-time (JIT) practices were widely adopted and organisations became increasingly dependent upon suppliers. This model, whilst undoubtedly of merit in stable market conditions, may become less viable as volatility of demand increases. The challenge in today's business environment is how best to combine 'lean' practices with an 'agile' response.

The globalisation of supply chains

There has been a dramatic shift away from the predominantly 'local for local' manufacturing and marketing strategy of the past. Now, through offshore sourcing, manufacturing and assembly, supply chains extend from one side of the globe to the other. For example, components may be sourced in Taiwan, sub-assembled in Singapore with final assembly in the US for sale in world markets.

Usually the motivation for offshore sourcing and manufacturing is cost reduction. However, that definition of cost is typically limited to the cost of purchase or manufacture. Only rarely are total supply chain costs considered. The result of these cost-based decisions is often higher levels of risk as a result of extended lead times, greater buffer stocks and potentially higher levels of obsolescence – particularly in short life-cycle markets. A further impetus to the globalisation of supply chains has come from the increase in cross-border mergers and acquisitions that we have witnessed over the last decade or so.

Focused factories and centralised distribution

One of the impacts of the implementation of the Single Market within the European Union and the consequent reduction in the barriers to the flow of products across borders has been the centralisation of production and distribution facilities. Significant scale economies can be achieved in manufacturing if greater volumes are produced on fewer sites. As highlighted in Chapter 9, some companies have chosen to 'focus' their factories – instead of producing the full range of products at each site, they produce fewer products exclusively at a single site. As a result, production costs may be lower but the product has to travel greater distances, often across many borders. Incidentally, at the same time, flexibility may be lost because these focused factories tend to be designed to produce in very large batches to achieve maximum scale economies.

Simultaneously with this move to fewer production sites is the tendency to centralise distribution. Many fast moving consumer goods manufacturers aim to serve the whole of the western European market through a few distribution centres, e.g. one in north-west Europe and one in the south.

The trend to outsourcing

One widespread trend, observable over many years, has been the tendency to outsource activities that were previously conducted within the organisation. No part of the value chain has been immune from this phenomenon; companies have outsourced distribution, manufacturing, accounting and information systems, for example. In some cases these companies might accurately be described as 'virtual' companies. There is a strong logic behind this based upon the view that organisations are more likely to succeed if they focus on the activities in which they have a differential advantage over competitors. This is leading to the creation of 'network organisations', whereby confederations of firms are linked together – usually through shared information and aligned processes – to achieve greater overall competitiveness. However, outsourcing also brings with it a number of risks, not least being the potential loss of control. Disruptions in supply can often be attributed to the failure of one of the links and nodes in the chain and, by definition, the more complex the supply network the more links there are and hence the greater the risk of failure. The case of Mattel, highlighted below, illustrates how this loss of control can significantly impact the standing and financial performance of a company.

Risk in the extended supply chain

'Mattel, the world's biggest toymaker, yesterday said the recall of more than 21m toys because of design flaws and potentially dangerous levels of lead paint in products made in China had hit profits and sales.

The maker of Barbie dolls and Fisher-Price toys said it had suffered a charge of about $40m because of the company's product scares, as sales were driven down $30–$50m by delayed shipments of toys and revoked import licenses.'[1]

Mattel, like many other western companies, had long moved much of its manufacturing offshore – a significant proportion of it to China, the world's largest toy exporter. Mattel used a number of contract manufacturing companies to produce a vast array of children's toys including Barbie fashion dolls and accessories, Fisher-Price toys, Sesame Street products, Winnie the Pooh and many others. In 2007 Mattel's worldwide sales were over US$5 billion.

In August 2007, a random product quality check revealed that some of their Chinese-manufactured products might contain potentially dangerous levels of lead paint whilst other products were found to contain small magnets which might be swallowed inadvertently by young children.

Whilst no actual cases of harm to children were reported, the impact of these events on Mattel's reputation has been significant. Part of the problem lay in the way in which Mattel handled the recall. Firstly, they may have over-reacted to the lead paint issue by recalling many toys that did not contravene US regulations on lead content in paint. Secondly, Mattel's initial reaction was to blame the Chinese manufacturers for these problems, only subsequently having to acknowledge that the issue with the magnets was caused by Mattel's design rather than by the manufacturer.

At a press conference in Beijing on 21 September 2007, Thomas Debrowski, a senior executive at Mattel, said 'Mattel takes full responsibility for these recalls and apologises to you, the Chinese people and all of our customers who received the toys'.[2]

The apology came too late for Zhang Shuhong, the Chief Executive of Lida Plastic Toys Co. Ltd in Guangdong, who committed suicide after laying off over 2,500 employees and halting production. Lida was a major contract manufacturer for Mattel whose factories were initially thought to have been the source of the lead paint problem.

The impact on Mattel's sales was felt most strongly in its biggest market – the United States – where sales of the iconic Barbie fell by 15 per cent. The total product recalls cost Mattel about $110 million in 2007;[3] however, the long term impact on Mattel's corporate reputation has yet to be quantified.

Whilst clearly there were issues surrounding the design process and quality control, the case of Mattel highlights the challenges that face any company where key business processes are outsourced. Whereas in the past the risk to an organisation's reputation lay mainly within the company, and hence was under its control, now that risk resides across an extended supply network. In the case of the lead paint problem it seems that the source of the problem was not even an immediate supplier but a second tier supplier, i.e. the company that supplied the paint to the first tier contract manufacturer.

References

1 *Financial Times*, 16 October 2007.
2 *Economist*, 29 September 2007.
3 *Financial Times*, 13 February 2008.

Reduction of the supplier base

A further prevailing trend over the last decade or so has been a dramatic reduction in the number of suppliers from which an organisation typically will procure materials, components, services, etc. In some cases this has been extended to 'single sourcing', whereby one supplier is responsible for the sole supply of an item. Several well-documented cases exist where major supply chain disruptions have been caused because of a failure at a single source. Even though there are many benefits to supplier base reduction it has to be recognised that it brings with it increased risk.

Sometimes a consolidation of the supply base happens through merger and acquisition. Since the rate of merger and acquisition has increased so dramatically over recent years, it follows that the supply base reduction will have accelerated for this reason alone.

Understanding the supply chain risk profile

Many organisations today are addressing the issues of what has come to be termed 'business continuity'. In practice, however, there tends to be a limited focus for much of business continuity management. There is a strong focus on IT and internal process management but often the wider supply risk dimension is not considered. This is paradoxical since it can be argued that the biggest risk to business continuity may be in the wider network of which the individual business is just a part.

To widen the focus on supply chain vulnerability it is suggested that a supply risk profile be established for the business. The purpose of the risk profile is to establish where the greatest vulnerabilities lie and what the probability of disruption is. In a sense this approach takes the view that:

Supply chain risk = Probability of disruption × Impact

Thus the risk profile attempts to seek out the 'critical paths' through a network where management attention should be especially focused. A weakness of this definition of risk is that it may lead to a failure to recognise that supply chains may be at their most vulnerable where the probability of occurrence is small but the potential impact could be catastrophic. For example, in May 2003 a tornado struck Jackson, Tennessee in the United States, severely damaging Procter & Gamble's sole factory in North America for the manufacture of Pringles. Production of this $1 billion a year sales revenue product was severely curtailed since P&G's only other manufacturing facility for Pringles is in Belgium.

To help identify the risk profile of a business it is helpful to undertake an audit of the main sources of risk across the network. This audit should examine potential risk to business disruptions arising from five sources:

1 *Supply risk*
   How vulnerable is the business to disruptions in supply? Risk may be higher due to global sourcing, reliance on key suppliers, poor supply management, etc.

2 *Demand risk*
   How volatile is demand? Does the 'bullwhip' effect cause demand amplification? Are there parallel interactions where the demand for another product affects the demand for ours?

3 *Process risk*
   How resilient are our processes? Do we understand the sources of variability in those processe, e.g. manufacturing? Where are the bottlenecks? How much additional capacity is available if required?

4 *Control risk*
   How likely are disturbances and distortions to be caused by our own internal control systems? For example, order quantities, batch sizes and safety stock policies can distort real demand. Our own decision rules and policies can cause 'chaos' type effects.

5 *Environmental risk*
   Where across the supply chain as a whole are we vulnerable to external forces? Whilst the type and timings of extreme external events may not be forecastable, their impact needs to be assessed.

Figure 10.2 summarises the connections between the five sources of risk.

Figure 10.2 Sources of risk in the supply chain

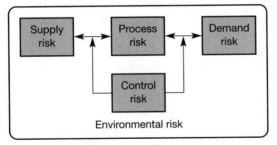

Source: Adapted from Mason-Jones, R. and Towill, D.R., 'Shrinking the supply chain uncertainty cycle', *Control*, September 1998, pp. 17–22

It is important for senior management to understand that the risk profile is directly and indirectly impacted by the strategic decisions that they take. Thus the decision, for instance, to transfer production from a western European factory to one in China should be examined in terms of how it may affect vulnerability from the five risk sources described above.

For multi-product, multi-market businesses the priority should be to identify the major profit streams and to concentrate on creating deep insights into how supply chain risk could impact those profit streams.

Mapping your risk profile Rather than cataloguing all the possible risks a company might face, the first stage in strategic risk management is to understand the company's internal processes in order to isolate the most relevant and critical threats. Once a company understands its own internal vulnerabilities, it can monitor the external environment for relevant danger signs and begin to develop mitigation and contingency strategies accordingly. Although companies may not be able to prevent disruptions, they can reduce their impact by understanding how their operations may be affected and by preparing for the possibilities. The goal is to develop operational resilience, foster the ability to recover quickly and plot alternative courses to work around the disruption.

Although global corporations are vulnerable to many of the same risks, each company has a unique risk profile.

There are six steps in developing this profile and appropriate management strategies.

1 *Prioritise earnings drivers*

Identify and map the company's earnings drivers, which provide operational support for the overall business strategy. These are the factors that would have the biggest impact on earnings if disrupted and a shock to any one could endanger the business. For example, in process industries, manufacturing is the major force behind earnings: wholesalers and retailers must prioritise inventory and logistics operations.

▶

▶ 2 *Identify critical infrastructure*

Identify the infrastructure – including processes, relationships, people, regulations, plan and equipment – that supports the firm's ability to generate earnings. Brand reputation, for example, might depend on product quality control processes, supplier labour practices and key spokespeople within the firm. Research and development might depend on specific laboratory locations, critical personnel and patent protection. Again, every company is unique and even companies in the same industry will prioritise their drivers differently. The goal is to identify the essential components required for the earnings driver. One way to do this is by asking 'What are the processes which, if they failed, would seriously affect my earnings?' Put another way, these are the factors that could end up in a footnote in an annual report explaining the rationale behind a charge against earnings.

3 *Locate vulnerabilities*

What are the weakest links, the elements on which all others depend? It could be a single supplier for a critical component, a border that 80 per cent of your products must cross to get to your key markets, a single employee who knows how to restore data if the IT system fails, or a regulation that makes it possible for you to stay in business. Vulnerabilities are characterised by:

● An element on which many others depend – a bottleneck

● A high degree of concentration – suppliers, manufacturing locations, material or information flows

● Limited alternatives

● Association with high-risk geographic areas, industries and products (such as war or flood zones, or economically troubled industries, such as airlines)

● Insecure access points to important infrastructure

Notice that the focus is still on the internal processes rather than potential external events. In many ways the impact of a disruption does not depend on the precise manner in which these elements fail. Whether your key supplier fails because of a fire in a plant, an earthquake, a terrorist attack or an economic crisis, you may have the same response plan.

4 *Model scenarios*

Best-practice organisations continuously assess their strengths and weaknesses by creating scenarios based on the full spectrum of crises highlighted earlier. In a recent *Harvard Business Review* article,[1] Ian Mitroff discussed his approach of spinning a 'Wheel of Crises' to challenge executives to think creatively and randomly. Using supply chain modelling tools to simulate the impact of crises is also useful in gauging risk levels for your trading partners.

5 *Develop responses*

After executives assess the impact of alternative crisis scenarios on the supply chain, they will have detailed knowledge of their operational vulnerabilities and how these soft spots relate to performance goals and earnings. Understanding these weak areas at the enterprise level will clarify critical decisions.

Completing a risk profile will also bring to light opportunities to reduce risk and indicate the value to be gained. Risk-mitigation plans can be put into two broad categories: redundancy and flexibility. Traditional risk-management approaches have focused heavily on redundant solutions, such as increasing inventory, preparing backup IT and telecommunications systems, and fostering long-term supplier contracts. While generally effective in protecting against potential risk, such approaches come with a higher cost – sometimes explicitly and sometimes hidden – that can potentially put organisations at a competitive disadvantage.

Flexible responses, however, utilise supply chain capabilities that not only manage risk but simultaneously increase an organisation's competitive capability. Examples include:

- Product design for agility – common components and delayed product differentiation
- Common, flexible and readily transferable manufacturing practices
- Lead-time reduction – duration and variability
- Dynamic inventory planning
- Supply chain visibility
- Cross-training of employees

Just as supply chain modelling tools and techniques can help assess the impact of crisis scenarios, they can also be used to evaluate the costs and benefits of alternative responses.

6 *Monitor the risk environment*

Each vulnerability will suggest a number of potential responses. The challenge is to ensure that the chosen response is proportional to the risk, in terms of both magnitude and likelihood. A company's risk profile is constantly changing: economic and market conditions change, consumer tastes change, the regulatory environment changes, as will products and processes. It is essential to redraw the company's risk map in tandem. Part of the mapping process includes identifying leading indicators based on the key supply chain vulnerabilities. Such an early warning system helps ensure that contingency plans are activated as soon as possible. Although a detailed assessment of a company's excellence in risk management is quite involved, a simple self-assessment can quickly identify the largest gaps.

References

1. 'Preparing for evil', *Harvard Business Review*, April 2003, pp. 109–115.

Managing supply chain risk

Figure 10.3 below suggests a seven-stage approach to the management of supply chain risk. Each of the seven stages is described in more detail in the following sections.

Figure 10.3 The supply chain risk management process

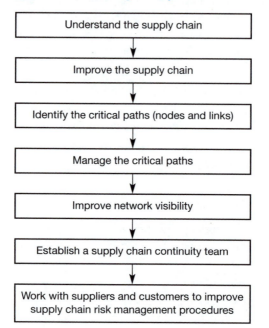

1 Understand the supply chain

There is in many companies an amazing lack of awareness of the wider supply/demand network of which the organisation is a part. Whilst there is often a good understanding of the downstream routes to market, the same is not always true of what lies upstream of first tier suppliers. First tier suppliers are often dependent themselves on second and even third tier suppliers for their continuity.

An example of this is provided by Chrysler which was reviewing the upstream supply chain for the Jeep Grand Cherokee's V8 engine.[4] The company mapped all the hundreds of component flows and found that one of these components – a roller lift valve manufactured by Eaton Corp. – was made from castings sourced from a local foundry. When the Chrysler team visited that foundry they discovered that the clay that was used to produce the castings came from a sole supplier who was losing money and thinking of exiting the business.

It is this detailed level of supply chain understanding that is necessary if risk is to be mitigated and managed. For complex supply chains or where complete mapping of the entire network is not practical it would be appropriate only to look in detail at the 'critical paths' – how these are identified is dealt with later.

2 Improve the supply chain

'Improving' the supply chain is all about simplification, improving process reliability, reducing process variability and reducing complexity. For more long-established businesses it is probably true to say that rarely have their supply chains been planned or designed in a holistic way. Rather they have developed organically in response to the needs and opportunities of the time. Suppliers may have been chosen because of their ability to meet the demands for lower price rather than because of the reliability of their supply chains for example.

Process variability can add to supply chain risk in a number of ways. Variation implies unstable processes with outcomes that are not always predictable. The use of six sigma methodology can be a powerful way to reduce variability in supply chain processes (see box).

Reducing process variability through six sigma methodology Conventional approaches to quality management were typically based upon 'inspection'. In other words, a sample of the output of a process would be taken on a periodic basis and if non-standard outputs were detected then remedial action would be taken. Not surprisingly, inspection-based quality management has proved to be less than satisfactory. Often non-conforming items would 'slip through the net' and, in any case, inspection is 'after the event'. Today, our thinking on quality management has changed. Now the recognition is that if we seek consistency in the quality of the output then the only way to achieve this is to ensure that the process that produces those outputs is under control.

Thus *process control* becomes the means by which *variation* in output is identified. Variation in any process is the problem. If everything in life or in business was totally constant or even predictable, then there would be few problems. The challenges arise because of variations. Hence it follows that if variation can be reduced then the consistency (and, by definition, the reliability) of the output can almost be guaranteed.

The six sigma way

The six sigma route to quality control emerged in the 1980s as Motorola searched for a robust quantitative approach that would drive variability out of manufacturing processes and thus guarantee the reliability of their products. The term 'six sigma' is largely symbolic, referring to a methodology and a culture for continuous quality improvement, as well as referring to the statistical goal, six sigma. The term 'sigma' (σ) is used in statistics to measure variation from the mean; in a business context the higher the value of sigma the more capable the process of delivering an output within customer specifications. The diagram below illustrates the difference between two processes: one with a low capability and the other with six sigma capability.

The *six sigma goal* (which in many cases is an aspirational one) is to squeeze out process variability until the process produces just 3.4 defects per million activities or 'opportunities'; this reduces waste and hence saves money whilst improving customer satisfaction. Whilst six sigma performance may be unattainable in many cases, it is used as a target.

▶

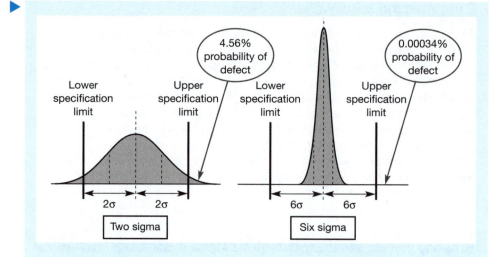

Six sigma is a data-driven continuous improvement methodology that seeks to bring processes under control and to improve process capability. The methodology itself follows the five-stage DMAIC cycle:

Define: What is it we are seeking to improve?

Measure: What is the current capability of the process? What averages, what variability in process output is evident?

Analyse: Map the process, use cause and effect analysis (Ishikawa) and prioritise for action.

Improve: Re-engineer the process, simplify.

Control: Improve visibility of the process. Use statistical process control and monitor performance.

Six sigma tools and techniques enable the proper execution of the DMAIC cycle and ensure that decisions are based on hard quantitative evidence.

SOURCE: CHRISTOPHER, M. AND RUTHERFORD, C., 'CREATING SUPPLY CHAIN RESILIENCE THROUGH AGILE SIX SIGMA', *CRITICAL EYE*, JUNE/AUGUST 2004

3 Identify the critical paths

Supply networks are in effect a complex web of interconnected 'nodes' and 'links'. The nodes represent the entities or facilities such as suppliers, distributors, factories and warehouses. The links are the means by which the nodes are connected – these links may be physical flows, information flows or financial flows. The vulnerability of a supply network is determined by the risk of failure of these nodes and links.

As there will be potentially thousands of nodes and links the challenge to supply chain risk management is to identify which of them are 'mission critical'. In other words, how severe would the effect of failure be on the performance of the supply chain? Companies need to be able to identify the critical paths that must be managed and monitored to ensure continuity.

Critical paths are likely to have a number of characteristics:

- Long lead time, e.g. the time taken to replenish components from order to delivery.
- A single source of supply with no short-term alternative.
- Dependence on specific infrastructure, e.g. ports, transport modes or information systems.
- A high degree of concentration amongst suppliers and customers.
- Bottlenecks or 'pinch points' through which material or product must flow.
- High levels of identifiable risk (i.e. supply, demand, process, control and environmental risk).

To help in identifying where the priority should be placed in supply chain risk management a useful tool is failure mode and effect analysis (FMEA). The purpose of FMEA is to provide a systematic approach to identifying where in a complex system attention should be focused to reduce the risk of failure. It is a tool more frequently associated with total quality management (TQM) but it is especially applicable to supply chain risk management. FMEA begins by looking at each node and link and asking three questions:

- What could go wrong?
- What effect would this failure have?
- What are the key causes of this failure?

The next step is to assess any possible failure opportunity against the following criteria:

- What is the severity of the effect of failure?
- How likely is this failure to occur?
- How likely is the failure to be detected?

A rating system such as the one shown below is then used to create a combined priority score by multiplying the three scores together.

Risk analysis scoring system	
S = Severity	1 No direct effect on operating service level
	2 Minor deterioration in operating service level
	3 Definite reduction in operating service
	4 Serious deterioration in operating service level
	5 Operating service level approaches zero
O = Likelihood of occurrence	1 Probability of once in many years
	2 Probability of once in many operating months
	3 Probability of once in some operating weeks
	4 Probability of weekly occurrence
	5 Probability of daily occurrence
D = Likelihood of detection	1 Detectability is very high
	2 Considerable warning of failure before occurrence
	3 Some warning of failure before occurrence
	4 Little warning of failure before occurrence
	5 Detectability is effectively zero

4 Manage the critical paths

Once the critical nodes and links have been identified the first question is how can the risk be mitigated or removed? At its simplest this stage should involve the development of contingency plans for actions to be taken in the event of failure. At the other extreme, re-engineering of the supply chain may be necessary. Where possible statistical process control should be used to monitor the critical stages along the pipeline.

'Cause and effect' analysis is another tool that can be used to identify the causes of problems with a view to removing or avoiding the causes. It seeks to separate symptoms from causes by a process of progressive questioning – sometimes known as 'Asking 'why' – five times' (see box).

CAUSE AND EFFECT ANALYSIS

Cause and effect analysis (also known as Root Cause Analysis) is used to gain an understanding of the real underlying causes of a problem. Typically it makes use of a sequential question and answer procedure often referred to as 'Asking 'why'– five times'. The idea is not to accept the immediate answer but to drill down as far as possible. For example, if the problem to be analysed is poor on-time delivery performance the questioning might go along the following lines:

1 Q   Why was this shipment delayed?
   A   There was no stock available

2 Q   Why was there no stock available?
   A   We failed to achieve the production plan

3 Q   Why did we fail to achieve the plan?
   A   There was a shortage of components

4 Q   Why was there a shortage?
   A   There is a bottleneck in in-bound inspection

5 Q   Why is there a bottleneck?
   A   We only have limited testing facilities

Now the real problem is revealed and appropriate action can be taken.

If bottlenecks are the cause of the problem then decisions will have to be made about the options. Can the bottlenecks be removed? Can they be reduced by adding capacity or by holding inventory? Sometimes the bottleneck may be a key supplier that is capacity constrained. If alternative sources are not available at short notice then it will be necessary to manage the bottleneck by carrying strategic inventory to enable the flow through the downstream nodes to be maintained.

Whilst the drive for commonality of components and standardisation of platforms in a manufacturing context helps reduce complexity, as was noted earlier, it can also add to risk if the component or platform comes from an external source. The case of Toyota described below highlights the potential danger.

Don't lean too far

In late 2009 and early 2010, owners of Toyota cars around the world were alarmed to learn that millions of vehicles were to be recalled for modification because of problems with the throttle pedal which was causing 'unintended acceleration' in some cases. Production of the affected models was halted whilst the sources of the problem were investigated. Sales of Toyota cars slumped leading to the loss of its position as the world's number one car manufacturer by volume.

What surprised many people was that this had happened to Toyota – a company which for years was held up as the icon of manufacturing excellence. It was suggested by some commentators that Toyota had become a victim of its own success – in other words as it grew significantly in size it was starting to lose control of vital parts of its supply chain.

▶

Toyota's rapid expansion in the decade prior to this recall had led to an increased reliance on tier one and tier two suppliers around the world. In many cases the suppliers were the sole suppliers of specific parts of sub-assemblies across several different models.

As the originator of 'lean' manufacturing, it was not surprising that Toyota had sought to achieve global economies of scale through its sourcing strategy. However, even though Toyota had close working relationships with its tier one suppliers, there was less understanding of what the potential risks were in the second and third tier of the supply chain.

Whilst there are many different views on the root causes of the recall problems impacting Toyota, it is quite possible that in seeking to achieve its goal of becoming the world's biggest car manufacturer it failed to control the complex extended enterprise upon which it had come to depend.

5 Improve network visibility

Many supply chains suffer from limited visibility. What this means is that a particular entity in the network is not aware of the status of upstream and downstream operations of the levels and flow of inventory as it progresses through the chain.

In such a situation it can often be weeks or months before problems become visible, by which time it may be too late to take effective action. The often cited case study of Nokia and Ericsson demonstrates the advantage that supply chain visibility can confer.

In March 2000 both Nokia and Ericsson were affected by a lightening strike on a semi-conductor factory in New Mexico, USA. This Philips-owned factory supplied the two companies with radio frequency chips for their mobile phones. The lightening strike caused a small fire leading to smoke damage that led to a disruption in production of this critical component. Because of Nokia's event management capability it was alerted to the potential problem that this breakdown in supply would entail. As a result it was able to take immediate action to find alternative sources of supply. On the other hand, Ericsson was slow to recognise that there was a problem and failed to act soon enough. As a result Ericsson lost significant sales revenue because of an inability to supply and soon afterwards decided to cease in-house manufacture of mobile phones.

We referred in Chapter 9 to the potential of supply chain event management (SCEM) to enable better identification of the occurence of unplanned events (or the non-occurrence of planned events). Tools such as these can significantly reduce supply chain uncertainty and thus reduce the need for additional inventory buffers. Another emerging technology that is enabling dramatic improvements in visibility is Radio Frequency Identification (RFID).

RFID tags enable a supply chain 'track and trace' capability to be created. Tags are either 'active' or 'passive'. Active tags transmit information to receiving stations and passive tags are read by scanners as they move through the chain. As the cost of these tags falls, and as more and more organisations require their suppliers to use them, then the adoption of this technology will accelerate. The impact, for example, of the decisions by Wal-Mart and the US Defense Department to utilise RFID has already had an impact on the rate of adoption.

A parallel technological development that will greatly assist the global management of assets in the supply chain is satellite tracking. Containers and trucks can be fitted with devices that enable the geographical position of the asset to be monitored by satellite, including information on variables such as temperature.

The challenge, as ever, is not technological but is the need to engender a greater willingness amongst supply chain entities to share information with each other, even if that information may not always be good news.

6 Establish a supply chain continuity team

All the foregoing stages in the supply chain risk management process require resources to undertake them. One way to do this is to create a permanent supply chain continuity team.

Many companies already have business continuity teams in place but, as was suggested earlier, often their focus is more limited and largely IT/IS focused. Other companies look at risk mainly from a financial perspective. All of these activities are necessary and essential but the argument here is that these teams should be expanded in their scope to take account of the fact that the biggest risk to business continuity lies in the wider supply chain.

Ideally these teams will be cross-functional and will have access to all the skills necessary to undertake the detailed analysis and implementation involved in the supply chain risk management process. The team should maintain a 'risk register', which identifies the possible points of vulnerability along with the actions that are to be taken to mitigate that vulnerability.

To ensure that high priority is given to supply chain risk management, the team should report to a board-level executive – ideally the supply chain director or vice-president if that person is on the board.

7 Work with suppliers and customers

Given the complexity of most supply networks, how can risk be better managed upstream and downstream of the focal firm? Ideally, if each entity in a network took responsibility for implementing risk management procedures of the type advocated here with their immediate first tier suppliers and customers then a far more resilient supply chain would emerge.

There are some good examples of collaborative working with both suppliers and customers to develop a greater understanding of the potential vulnerabilities in specific industries. At BAe Systems – a major aerospace company – they have a strategic supplier management process with about 200 key suppliers based upon an industry initiative 'Supply Chain Relationships in Action' (SCRIA). BAe put small teams into these key suppliers to find ways of aligning supply chain processes and improving visibility. With their biggest suppliers such as Rolls-Royce there is ongoing contact right up to board level.

This approach is akin to the idea of *supplier development*, which has been quite widely adopted in the automotive sector. Going beyond this there is an opportunity to draw from the experience of companies which have insisted that their suppliers meet rigorous quality standards in terms of the products that they supply. The same practice could be applied in supply chain risk management by requiring suppliers to monitor and manage their supply chain vulnerabilities. In this way a 'snowball effect' might be achieved, with each supplier working with their first tier suppliers to implement supply chain risk management procedures.

Target Stores, the North American retailer, requires its suppliers to sign an agreement that they will comply with Target's requirements on supply chain security and risk management. Pfizer, the pharmaceutical company, also has clearly established performance standards for its suppliers in terms of supply chain risk management which are audited continuously.

Achieving supply chain resilience

Because even the best managed supply chains will hit unexpected turbulence or be affected by events that are impossible to forecast, it is critical that *resilience* be built into them. Resilience implies the ability of a system to return to its original or desired state after being disturbed.[5] Resilient processes are flexible and agile and are able to change quickly. In this latter respect it is important to realise that velocity alone is not enough – it is acceleration or the ability to ramp up or down quickly that matters so far as resilience is concerned. Supply chain resilience also requires 'slack' at those critical points that constitute the limiting factors to changes in the rate of flow.

Access to information as rapidly as possible is also a prerequisite for resilience as we observed in the case of Nokia and Ericsson. Through collaborative working this information can be converted into supply chain *intelligence*. Because networks have become more complex they will rapidly descend into chaos unless they can be connected through shared information and knowledge. The aim is to create a supply chain community whereby there is a greater visibility of upstream and downstream risk profiles (and change in those profiles) and a shared commitment to mitigate and manage those risks.

Finally, supply chain resilience requires a recognition that when strategic decisions are taken, such as relocating facilities or changing sources of supply, then the impact of those decisions on the supply chain risk profile must be fully understood. Based upon that analysis it may be necessary to re-engineer the supply chain, or parts of it, to ensure the mitigation or removal of that risk. Figure 10.4 attempts to summarise the different requirements that need to be in place if supply chain resilience is to be improved.

A report by A.T. Kearney[6] suggested a number of stages to supply chain risk management excellence (see Table 10.1). Stage 1 companies have a very limited definition of risk, largely confined to financial, property and IT issues. At the other extreme, stage 4 companies have a supply chain wide perspective and have active programmes for risk mitigation.

Figure 10.4 Creating the resilient supply chain

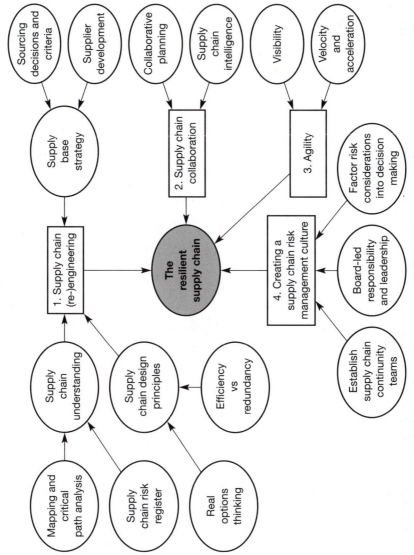

Table 10.1 Stages of excellence in supply chain risk management

Dimension	Stage 1	Stage 2	Stage 3	Stage 4
Responsibility level	• Functional or departmental skills	• Business unit	• Corporate (chief risk officer)	• Extended enterprise (board level)
Scope of risk	• Market risks (foreign exchange credit, commodity) • Property or safety risk • IT security	• Market risk • Property or safety risks • Operational risk • IT disruption • Easily quantified risks	• All enterprise risks • Business continuity • Country risk • Key business processes • Day-to-day risks	• Strategic risks • Operational resilience • Global business environment • Organisational or cultural component of risk management
Risk-mitigation tools	• Financial derivatives, property insurance	• Incident data and trend analysis • Supplier contract reviews • Self-assessment	• Contingency planning • Scenario analysis • New business and new venture audits • Risk adjusted performance measures	• Advance warning systems • Back-up of processes as well as data • Quarterly drills that include key partners
Motivation	• Follow regulations, reduce financial exposure	• Avoid operational disruptions, avoid costs of accidents	• Protect brand image, maintain earnings stability	• Create competitive advantage, generate shareholder value
Updates to risk plan	• Never	• After major incidents	• Annually	• Quarterly
Supply chain	• Buffer inventories • Excess capacity	• Alternative suppliers • Recovery plans – select scenarios	• Co-ordinated forecasts throughout supply chain • 'What if' modelling • Agility: products and processes	• Supply chain transparency • 'War gaming' • Dynamic reserves of critical components
Collaboration	• Focus Internally	• Communicate policies to suppliers	• Collaborate with suppliers, industry associations	• Lead industry initiatives, collaborate with goverment

Source: Supply Chains in a Vulnerable, Volatile World. Copyright A.T. Kearney, 2003. All rights reserved. Reprinted with permission

References

1 Singhal, V.R. and Hendricks, K., 'How supply chain glitches torpedo shareholder value', *Supply Chain Management Review*, January/ February 2002.

2. *McKinsey Quarterly*, 'Understanding supply chain risk', October 2006.

3. Cranfield School of Management, *Supply Chain Vulnerability*, report on behalf of DTLR, DTI and Home Office, 2002.

4. Houghton, T., Markham, B., and Tevelson, B., 'Thinking strategically about supply chain management', *Supply Chain Management Review*, September–October 2002.

5. Cranfield School of Management, *Creating Resilient Supply Chains: A Practical Guide*, Report on behalf of the Department for Transport, 2003.

6. A.T. Kearney, *Supply Chains in a Vulnerable, Volatile World*, 2003.

The era of network competition

11

- The new organisational paradigm

- Collaboration in the supply chain

- Managing the supply chain as a network

- Seven major business transformations

- The implications for tomorrow's logistics managers

- Supply chain orchestration

- From 3PL to 4PL™

Throughout this book the emphasis has been upon the achievement of competitive advantage through excellence in logistics and supply chain management.

An increasing number of organisations can be identified in which logistics and supply chain management are quite clearly recognised as major strategic variables. Companies like Xerox, Dell, Nokia, Zara and 3M have invested significantly in developing responsive logistics capability. Whilst their success in the marketplace is due to many things there can be no doubting the role that logistics and supply chain management have played in achieving that success.

Each year AMR Research – a company specialising in supply chain management analysis and research – has conducted a study of leading supply chains and has sought to understand what constitutes the key drivers of supply chain excellence. Using hard quantitative data and qualitative assessment from a panel of experts, AMR produces an annual ranking of the 'top 25 supply chains'.[1] Based on an analysis of the leading companies in the survey the have identified six consistent characteristics exhibited by those companies:

- *Outside-in focus*
  Leading supply chains are designed from the customer backwards and are demand-driven.

- *Embedded innovation*
  This implies a close integration between product design, manufacturing and logistics to ensure that the supply chain begins on the drawing board.
- *Extended supply chain*
  A recognition that in today's world of global supply chains and outsourcing that the close management of relationships from end-to-end is essential.
- *Balanced Metrics*
  In order to achieve high levels of agility and responsiveness there has to be a realisation that there will be trade-offs across the business. To achieve the best overall outcomes requires a set of key performance indicators (KPIs) that reflect the need for balance.
- *Attitude*
  A culture that extends across the organisation based on the recognition that internal silos must be removed and that external relationships need to be managed in a spirit of partnership
- *Supply chain talent*
  Supply chains are as much about people as anything. Leading companies actively seek to develop the skills and capabilities that will enable success on the previous five elements.

The new organisational paradigm

It will be apparent that to achieve success in all of these areas will require significant change within the company. It requires a transformation that goes beyond redrawing the organisation chart and entails a cultural change that must be driven from the top. In fact the basic principles that have traditionally guided the company must be challenged and what is required is a shift in the basic paradigms that have underpinned industrial organisations for so long.

The need for new business models

Most of us work in organisations that are hierarchical, vertical and functionally defined. The organisation chart for the typical company resembles a pyramid and provides a clear view of where everyone fits in relation to each other and will also normally reflect reporting relationships. In essence, the conventional organisation structure is little changed since the armies of the Roman Empire developed the precursor of the pyramid organisation.

> Most of us work in organisations that are hierarchical, vertical and functionally defined.

Whilst there can be no doubting that this organisational model has served us well in the past, there are now serious questions about its appropriateness for the changed conditions that confront us today. Of the many changes that have taken place in the marketing environment, perhaps the biggest is the focus upon 'speed'. Because of shortening product life cycles, time-to-market becomes ever more critical. Similarly, the dramatic growth of just-in-time (JIT) practices in manufacturing means that those companies wishing to supply into that environment have to develop systems capable of responding rapidly and flexibly to customers' delivery requirements, Indeed, the same is true in almost every market today as organisations seek to reduce their inventories, and hence a critical requirement of a supplier is that they are capable of rapid response.

The challenge to every business is to become a responsive organisation in every sense of the word. The organisation must respond to changes in the market with products and services that provide innovative solutions to customers' problems; it must respond to volatile demand and it must be able to provide high levels of flexibility in delivery.

Perhaps one of the most significant breakthroughs in management thinking in recent years has been the realisation that individual businesses no longer compete as stand-alone entities, but rather as supply chains. We are now entering the era of 'network competition', where the prizes will go to those organisations that can better structure, co-ordinate and manage the relationships with their partners in a network committed to delivering superior value in the final marketplace.

The emergence of the 'network organisation' is a recent phenomenon that has given rise to much comment and analysis. These 'virtual' organisations are characterised by a confederation of specialist skills and capabilities provided by the network members. It is argued that such collaborative arrangements provide a more effective means of satisfying customer needs at a profit than does the single firm undertaking multiple value-creating activities. The implications of the network organisation for management are considerable and, in particular, the challenges to logistics management are profound.

Making networks more effective in satisfying end-user requirements demands a high level of co-operation between organisations in the network, along with the recognition of the need to make inter-firm relationships mutually beneficial. Underpinning the successful network organisation is the value-added exchange of information between partners, meaning that information on downstream demand or usage is made visible to all the upstream members of the supply chain. Creating 'visibility' along the pipeline ensures that the manufacture and delivery of product can be driven by real demand rather than by a forecast and hence enables all parties in the chain to operate more effectively.

Supply chain management is concerned with achieving a more cost-effective satisfaction of end customer requirements through buyer/supplier process integration. This integration is typically achieved through a greater transparency of customer requirements via the sharing of information, assisted by the establishment of 'seamless' processes that link the identification of physical replenishment needs with a 'just-in-time' response.

In the past it was more often the case that organisations were structured and managed on the basis of optimising their own operations with little regard for the way in which they interfaced with suppliers or, indeed, customers. The business model was essentially 'transactional', meaning that products and services were bought and sold on an arm's-length basis and that there was little enthusiasm for the concept of longer-term, mutually dependent relationships. The end result was often a high-cost, low-quality solution for the final customer in the chain.

This emerging competitive paradigm is in stark contrast to the conventional model. It suggests that in today's challenging global markets, the route to sustainable advantage lies in managing the complex web of relationships that link highly focused providers of specific elements of the final offer in a cost-effective, value-adding chain.

The key to success in this new competitive framework, it can be argued, is the way in which this network of alliances and suppliers are welded together in partnership to achieve mutually beneficial goals.

Collaboration in the supply chain

It will be clear that one of the key ingredients of supply chain management excellence is a high level of collaboration across the network.

The benefits of collaboration are well illustrated by the often quoted example of the 'prisoner's dilemma'. The scenario is that you and your partner have been arrested on suspicion of robbing a bank. You are both put in separate cells and not allowed to communicate with each other. The police officer tells you both independently that you will be leniently treated if you confess, but less well if you do not!

In fact the precise penalties are given to you as follows:

Option 1:   You confess but your partner doesn't.

Outcome: You get one year in jail for co-operating but your partner gets five years.

Option 2:   You don't confess but your partner does.

Outcome: You get five years in jail and your partner gets only one year for co-operating.

Option 3:   Both of you confess.

Outcome: You get two years each.

Option 4:   Neither of you confess.

Outcome: You both go free.

These options and outcomes can be summarised in the matrix in Figure 11.1.

What is the most likely outcome? If neither you nor your partner really trusts the other, particularly if previous experience has taught you to be wary of each other, then both of you will confess. Obviously the best strategy is one based on trust and hence for neither party to confess!

Figure 11.1 The prisoner's dilemma: penalty options (years in jail)

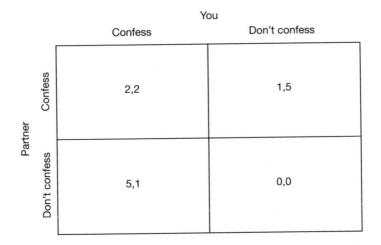

This simple example provides a good analogy with the real world. The conventional wisdom of purchasing has tended towards the view that multiple sources of supply for a single item are to be preferred. In such situations, it is argued, one is unlikely to become too reliant upon a single source of supply. Furthermore we can play one supplier off against another and reduce the cost of purchases. However, such relationships tend to be adversarial and, in fact, sub-optimal.

One of the first things to suffer when the relationship is based only upon negotiations about price is quality. The supplier seeks to minimise his costs and to provide only the basic specification. In situations like this the buyer will incur additional costs on in-bound inspection and rework. Quality in respect of service is also likely to suffer when the supplier does not put any particular priority on the customer's order.

At a more tangible level those customers who have moved over to synchronous supply with the consequent need for JIT deliveries have found that it is simply impractical to manage in-bound shipments from multiple suppliers. Similarly the communication of orders and replenishment instructions is so much more difficult with multiple suppliers.

The closer the relationship between buyer and supplier the more likely it is that the expertise of both parties can be applied to mutual benefit. For example, many companies have found that by close co-operation with suppliers they can improve product design, value-engineer components, and generally find more efficient ways of working together.

This is the logic that underlines the emergence of the concept of 'co-makership' or 'partnership sourcing'. Co-makership may be defined as:

The development of a long-term relationship with a limited number of suppliers on the basis of mutual confidence.

The basic philosophy of co-makership is that the supplier should be considered to be an extension of the customer's operations with the emphasis on continuity and a 'seamless' end-to-end pipeline. As the trend to outsourcing continues so must the move towards co-makership. Nissan Motors in the UK have been one of the leading advocates of this concept. A key element of their approach is the use of 'supplier development teams', which are small groups of Nissan specialists who will help suppliers to achieve the requirements that Nissan places upon them. The overall objective of the supplier development team is to reduce the costs and increase the efficiency for both parties – in other words a 'win-win' outcome. Because the cost of materials in an automobile can be as high as 85 per cent, anything that can reduce the costs of purchased supplies can have a significant effect on total costs.

Figure 11.2 depicts a not-untypical situation where a car manufacturer's purchased materials are 85 per cent of total costs. This is then exploded further where it is shown that the material costs of the component supplier are a figure closer to the average for manufacturing industry of 40 per cent. Of the remaining 60 per cent ('supplier value added'), 80 per cent of that figure might be accounted for by overheads, of which typically 30 per cent or so would be accounted for by the supplier's logistics costs (i.e. inventory, set-up costs transport, warehousing, etc.).

Figure 11.2 The impact of suppliers' logistics costs on the costs of a car

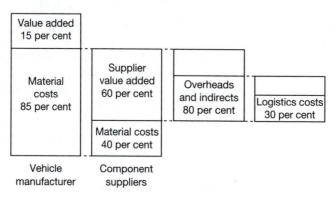

What this implies is that approximately 12 per cent of the cost of materials to the car manufacturer are accounted for by the supplier's logistics costs (i.e. 85 per cent × 60 per cent × 80 per cent × 30 per cent). When it is realised that a proportion of the supplier's logistics costs are caused by the lack of integration and partnership between the car manufacturer and the supplier, it becomes apparent that a major opportunity for cost reduction exists.

Under the traditional adversarial relationship the vehicle manufacturer would seek to reduce the material cost by squeezing the profit margin of the component suppliers. The co-makership approach is quite different – here the vehicle manufacturer seeks instead to reduce a supplier's costs, not their profits. Through collaboration and closely integrated logistics planning mechanisms the two parties seek to achieve a situation where there are benefits to both parties. Companies like Nissan Motors in the UK have shown that this is not a utopian dream but can be a practical reality.

The principle of co-makership can be extended in both directions in the supply chain – upstream to suppliers and downstream to distributors, retailers and even end users. The prizes to be won from successful co-makership potentially include lower costs for all parties through reduced inventories and lower set-up costs as a result of better schedule integration. The implications for competitive strategy are profound. The new competitive paradigm is that supply chain competes with supply chain and the success of any one company will depend upon how well it manages its supply chain relationships.

Managing the supply chain as a network

The new competitive paradigm that we have described places the firm at the centre of an interdependent network – a confederation of mutually complementary competencies and capabilities – which competes as an integrated supply chain against other supply chains.

To manage in such a radically revised competitive structure clearly requires different skills and priorities to those employed in the traditional model. To achieve market leadership in the world of network competition necessitates a focus on network management as well as upon internal processes. Of the many issues and challenges facing organisations as they make the transition to this new competitive environment, the following are perhaps most significant.

1 Collective strategy development

Traditionally, members of a supply chain have never considered themselves to be part of a marketing network and so have not shared with each other their strategic thinking. For network competition to be truly effective a significantly higher level of joint strategy development is required. This means that network members must collectively agree strategic goals for the network and the means of attaining them.

2 Win-win thinking

Perhaps one of the biggest challenges to the successful establishment of marketing networks is the need to break free from the often adversarial nature of buyer/supplier relationships that existed in the past. There is now a growing realisation that co-operation between network partners usually leads to improved performance generally. The issue then becomes one of determining how the results of that improved performance can be shared amongst the various players. 'Win-win' need not mean 50/50, but at a minimum all partners should benefit and be better off as a result of co-operation.

3 Open communication

One of the most powerful drivers of change in marketing networks has been the advent of information technology, making the exchange of information between supply chain partners so easy and so advantageous. The Internet has provided a ubiquitous platform to enable end-to-end pipeline visibility to become a reality. With all parties 'singing from the same song sheet' a much more rapid response to marketplace changes is achieved with less inventory and lower risks of obsolescence. For network marketing to work to its fullest potential, visibility and transparency of relevant information throughout the supply chain is essential. Open-book accounting is another manifestation of this move towards transparency by which cost data is shared upstream and downstream and hence each partner's profit is visible to the others. Building this network-based approach to competitive advantage clearly requires a number of significant changes to the way in which the business is run and the 'mindsets' of those who manage it. Some of these fundamental changes are addressed in the following section.

Seven major business transformations

1 From supplier-centric to customer-centric

Traditionally supply chains have been designed from the 'factory outwards' rather than from the 'customer backwards'. The emphasis in the past was on how to ensure that a batch-oriented production process could most efficiently distribute its output. Thus the goal in supply chain design was often cost minimisation. In today's highly competitive marketplace the goal must change to the attainment of higher levels of customer responsiveness. Thus agility rather than cost becomes the key driver.

2 From push to pull

Closely linked to the first transformation is the idea of moving from a 'production push' mentality which seeks to optimise operations through level scheduling and long planning horizons to a 'demand pull' philosophy in which, ideally, nothing is made, sourced or moved until there is a demand for it. This in essence is the Japanese 'Kanban' principle, with the modification that the quantities triggered by the Kanban should be variable depending on demand. Clearly the success of such a system requires the highest level of flexibility of all the supply chain's resources, including people.

3 From inventory to information

Logistics and supply chain management have conventionally been forecast-driven rather than demand-driven. In other words, the focus has been to look ahead over a planning horizon and to predict demand at a point in time and then to build inventory against that forecast. As markets become more volatile and turbulent so too have they become harder to predict. The risk of over- or under-stocking increases. The challenge today is to enable supply chains to become demand-driven as a result of better visibility of real demand. Real demand occurs at the end of the supply chain and if that information can be captured and shared upstream then the dependency on inventory reduces.

4 From transactions to relationships

There is a growing recognition that the route to sustained profitability is through building long-term relationships with selected customers. The focus in the past was on volume and market share and the company was transactional in its orientation. Today, customer retention is a key measure of success in the world of relationship marketing. One of the drivers of improved customer retention is the delivery of superior customer service. Hence there is a very clear connection between logistics and customer retention. Managing customer relationships has become a critical business process as organisations seek to improve the quality of their earnings.

5 From 'trucks and sheds' to 'end-to-end' pipeline management

Over the last two decades there has been a dramatic broadening of the scope of logistics and supply chain management in many organisations. Previously logistics – or, more properly, distribution management – was seen as being primarily a concern with transportation and warehousing. As such, the focus of managerial effort tended to be on cost minimisation and the 'optimisation' of networks and resources. Whilst the need for efficient distribution is still as strong now as in the past, there is a widely held view that the real task of supply chain management is to co-ordinate the wider end-to-end pipeline. In-bound logistics is just as critical as the distribution of final product under this paradigm and the emphasis is now on time compression from one end of the supply chain to the other.

6 From functions to processes

Only recently have companies come to challenge the primacy of functions in the organisational structure. Traditionally the business has been organised around functions and those functions have provided a convenient mechanism for the allocation of resources and for the promotion of personnel. The classic business organisation could be described as 'vertical' with a multi-layered hierarchical decision-making structure. However, in today's turbulent business environment questions are increasingly being asked about the ability of such organisations to respond rapidly to the fast-changing needs of the market. It is now suggested that the emphasis in organisations should be upon the key business processes that create value for customers. These processes, by definition, are cross-functional and market-facing. They are, more than likely, team-based and they draw their members from the functions whose roles are now transformed to 'centres of excellence'.

7 From stand-alone competition to network rivalry

The conventional business model has always been that companies succeed or fail on the basis of their own resources and competencies. However, as the trend to outsourcing has increased, there has come a realisation that the competitive vehicle is no longer the individual firm but rather the supply chain of which that firm is a member. Whereas once a single firm might encompass almost the whole supply chain, today that is no longer the case. Instead, today the company finds itself a member of an 'extended enterprise'. This extended enterprise is in reality a complex network of specialist providers of resources and competencies. The companies that will be the most successful in this era of network competition will be those that are best able to utilise the resources and competencies of other partners across the network.

The implications for tomorrow's logistics managers

Transformations of the type outlined above have significant implications for the type of skills profile that will characterise successful logistics and supply chain managers.

Table 11.1 suggests some of the elements of the necessary skills profile that flow from the seven business transformations.

This is only indicative, but what it does suggest is that there is a real need for formal education and training in areas as diverse as information systems and change management. The skills that are indicated cannot be acquired solely through osmosis and experience; the foundation for mastery of these skills must be gained through appropriate management education programmes.

The following quotation from an article in the *Harvard Business Review* neatly summarises the issue:

> *Despite years of process breakthroughs and elegant technology solutions, an agile, adaptive supply chain remains an elusive goal. Maybe it's the people who are getting in the way ... Supply chains it seems are really about talent, not technology, especially as the marketplace grows ever more complex.*

> *SOURCE*: J. KIRBY[2]

This is the challenge for today's logistics educators: how to establish programmes that have the breadth as well as the depth to create 'T-shaped' managers.

'T-shaped' managers are so called because of their skills profile. Even though they have a specific specialism (the down-bar of the T) with in-depth knowledge and capability, they also have a significant understanding of the other key business functions (see Figure 11.3). This breadth of understanding is critical for the supply chain manager of the future, given the need to think and manage 'horizontally', i.e. across functions and between businesses.

Table 11.1 The key business transformations and the implications for management skills

Business transformation	Leading to	Skills required
From supplier-centric to customer-centric	The design of customer-driven supply chains	Market understanding; customer insight
From push to pull	Higher levels of agility and flexibility	Management of complexity and change
From inventory to information	Capturing and sharing information on real demand	Information systems and information technology expertise
From transactions to relationships	Focus on service and responsiveness as the basis for customer retention	Ability to define, measure and manage service requirements by market segment
From 'trucks and sheds' to 'end-to-end' pipeline management	A wider definition of supply chain cost	Understanding of the 'cost-to-serve' and time-based performance indicators
From functions to processes	The creation of cross-functional teams focused on value creation	Specific functional excellence with cross-functional understanding; team working capabilities
From stand-alone competition to network rivalry	More collaborative working with supply chain partners	Relationship management and 'win-win' orientation

Figure 11.3 Creating a T-shaped skills profile

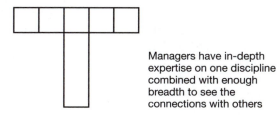

Effective process management requires significant cross-functional skills

Managers have in-depth expertise on one discipline combined with enough breadth to see the connections with others

Supply chain orchestration

With the emergence of the virtual organisation and the extended enterprise comes a heightened requirement for some way of managing the complexity that is inevitably created. Consider for a moment the difference between the supply chain at Ford during the time of Henry Ford with Ford's supply chain today. Henry Ford had an integrated supply chain because in effect he owned most of it. As well as manufacturing the vast majority of all the components that went into the vehicle, the company also owned steel mills, rubber plantations and mahogany forests! Today's Ford could not be more different. Most of the component manufacturing business was floated off as a separate company, Visteon, and the steel mills have long since gone. Instead Ford is at the centre of a network of specialist service providers, first tier suppliers and collaborative alliances. The task of managing, co-ordinating and focusing this value-creating network might usefully be termed *supply chain orchestration*.

The idea of orchestration is that there has to be a common agreed agenda driving the achievement of the supply chain goals. This itself implies that there must be a supply chain strategy that is subscribed to by the entities in the chain. By the very nature of things, the orchestrator will probably be the most powerful member of the network, i.e. a Wal-Mart or a Dell, but not necessarily. Innovative organisations can utilise their superior supply chain capabilities to act as orchestrators, as the Li and Fung case study below demonstrates.

Li and Fung: supply chain orchestrator

Li and Fung (L&F) is a long established Hong Kong-based trading company, orchestrating one of the largest and most successful of all outsourced manufacturing networks. It supplies apparel, accessories, sporting equipment, household goods and toys to retail chains located mostly in North America and Europe.

L&F does not manufacture anything in-house, but as network co-ordinator it oversees the manufacturing and delivery processes end-to-end. Its *modus operandi* is, however, in sharp contrast to automotive industry-style supplier management programmes. L&F does not micro manage or monitor each and every process of a handful of first tier suppliers. Nor does it control its network through intricately worded contracts or sophisticated IT capabilities. The secret of L&F's success is that it has learned how to manage outsourced operations through hands-off relationships with over 7,500 trusted and very specialised manufacturing organisations, working with up to 2,500 at any time. L&F's suppliers are located in around 40 countries, stretching across South East Asia, into China, the Indian subcontinent, the Mediterranean, Africa and across to the Americas. Together the suppliers represent a highly flexible and highly skilled resource pool, able to meet the requirements of almost any customer. L&F ensures their loyalty by pre-booking between 30 and 70 per cent of the selected suppliers' capacity each season and rewarding high performers with more business.

When an order is received, L&F is able to draw on this vast array of talent, selecting yarn from one country, to be woven and dyed in another, cut in a third and assembled in a fourth, before being shipped to retailers elsewhere. For each stage of manufacture and distribution it carefully picks the organisation best able to undertake that particular value-adding activity, but then leaves the company to determine exactly how that should be achieved. For each value-adding step, L&F will provide specifications for the work – relating to what must be achieved – but not how – and the deadline by which the supplier must have shipped the work to its next destination. In doing so L&F gets the benefits of control without stifling innovation. It gets the product or service it requires, but leaves it to the supplier to determine the most efficient way of achieving it. If a quality problem or some logistical difficulty arises, then the network is flexible enough for production to be transferred very quickly to an alternative source or location.

L&F is constantly searching for new companies to add to the network, as well as new product opportunities. Over 100 years of experience has provided the company with a deep knowledge of its business and the ability to identify those organisations that have the right capabilities to enhance and sustain the growth and diversity of the network. Co-ordination costs are high, but L&F has demonstrated that these are more than offset by the advantages of flexibility offered by its loosely coupled network.

Another model for the co-ordination of complex networks that has been proposed is the idea of a 4PL™ or a lead logistics service provider.

From 3PL to 4PL™

Third-party logistics service providers are companies that provide a range of logistics activities for their clients. They might operate distribution centres, manage the delivery of the product through their transport fleets or undertake value-adding services such as re-packing.

The idea of the fourth-party logistics service provider was originated by the consulting company Accenture. The underpinning principle was that because modern supply networks are increasingly global and certainly more complex, the capabilities to manage the network probably do not exist in any one organisation. In such situations, there is a need for an organisation – possibly coming together with the focal firm through a joint venture – that can use its knowledge of supply chains and specialist third-party service providers to manage and integrate the complete end-to-end supply chain.

The 4PL™ would assemble a coalition of the 'best of breed' service providers and – using its own information systems capability – ensure a cost-effective and sustainable supply chain solution. Figure 11.4 summarises the principle behind the 4PL™ concept.

Figure 11.4 The 4PL™ Concept

Primary client's contribution
- Start-up equity
- Assets
- Working capital
- Operational expertise
- Operational staff
- Procures logistics services from 4PL organisation

3PL service providers' contribution
- Transportation services
- Warehouse facilities

Partner's contribution
- Set-up equity
- Logistics strategy
- Re-engineering skill
- Best practice benchmarks
- IT development
- Customer service management
- Supplier management
- Logistics consultancy

Key characteristics
- Hybrid organisation – formed from a number of different entities
- Typically established as a JV or long-term contract
- Alignment of goals of partners and clients through profit sharing
- Responsible for management and operation of entire supply chain
- Continual flow of information between partners and 4PL organisation
- Potential for revenue generation

Souce: Accenture

In this particular business model a joint venture (JV) has been formed between the client and the partner. As well as putting in equity the client will also transfer its existing logistics assets (e.g. distribution centres) to the JV. Probably too, the staff who manage and run the existing logistics system will move to this new company. The partner's contribution might include, as well as start-up equity, its information systems capability, its strategy development skills and its process re-engineering skills.

The JV will then identify those specialist providers of logistics services who between them will execute the different activities in the supply chain. Using its information systems the JV now becomes the supply chain orchestrator and delivers to the client, against agreed service and cost goals, a complete network management capability.

Whether the 4PL™ be a joint venture or some other model there are four key components that must be in place:

- Systems architecture and integration skills
- A supply chain 'control room'
- Ability to capture and utilise information and knowledge across the network
- Access to 'best of breed' asset providers

Figure 11.5 summarises these key requirements.

Figure 11.5 Four key components a 4PL must assemble

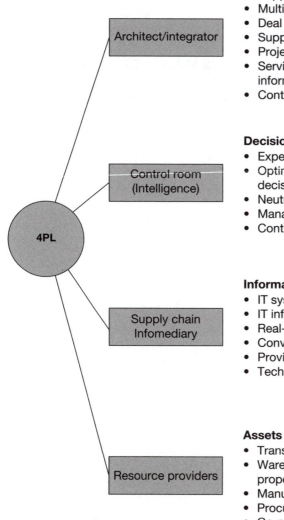

Change Leader
- Supply chain visionary
- Multiple customer relationship
- Deal shaper and maker
- Supply chain re-engineers
- Project management
- Service, systems and information integrator
- Continuous innovation

Decision makers
- Experienced logisticians
- Optimisation engines and decision support
- Neutral positioning
- Manage multiple 3PLs
- Continuous improvement

Information nervous system
- IT system integration
- IT infrastructure provision
- Real-time data to information
- Convert data to information
- Provide info to point of need
- Technical support

Assets
- Transportation asset provider
- Warehouse, cross-dock, property facility
- Manufacturing – outsourcing
- Procurement service
- Co-packing service

Souce: Accenture

We are seemingly entering an era where the rules of competition will be significantly different from those that prevailed in the past. A new paradigm of competition is emerging in which the supply chain network increasingly will provide a source of sustainable advantage through enhanced customer value.

If such an advantage is to be achieved, then it is critical for the organisation to review the way in which it currently delivers value to its customers and to consider whether the time has come to reconfigure the chain to utilise the strengths of other players in the supply chain. One thing is for certain, companies that believe that they can continue to conduct 'business as usual' will find that their prospects for success in tomorrow's marketplace will decline rapidly.

References

1. O'Marah, K. and Hofman, D., 'Top 25 supply chains', *Supply Chain Management Review*, October 2009.
2. Kirby, J., 'Supply chain challenges: building relationships', *Harvard Business Review*, Vol. 81, No. 7, 2003, pp. 65–73.

Overcoming the
barriers to supply
chain integration

12

- Creating the logistics vision

- The problems with conventional organisations

- Developing the logistics organisation

- Logistics as the vehicle for change

- Benchmarking

The transition to the twenty-first century seems to have been accompanied by ever higher levels of change in the business environment. Companies that were market leaders a decade ago have in many cases encountered severe reversals of fortune. Mergers and takeovers have changed the shape of many markets and the advent of regional and global competition have changed for all time the rules of the game. On top of all this, as we have noted, has been a growing demand from the marketplace for ever higher levels of service and quality. These pressures have combined to produce a new imperative for the organisation: the need to be responsive.

The responsive organisation not only seeks to put the customer at the centre of the business, but it also designs all its systems and procedures with the prime objective of improving the speed of response and the reliability of that response. Traditional organisations have grown heavy with layer upon layer of management and bureaucracy. Such companies have little chance of remaining competitive in the new marketplace. Neither is it sufficient to rely upon restructuring the organisation through removing layers of management, i.e. 'flattening' the organisational chart – as many companies are now seeking to do – if such 'de-layering' is not accompanied by equivalent change to the networks and systems that deliver service to the customer.

> Traditional organisations have grown heavy with layer upon layer of management and bureaucracy.

Creating the logistics vision

Making service happen is the ultimate challenge. Whilst it is by no means easy to develop strategies for service that will lead to improved competitive performance, the hardest task is to put that strategy into action. How do we develop an organisation that is capable of delivering high-quality service on a consistent, ongoing basis?

These days most companies are familiar with the idea of 'mission statements' as an articulation of the vision of the business. The mission statement seeks to define the purpose of the business, its boundaries and its aspirations. It is now by no means uncommon for organisations to have such statements for the business as a whole and for key constituent components. What some companies have found is that there can be significant benefits to defining the logistics vision of the firm.

The purpose of the logistics vision statement is to give a clear indication of the basis on which the business intends to build a position of advantage through closer customer relationships. Such statements are never easy to construct. There is always the danger that they will descend into vague 'motherhood' statements that give everyone a warm feeling but provide no guidelines for action.

Ideally the logistics vision should be built around the simple issue of 'How do we intend to use logistics and supply chain management to create value for our customers?' To operationalise this idea will necessitate a detailed understanding of how customer value is (or could be) created and delivered in the markets in which the business competes. Value chain analysis will be a fundamental element in this investigation, as will the definition of the core competencies and capabilities of the organisation. Asking the questions 'What activities do we excel in?' and 'What is it that differentiates us from our competitors?' is the starting point for creating the logistics vision statement.

The four elements of logistics-derived customer value highlighted later in this chapter are 'Better, Faster, Cheaper, Closer' and the criterion for a good logistics vision statement is that it should provide the roadmap for how these four goals are to be achieved.

The problems with conventional organisations

Amongst experienced observers and commentators of the logistics management process there is general agreement that the major barrier to the implementation of the logistics concept is organisational. In other words, a major impediment to change in this crucial managerial area is the entrenched and rigid organisational structure that most established companies are burdened with.

There is a great danger that those companies that do not recognise the need for organisational change, or that lack the will to make it happen, will never achieve the improvements in competitive advantage that integrated logistics management can bring. The argument advanced here is that the demands of the marketplace for enhanced service provision combined with dramatically heightened competition call for a paradigm shift in the way in which we think about our organisations.

The concept of integrated supply chain management, whereby flows of information and material between source and user are co-ordinated and managed as a system, is now widely understood, if not widely implemented. The logic of linking each step of the process as materials and products move towards the customer is based upon the principles of optimisation. In other words, the goal is to maximise customer service whilst simultaneously minimising costs and reducing assets locked up in the logistics pipeline.

However, in the conventional organisation this poses an immediate problem. Most companies are organised on a functional basis. In other words, they have created a division of responsibility by function, so we might find a purchasing function, a production function, a sales function and so on. Typically the organisation chart would look like that in Figure 12.1.

Figure 12.1 The functional organisation

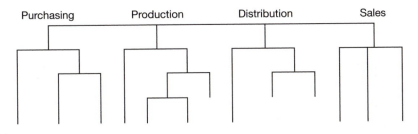

Each of the 'vertical' functions in the conventional organisation is normally headed by senior managers who come to regard their functional area as their 'territory'. Indeed in many companies these functional heads are 'barons' who wield considerable power and who jealously guard those territories from what they perceive as unwarranted incursions from other functional barons.

Further reinforcing the functional or vertical orientation in the conventional organisation is the budgeting system. Typically, each function will be driven by a budget that seeks to control the resources consumed by those functions. It is almost as if the company is working on the assumption that the prime purpose of any enterprise is to control the consumption of resources. In fact, the leading-edge companies have long since realised that the sole purpose of the business is to create profitable outputs and that outputs, not inputs, should form the basis both for the way we organise and for the way we plan and control.

We will look in detail later at the alternative models for organisation and for planning and control, but first let us highlight some of the real problems that the conventional organisation creates that hamper the successful implementation of integrated logistics management.

Inventory builds up at functional boundaries

If individual functions are encouraged to 'optimise' their own costs – because of the budgeting system – then this will often be at the expense of substantially increased inventory across the system as a whole. What happens if, say, production seeks to minimise the unit costs of production by maintaining long production runs with large batch quantities is the creation of more inventory than is normally required for immediate requirements. Likewise, if purchasing management seeks low material costs through bulk purchases then again the inventory of raw materials ahead of production will often be excessive. Similar buffers of inventory will exist right across the supply chain at boundaries within organisations and, indeed, at boundaries between organisations.

Not only is this increased inventory a financial burden and a further strain on working capital, it also obscures our 'visibility' of final demand. Thus upstream activities may not have any clear view of what the real demand is downstream, as all they see is a reorder-point-generated order hitting them at short notice (or, more often than not, no notice at all). Figure 12.2 illustrates this point.

Figure 12.2 Inventory hides demand

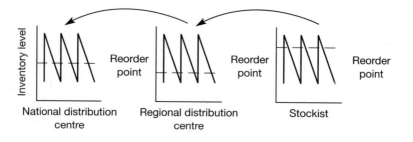

Pipeline costs are not transparent

Closely related to the preceding issue is the problem of cost 'transparency'. What this means is that costs relating to the flows of material across functional areas are not easy to measure. Hence the real costs to serve different customers with different product mixes are rarely revealed.

Once again the problem is that the conventional organisation will normally only identify costs on a functional basis, and even then at a fairly high level of aggregation. Hence we may well know our transport costs in total but not necessarily how they vary by customer category or by delivery characteristics, e.g. central delivery to a regional distribution centre or local delivery to a supermarket. Where attempts to estimate the costs of outputs are made they usually require, out of necessity, crude allocation procedures. As we noted in Chapter 3, there has recently been much interest in 'throughput accounting' and 'activity-based costing', both of which are attempts to pin down costs as they occur and hence to make the total pipeline costs easier to identify. The problem need not exist, it is only a problem because the costing systems we have are designed to monitor functional or input costs rather than flow or output costs. Figure 12.3 makes this point.

Figure 12.3 Alternative cost concepts

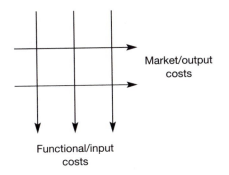

Market/output costs

Functional/input costs

Functional boundaries impede process management

The process of satisfying customer demand begins with in-bound supply and continues through manufacturing or assembly operations and onwards by way of distribution to the customer. Logically the ideal way to manage this process is as a complete system, not by fragmenting it into watertight sections. Yet that is more or less what happens in the conventional business, as we have seen. Not only is this inefficient, it actually leads to a loss of effectiveness in competitive terms.

Many of the variations in the order-to-delivery cycle, for example, are caused by the variability that inevitably arises in the inefficient procedures that have to be created to manage the interfaces between functions. The time taken to process orders, for instance, is often extended purely because of the paperwork, checking and rechecking, that conventional systems generate. Because organisations grow organically they tend to add to existing processes in a patchwork manner rather than taking a 'clean piece of paper' approach. As a result the systems in use tend to owe more to history than to any concept of holistic management. This phenomenon is further compounded by the inability of managers to detach themselves from their familiar surroundings and to see the 'big picture'. Instead there is a natural tendency to focus on piecemeal improvements within their own narrow functional area.

To achieve a smooth-flowing logistics pipeline requires an orientation that facilitates end-to-end process management. The principle can be compared to the management of an industrial process, say an oil refinery, where to ensure the achievement of optimum efficiency the entire process is managed and controlled as a system, not as a series of adjacent, independent activities.

The cost to an organisation, and indeed to the economy as a whole, of these fragmented processes can only be guessed at, but it must be huge.

Conventional organisations present many faces to the customer

Perhaps the most damning criticism of the traditional organisation is that it does not present a 'single face' to the customer. Rather than the customer having to do business with just one organisation, in effect they deal with many.

This criticism goes beyond the obvious problems that arise when a customer, seeking, say, information on an order, is passed from one section of the company to another – although that is a common enough occurrence. The real problem is that no one person or department is empowered to manage a customer from enquiry through to order delivery – in other words, to service the customer.

Consider for a moment how the conventional organisation processes orders. Typically there will be a sequence of activities beginning with order entry. The point of entry may be within the sales or commercial function but then it goes to credit control, from where it may pass to production planning or, in a make-to-stock environment, to the warehouse. Once the order has been manufactured or assembled it will become the responsibility of distribution and transport planning. At the same time there is a separate process involving the generation of documents such as bills of lading, delivery notes, invoices and so on. The problem is that these activities are sequential, performed in series rather than in parallel. Each function performs its task and then passes the order on to the next function; at each step it is as if the order is 'thrown over the wall'. Figure 12.4 depicts this classic process.

Figure 12.4 Managing the order

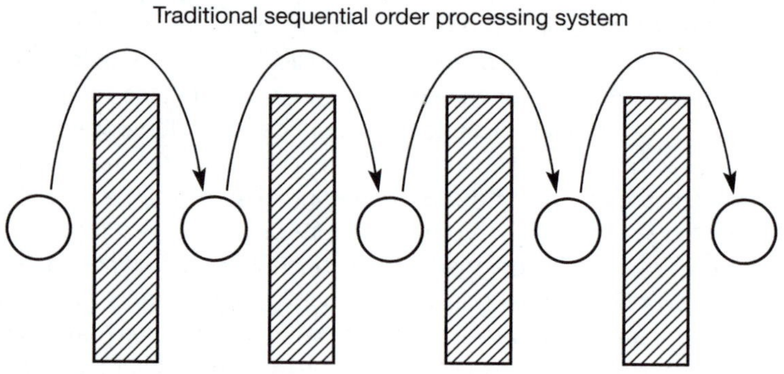

Traditional sequential order processing system

Developing the logistics organisation

Some commentators have suggested that the solution to the problems outlined above lies in creating a higher level of authority in the form of a logistics function that links together the purchasing, production and distribution tasks. Appealing as this may appear at first sight, it will not solve the underlying conflicts that the traditional organisation creates. It merely adds another layer of management. At a time when the trend is towards 'flattening' organisations, this solution is unlikely to gain ground.

Instead radical solutions must be sought which may require a restructuring of the conventional 'vertical' organisation and lead to the creation of a 'horizontal', or market-facing, business. Figures 12.5 and 12.6 contrast the 'vertical' with the 'horizontal' organisation.

Figure 12.5 Vertical organisations focus

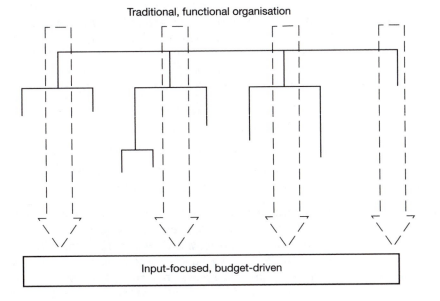

Traditional, functional organisation

Input-focused, budget-driven

Figure 12.6 Horizontal organisational focus

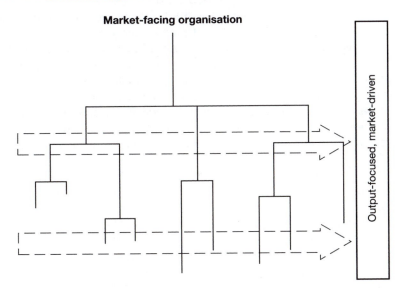

Market-facing organisation

Output-focused, market-driven

The horizontal organisation has a number of distinguishing characteristics. It is:

- Organised around processes
- Flat and de-layered
- Built upon multi-functional teams
- Guided by performance metrics that are market-based

It is the focus on processes rather than functions that is the key to the horizontal organisation. The basic precept of process management is that it is through processes that customer value is created. Hence the logic of seeking to manage processes on an integrated basis.

In most organisations there will only be a limited number of core processes and the following are likely to be central to most businesses:

- Innovation (including new product development)
- Consumer development (primarily focused on building loyalty with end users)
- Customer management (creating relationships with intermediaries)
- Supplier development (strengthening upstream and alliance relationships)
- Supply chain management (the cash-to-cash process)

Typically, companies that focus upon process management have recognised that they are best managed by cross-functional teams. These teams will comprise specialists drawn from the functional areas (which now become 'centres of excellence') and will be led by 'integrators' whose job it is to focus the process team around the achievement of market-based goals. In such organisations a different type of skills profile is clearly required for managers at all levels. Equally the reward systems need to change as the horizontal organisation by definition is flatter and hence the traditional upward promotion opportunities are fewer.

Making the change from the 'vertical' to the 'horizontal' poses many challenges and yet it is critical to the implementation of a market-driven logistics strategy.

The achievement of this transformation might begin by the recognition that logistics is essentially a planning orientation – in other words the logistics management process entails the linking of production plans with materials requirements plans in one direction and distribution requirements plans in the other. The aim of any organisation should be to ensure that production produces only what the marketplace requires whilst purchasing supplies production with what it needs to meet its immediate requirements. How can this fairly obvious idea be converted into reality?

The key lies in the recognition that the order and its associated information flows should be at the heart of the business. It may be a truism but the only rationale for any commercial organisation is to generate orders and to fulfil those orders. Everything the company does should be directly linked to facilitating this process, and the process must itself be reflected in the organisational design and in its planning and control systems.

All of this leads to the conclusion that the order fulfilment process should be designed as an integrated activity across the company with the conventional functions of the business supporting that process. To assist this transition the development of a customer order management system is a vital prerequisite.

A customer order management system is a planning framework that links the information system with the physical flow of materials required to fulfil demand. To achieve this requires the central management of forecasts, requirements plans, material and production control, and purchasing.

At the heart of the customer order management system is a requirements plan that is market-driven. The inputs to this plan include data and information relating to enquiries and orders, price changes, promotional activity and product availability. This information provides the basis for the forecast that then drives the requirements plan. Alongside this is a process for the fulfilment of current orders. They are not separated but closely integrated through the information system.

Order fulfilment groups

Given that the process of managing orders can be refined along the lines described above, what scope exists for improving the 'process architecture'?

Several companies have experimented with the idea of a cross-functional, cross-departmental team to take responsibility for the management of orders. This team may be termed the order fulfilment group. The idea behind such a group is that rather than having an organisational structure for order management where every activity is separated with responsibility for each activity fragmented around the organisation, instead these activities should be grouped together both organisationally and physically. In other words, instead of seeing each step in the process as a discrete activity we cluster them together and bring the people involved together as well – ideally in a single open-plan office. Thus the order fulfilment group might comprise commercial or sales office people, credit control and accounts, the production scheduler and transport scheduler – indeed anyone involved in the crucial business process of *converting an order into cash*.

It is likely that in a large business serving many different customers a number of these teams may be required. Indeed for the biggest, most important accounts it is probable that a single dedicated team will be required to manage the relationship.

The effect that such groups can have is often dramatic. Because all the key people in the order fulfilment process are brought together and linked around a common entity – the order – they are better able to sort out problems and eliminate bottlenecks. Order cycle times can be dramatically reduced as teamwork prevails over interdepartmental rivalry. New ways of dealing with problems emerge, more non-value-added activities are eliminated and customer service problems – when they arise – can quickly be resolved, since all the key people are in close connection with each other.

Schonberger[1] gives a number of examples of how the concept of a manufacturing 'cell' – where linked actions are performed in parallel by multi-functional teams – can work just as effectively in order processing. One of the cases he quotes, Ahlstrom, a Finnish company, has reduced lead times in order processing from one week to one day, and variation in total lead time has dropped from up to six weeks to one week. Another case was that of Nashua Corporation in North

America, where order entry lead time has been reduced from eight days to one hour, with a 40 per cent reduction in space and a 70 per cent reduction in customer claims.

This approach has been likened to a game of rugby rather than a relay race! What this means is that a team of closely integrated colleagues run up the field together passing the ball as they run. In a relay race no one can run until they receive the baton from the preceding person in the chain. The end result is that this vital part of the service process can be speeded up whilst simultaneously improving the quality of the output, hence a major competitive advantage is achieved.

In a manufacturing context the customer order management system must be closely linked to production planning and the materials requirements plan. Ideally all the planning and scheduling activities in the organisation relating to the order and its satisfaction should be brought together organisationally.

> As markets, technologies and competitive forces change at ever increasing rates the imperative for organisational change becomes more pressing.

Logistics as the vehicle for change

As markets, technologies and competitive forces change at ever increasing rates the imperative for organisational change becomes more pressing. The paradox is that because organisational structures are rigid, even ossified, they do not have the ability to change at anything like the same rate as the environment in which they exist.

The trend towards globalisation of industry, involving as it does the co-ordination of complex flows of materials and information from a multitude of off-shore sources and manufacturing plants to a diversity of markets, has sharply highlighted the inappropriateness of existing structures. What we are discovering is that the driving force for organisational change is logistics.

To compete and survive in these global markets requires a logistics-oriented organisation. There has to be nothing less than a shift from a functional focus to a process focus. Such a radical change entails a regrouping within the organisation so that the key tasks become the management of cross-functional work flows. Hewlett Packard is an example of a company that has restructured its organisation around market-facing processes, rather than functions. Order fulfilment has been recognised as a core process and so, on a global scale, there is one order management system architecture that links order entry, order management and factory order/shipment processing. This core process is supported by a common information system that provides 'end-to-end' visibility of the logistics pipeline from order through to delivery.

In fact it is through such breakthroughs in information technology that the type of organisational change we are describing has been made possible. The information network now defines the organisation structure. In other words, the information that flows from the marketplace at one end of the pipeline to supply points at the other will increasingly shape the organisation – not the other way round.

Such a change will be accelerated by the trend, commented upon earlier in this book, for companies to focus on what might be termed 'core competencies' and to outsource everything else. In other words, the business of tomorrow will most likely only perform those activities in the value chain where they believe they have a differential advantage, and all other activities will be performed by partners, co-makers and logistics service providers. In cases such as this the need for co-ordination of information and materials flows between entities in the supply chain becomes a key priority, further highlighting the central role of logistics as a process-oriented management task.

In this brief review of the challenges facing the organisation in a changed environment we have emphasised the need to break down the 'walls' that traditionally have fragmented the organisation and impeded the cost-effective achievement of customer service requirements. Clearly there is a need for 'pattern breaking' on a major scale. The only way such significant change will be achieved is through leadership from the very top of the organisation. It is no coincidence that the handful of companies that have achieved excellence in logistics have been through a process of change that was driven from the top. Companies like Xerox, Hewlett Packard, Nokia and Philips have experienced, and are still experiencing, often painful change as they transform themselves from functionally based businesses to market-facing businesses. Whilst the impetus for change differs from company to company, the engine of change has been the same – the search for superior performance through logistics management.

Benchmarking

The intense level of competitive activity encountered in most markets has led to a new emphasis on measuring performance not just in absolute terms, but rather in terms relative to the competition, and beyond that to 'best practice'.

In the past it was usually deemed to be sufficient simply to measure internal performance. In other words, the focus was on things such as productivity, utilisation, cost per activity and so on. Whilst it is clearly important that such things continue to be measured and controlled it also has to be recognised that such measures only have meaning when they are compared against a relevant 'metric' or benchmark. What should be the metric that is used in assessing logistics and supply chain performance?

There are in fact several dimensions to the measurement problem. The first key point to make is that the ultimate measuring rod is the customer, hence it is customers' perceptions of performance that must be paramount. Secondly, it is not sufficient just to compare performance to that of immediate competitors. We must also compare ourselves to the 'best in the class'. Thirdly, it is not just outputs that should be measured and compared but also the processes that produce that output. These three ideas lie at the heart of what today is termed competitive benchmarking.

Competitive benchmarking might simply be defined as the continuous measurement of the company's products, services, processes and practices against the standards of best competitors and other companies that are recognised as leaders. The measures that are chosen for the comparison must directly or indirectly impact upon customers' evaluation of the company's performance.

One of the earliest firms to adopt benchmarking was the Xerox Corporation which used it as a major tool in gaining competitive advantage. Xerox first started benchmarking in manufacturing activity with a focus on product quality and feature improvements. Following success in the manufacturing area, Xerox's top management directed that benchmarking be performed by all cost centres and business units across the company.

Initially there was some difficulty in performing benchmarking in departments such as repair, service, maintenance, invoicing and collection and distribution, until it was recognised that the 'product' was, in fact, a process. It was this process that needed to be articulated and compared with that used in other organisations. By looking at competitors' processes step-by-step and operation-by-operation, Xerox was able to identify best methods and practices in use by competitors.

Initially benchmarking activities were concentrated solely on competitors until it became clear that Xerox's objective in achieving superior performance in each business function was not being obtained by looking only at competitors' practices.

The objective of creating competitive advantage involves outperforming rather than matching the efforts of competitors. This, together with the obvious difficulties in gaining all the information required on competitors and their internal systems and processes, led to a broader perspective on benchmarking being adopted. Thus benchmarking was expanded from a focus solely on competitors to a wider, but selective, focus on the processes of top performing companies regardless of their industry sector.

Xerox has successfully used this broader perspective on benchmarking as a major element in increasing both quality and productivity. Collaborative co-operation between firms in non-competing industries offers significant opportunity in this regard. For example, in the Xerox logistics and distribution unit, annual productivity has doubled as a result of benefits obtained from non-competitive collaborative benchmarking.

Camp[2] has identified a number of benefits that a company derives from benchmarking. These include the following:

- It enables the best practices from any industry to be creatively incorporated into the processes of the benchmarked function.

- It can provide stimulation and motivation to the professionals whose creativity is required to perform and implement benchmark findings.

- Benchmarking breaks down ingrained reluctance of operations to change. It has been found that people are more receptive to new ideas and their creative adoption when those ideas did not necessarily originate in their own industry.

- Benchmarking may also identify a technological breakthrough that would not have been recognised, and thus not applied, in one's own industry for some time to come.

What to benchmark?

One useful framework for benchmarking is that devised by a cross-industry association – The Supply Chain Council.[3] Their model, known as SCOR (Supply Chain Operations Reference), is built around five major processes – Plan–Source–Make–Deliver–Return – and covers the key supply chain activities from identifying customer demand through to delivering the product and collecting the cash. The aim of SCOR is to provide a standard way to measure supply chain performance and to use common metrics to benchmark against other organisations.

Identifying logistics performance indicators

One benefit of a rigorous approach to logistics and supply chain benchmarking is that it soon becomes apparent that there are a number of critical measures of performance that need to be continuously monitored. The idea of 'key performance indicators' (KPIs) is simple. It suggests that, whilst there are many measures of performance that can be deployed in an organisation, there are a relatively small number of critical dimensions that contribute more than proportionately to success or failure in the marketplace.

Much interest has been shown in recent years in the concept of the 'Balanced Scorecard'.[4] The idea behind the Balanced Scorecard is that there are a number of key performance indicators – most of them probably non-financial measures – that will provide management with a better means of meeting strategic goals than the more traditional financially oriented measures. These KPIs derive from the strategic goals themselves. Thus the intention is that the balanced scorecard will provide ongoing guidance on those critical areas where action may be needed to ensure the achievement of those goals.

These ideas transfer readily into the management of logistics and supply chain strategy. If suitable performance measures can be identified that link with the achievement of these strategic goals they can become the basis for a more appropriate scorecard than might traditionally be the case.

A logical four-step process is suggested for constructing such a scorecard:

Step 1: Articulate logistics and supply chain strategy

How do we see our logistics and supply chain strategy contributing to the overall achievement of corporate and marketing goals?

Step 2: What are the measurable outcomes of success?

Typically, these might be summarised as 'Better, Faster, Cheaper, Closer'. In other words, superior service quality, achieved in shorter time-frames at less cost to the supply chain as a whole, built on strong relationships with supply chain partners.

Step 3: What are the processes that affect these outcomes?

In the case of 'Better, Faster, Cheaper, Closer', the processes that lead to 'perfect order achievement', shorter pipeline times, reduced cost-to-serve and stronger relationships need to be identified.

Step 4: What are the drivers of performance within these processes?

These activities are the basis for the derivation of the key performance indicators. Cause and effect analysis can aid in their identification.

In this framework the four key outcomes of success are suggested to be: Better, Faster, Cheaper, Closer. This quartet of interconnected goals are almost universal in their desirability. They are significant because they combine customer-based measures of performance in terms of total quality with internal measures of resource and asset utilisation.

The idea behind the logistics scorecard is to produce a number of measures against each of the four broad aims. There should be no more than 20 measures in total since the aim is to focus on the major drivers of excellence in each area. Like any dashboard or cockpit, there is a need for simplicity and to focus on the 'mission critical' measures. Figure 12.7 summarises this idea.

Figure 12.7 Creating the logistics scorecard

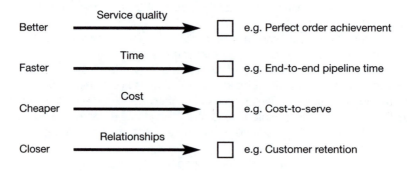

As the old cliché reminds us: 'What gets measured, gets managed.' Hence it is important to ensure that the logistics scorecard is designed to encourage the actions and behaviour that will lead to the fulfilment of the 'logistics vision' that we earlier described. Indeed it can be argued that if organisational change is necessary, the place to begin that change process is with a review of the performance measures currently in use. Many companies seek to be responsive and market-facing and yet they still use performance metrics that relate to internal efficiencies. As a result they are unlikely ever to change.

References

1. Schonberger, R.J., *Building a Chain of Customers*, The Free Press, 1990.
2. Camp, R., *Benchmarking: The Search For Industry Best Practices That Lead to Superior Performance*, ASQC Quality Press, 1989.
3. For further details of the SCOR model, visit www.supply-chain.org.
4. Kaplan, R.S. and Norton, D.P., *The Balanced Scorecard*, Harvard Business School Press, 1996.

Creating a sustainable supply chain

13

- The triple bottom line

- Greenhouse gases and the supply chain

- Reducing the transport-intensity of supply chains

- Peak oil

- Beyond the carbon footprint

- Reduce, reuse, recycle

- The impact of congestion

Perhaps one of the biggest issues to rise to prominence across every aspect of business and society in the opening years of the twenty-first century has been 'sustainability'. The growing concern with the environment, in particular the possibility of climate change through global warming, has led to a focus on how human and economic activity has the potential to adversely impact the long-term sustainability of the planet.

The definition of sustainability that is most widely used originates from the United Nations Brundtland Commission, which reported in 1987. Sustainability, the Commission suggested, was about

meeting the needs of the present without compromising the ability of future generations to meet their own needs.[1]

The triple bottom line

This definition can be further augmented by adopting the parallel idea of the 'triple bottom line'.[2] The triple bottom line concept emphasises the importance of examining the impact of business decisions on three key arenas:

Environment (e.g. pollution; climate change; the depletion of scarce resources, etc.)

Economy (e.g. effect on people's livelihoods and financial security; profitability of the business, etc.)

Society (e.g. poverty reduction; improvement of working and living conditions, etc.)

These three elements – the 3Ps of people, profit and planet – are inevitably intertwined and they serve to remind us that for a business to be truly sustainable, it must pay regard to the wider impact of the activities it undertakes if it seeks to remain viable and profitable (see Figure 13.1).

Figure 13.1 The triple bottom line: planet, people, profit

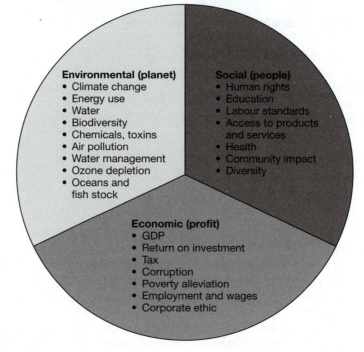

Source: Accenture

In the context of supply chains we can build on the triple bottom line philosophy to encompass the wider idea that sustainability is concerned with ensuring the long-term viability and continuity of the business as well as contributing to the future well-being of society. Indeed, it can be argued that these two goals are mutually supportive, i.e. supply chain strategies that benefit the wider environment are likely also to involve the business in less cost in the long term as the result of a better use of resources. For example, one element in a 'green' supply chain might involve utilising transport capacity more efficiently through better routing and scheduling. In so doing, not only is the environmental impact of transport reduced, but also the cost to the company.

Because the supply chain underpins the efficient and effective running of the business it can provide a useful framework for exploring opportunities for improving sustainability. If we adopt the philosophy advocated in Chapter 8 that the supply chain 'begins on the drawing board', i.e. that product design decisions impact subsequent supply chain costs, it makes sense to look at sustainability across the entire product life cycle. In other words, we need to understand the impact on sustainability of everything we do from product design through to end-of-life disposal.

Greenhouse gases and the supply chain

Recent years have seen a considerable growth of awareness of the potential harm to the environment that can be caused by so-called 'greenhouse gases'. These gases include carbon dioxide, methane and nitrous oxide and various fluorocarbons. Generically these emissions as they relate to an activity are often referred to as its 'carbon footprint'. As a result of increased economic activity around the world, the level of these greenhouse gases has risen significantly over the years. It is estimated that current levels are around 430 parts per million compared to 280 parts per million before the Industrial Revolution.

A view that is held by many, although not all, commentators is that this increase in greenhouse gas levels has been, and is, a major cause of climate change. A number of influential reports, e.g. that produced by Sir Nicholas Stern in the UK[3] and the work of Al Gore in the USA,[4] have brought these issues to the attention of governments, industry and the wider public on a global scale. Even though it has proved difficult to get universal agreement on the best means for reducing greenhouse gas emissions, there is a widespread acknowledgement that action is required.

For supply chain managers this is a particular call to action since some of the major causes of greenhouse gases arise from industrial activities such as manufacturing, energy production and transportation. In the specific case of freight transport, for example, it is acknowledged that as a result of the globalisation of supply chains we are now moving products greater distances than ever before with a consequent impact on the carbon footprint. The example of the laptop used by Thomas Friedland, the author of The World is Flat,[5] is a case in point. He estimated that the approximately 400 different components in his Dell computer had travelled hundreds of thousands of miles from all their different sources and through the assembly and distribution process to reach him.

In recent years there has been a growing awareness amongst consumers of the issue of 'food miles' – in other words how far food travels from its origin to the point of final consumption – and what the impact of this might be on carbon emissions. The item highlighted below is indicative of this growing concern.

12,000-mile round trip to have seafood shelled

A seafood firm was accused of 'environmental madness' yesterday for choosing to send langoustines on a 12,000-mile round trip to Thailand to have their shells removed.

After the shellfish are caught in Scottish waters they will be frozen and shipped to the Far East where they will be peeled by hand and sent back to be sold as scampi. The move by Young's Seafood is costing 120 jobs at a plant in Annan, south-west Scotland, where the langoustines have been peeled mechanically.

The firm claims that removing the shells by hand enhances the taste, but UK wage costs – at £6 an hour, compared with about 25p an hour in Thailand – are prohibitive.

Friends of the Earth Scotland said the move was 'madness and would add to global warming'.

SOURCE: CRAMB, A., '12,000-MILE ROUND TRIP TO HAVE SEAFOOD SHELLED', *DAILY TELEGRAPH*, 16 NOVEMBER 2006

Whilst at the moment the environmental costs incurred as a result of commercial activity are not generally borne by the companies that cause them, this will almost certainty change as a result of carbon taxes, emission trading schemes and regulatory change. Hence the need for supply chain managers to think hard about alternative strategies.

Carbon and the supply chain

The volume of global trade has more than doubled in the last decade – reaching six times the rate of growth of the world's gross domestic product (GDP) during the same period of time. This phenomenon has been facilitated by relatively cheap energy, with low attention given to the impact on climate change. Consider that the global fleet of ocean-going ships accounts for more CO_2 emissions than any of all but six countries worldwide. Yet none of this environmental impact is reflected in shipping prices.

With estimated economic damage of about US$85 for each ton of carbon dioxide, capping greenhouse gas (GHG) emissions and putting a price tag on them becomes inevitable. Indeed, under the European Union emissions trading scheme (EU ETS), such a setup is already in effect for certain industries. Similar schemes are popping up across the United States in separate groups of states and in other major industrial economies worldwide.

Going forward, firms should expect to be charged for their CO_2 emissions. And most certainly, this charge will force a change in the way companies run their supply chains. Common practices of the last century – like long distance airfreight, small batch size, just-in-time concepts and energy-intensive production in countries with low environmental standards – will likely go by the economic and political wayside. Reducing the supply chain's carbon footprint will become an inescapable obligation.

The choice will be either to delay – or to embrace – the climate challenge as a chance to restructure the supply chain for the economic and environmental good. The companies that act now can reap advantages that may be denied to those that wait for the regulatory hand. These benefits include the mindshare of growing ethical consumer markets; the attraction and retention of top talent; and more sustainable growth overall

SOURCE: BUTNER, K., GEUDER, D., AND HITTNER, J., *MASTERING CARBON MANAGEMENT: BALANCING TRADE-OFFS TO OPTIMISE SUPPLY CHAIN EFFICIENCIES*, IBM GLOBAL SERVICES, 2008, REPRINT COURTESY OF INTERNATIONAL BUSINESS MACHINES CORPORATION © 2008 INTERNATIONAL BUSINESS MACHINES CORPORATION

Reducing the transport-intensity of supply chains

As global economic growth continues, so too does international trade increase and hence transport. The continued upward trend in global sourcing has inevitably led to products travelling greater distances. The end result is an increase in what might be termed the *transport-intensity* of the supply chain. Transport intensity can be measured in a number of ways, but at its simplest it is a reflection of the miles/kilometres travelled per unit of product shipped. Since the transport of raw material and finished goods globally is estimated to consume 15 million barrels of oil each day – almost one fifth of the world's daily production[6] – there is clearly a correlation between transport intensity and a supply chain's carbon footprint. Not only is there an economic benefit to be gained by improving transport intensity but also a potential positive environmental impact – this is the concept of *eco-efficiency*,[7] which is now rapidly becoming a major issue in global commerce.

What practical steps can organisations take to improve the transport-intensity of their supply chains?

- *Review product design and bill of materials*
  Product design can impact transport-intensity through the physical characteristics of the product, its density, the choice of materials (including packaging materials), the ease of recycling, reuse and end-of-life disposal.

- *Review sourcing strategy*
  As we have previously noted, many sourcing decisions have led to a migration to low-cost country locations. This often has led to products being moved greater distances. Global sourcing decisions will increasingly need to factor the carbon footprint into the total cost of ownership.

- *Review transport options*
  Clearly different transport modes have different impacts on carbon and other emissions. The design of vehicles and vessels is also increasingly influenced by the need to improve fuel efficiency. There are also arguments for increasing the size of vehicle or the vessel to achieve lower transport intensity per unit. For example, new-generation container ships such as the *Emma Maersk*.

- *Improve transport utilisation*

  Research has highlighted that vehicle capacity is often poorly utilised. It is suggested that empty running because of the lack of return loads means that up to a third of the trucks on the roads of Europe are running empty! More use of shared distribution, better vehicle routing and scheduling, and better loading can also dramatically improve transport-intensity.

- *Use postponement strategies*

  If standard, generic products can be shipped in bulk from their point of origin and then assembled, customised or configured for local requirements nearer the point of use, there may be an opportunity to reduce overall transport-intensity.

Sharing distribution to reduce 'empty miles'

Recently a number of initiatives have been launched to improve transport capacity utilisation through shared distribution. There is a growing realisation in many companies that it may make good economic and environmental sense to share transport with other organisations – including competitors.

In the USA the Voluntary Inter-industry Commerce Solutions Association (VICS) has brought together major retailers, manufacturers and trucking companies to create an 'Empty Miles' programme. The objective of this collaborative initiative is to improve the utilisation of truck capacity by sharing transport arrangements. Because many trucks return empty to their point of origin after having made a delivery, this scheme provides the means to match the availability of space on a particular route with the transportation requirements of participating retailers and manufacturers. One of the scheme's biggest users is the retailer J.C.Penney who were able to save $5.6million in transport costs in 2009 as well as achieving a significant reduction in carbon emissions (1).

Similarly in the UK the Institute of Grocery Distribution (IGD) has been supporting an initiative in which forty of Britain's major retailers and manufacturers have agreed to share their transport. In the first three years that the scheme was running it was estimated that 120 million road miles had been eliminated which is the equivalent of removing 2,000 lorries from the UK's roads thus conserving 60 million litres of diesel fuel per year (2).

These examples highlight the opportunities that exist for making dramatic improvements in vehicle utilisation thus reducing supply chain costs whilst shrinking the carbon footprint. Increasingly these asset-sharing arrangements between supply chain partners will become more common as companies recognise that it is no longer tenable to tolerate the situation that has prevailed for decades whereby between a quarter and a third of trucks on the road were actually empty.

References:

(1) Karen Tilley, 'Retailers Teaming Up to Cut 'Empty Miles' and Transport Costs' *Wall street Journal*, June 9, 2010

(2) Institute of Grocery Distribution, www.igd.com/ecr February 19, 2010

A further incentive to reduce the transport-intensity arises from the continued upward pressure on oil-based fuel costs, which will only intensify as oil reserves become depleted.

Peak oil

The concept of 'peak oil' originated as far back as 1956 when Dr Marion King Hubbert, a geologist at Shell, first coined the phrase. What he recognised was that all oil production, whether from an individual field, a country or the entire world, follows a normal distribution, i.e. a bell-shaped curve. All the current indications are that we have reached the top of that curve, or that we shortly will. Even with new discoveries, the total amount of oil reserves will still be in decline once the peak has passed.

At the moment the world demand for oil is approximately 85 million barrels a day, which by chance is about the current daily output of all the working fields. However, whilst output will inevitably decline as 'peak oil' is passed, world demand is likely to grow – particularly fuelled by economic growth in countries such as India and China. The gap between demand and supply will get larger by the day.

Some commentators have suggested that the gap between the demand and supply for oil will be filled by the discovery of new oil fields or the development of new fuels (e.g. bio-fuels). However, such is the likely deficit that it is estimated that we would need to find new reserves of oil (or create alternative fuels) equivalent to five Saudi Arabias over the next 20 years. Simple economics tells us that the only way that the gap will actually be closed is by the price mechanism. In other words, the cost of oil will increase dramatically to reflect the shortfall in supply.

Today's supply chains are more energy intensive than before because they are more transport intensive than they used to be. There are a number of reasons for this including:

- Focused factories and centralised distribution – as a result of rationalising production and distribution, many companies are now having to serve customers at a greater distance.

- Global sourcing and offshore manufacturing – the well-established trend to low-cost country sourcing and manufacturing has meant that supply chains are significantly extended and products travel much further.

- Just-in-time deliveries – as more customers demand just-in-time deliveries from their suppliers, it is inevitable that shipment sizes reduce whilst delivery frequencies increase.

When many of today's supply chains were originally designed, the cost of oil was a fraction of what it is today. For example, in December 1998 a barrel of crude oil sold for about US$9.64; in July 2008 – ten years later – it rose to an all-time high of $147.27.

It is quite possible that if oil prices continue to rise over time, current supply chain arrangements will prove to be too expensive. There is clearly a need for supply chain strategists to review their network configurations and to ask 'what if' questions based upon worst-case scenarios of transport costs.

Beyond the carbon footprint

Whilst there is an understandable concern that the supply chain's carbon footprint should be minimised, it must also be recognised that supply chain decisions have a wider impact on resources generally. Rather than limiting the focus of attention to reducing greenhouse gas emissions, it is important to recognise the effect of economic activity on the use of scarce resources across the value chain as a whole. Decisions that are taken at every stage in a company's value chain can have significant implications for resource requirements and for the wider environment. Figure 13.2 highlights some of the potential linkages.

Figure 13.2 Supply chain decisions impact the resource footprint

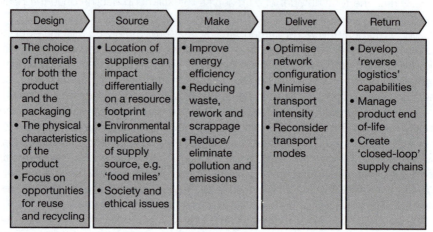

Design	Source	Make	Deliver	Return
• The choice of materials for both the product and the packaging • The physical characteristics of the product • Focus on opportunities for reuse and recycling	• Location of suppliers can impact differentially on a resource footprint • Environmental implications of supply source, e.g. 'food miles' • Society and ethical issues	• Improve energy efficiency • Reducing waste, rework and scrappage • Reduce/eliminate pollution and emissions	• Optimise network configuration • Minimise transport intensity • Reconsider transport modes	• Develop 'reverse logistics' capabilities • Manage product end of-life • Create 'closed-loop' supply chains

Because so many natural resources are being depleted at an increasing rate, it is important that businesses understand these linkages. Some examples of the resource implications of supply chain decisions are described below.

Design

We have previously argued that the supply chain 'starts on the drawing board', meaning that decisions that are taken regarding the design of the product can have a significant impact across the supply chain. This is particularly true when considering the supply chain's 'resource footprint'. More and more companies are actively seeking to reduce the amount of packaging material that is used, for example, but there can be other, less obvious ways to improve resource sustainability. If those managers responsible for new product development are not aware of the resource implications of their design decisions, this may lead to the launch of products with a bigger than desirable resource footprint. For example, many high-tech products rely for their functionality on scarce materials such as the so-called 'rare earth metals' (e.g. dysprosium and neodymium) whose future availability may increasingly be limited.

Source

'Sustainable sourcing' is emerging as a fundamental element of best practice procurement. One reason for this is that it is estimated that for a manufacturer somewhere between 40 and 60 per cent of their total carbon footprint lies upstream of their operations, whilst for retailers it can be as high as 80 per cent.[8] Depending on where and how those upstream materials and products are sourced and made, there can be major differences in resource consumption. For example, SAB Miller, one of the world's biggest beer producers, compared its 'water footprint' in two different countries – South Africa and the Czech Republic. It found that the water used in crop production accounted for the vast majority of the total water footprint, but the South African footprint was greater than the Czech footprint because of a greater reliance on irrigation and higher levels of evaporation required to grow the crops used in South Africa. It actually required 155 litres of water to produce a litre of beer in South Africa against 45 litres of water required to produce a litre of beer in the Czech Republic.[9]

Make

Manufacturing processes affect the resource footprint primarily through their use of energy, their relative efficiency and the creation and disposal of waste and toxic materials/effluents. In this age of outsourcing and offshore manufacturing it may not always be apparent to the customer what impact manufacturing strategy decisions can have on supply chain sustainability. However, it is evident that there are big differences in the energy efficiency of different factories and also in the waste they generate and how they dispose of it. Even the source of energy has sustainability implications. For example a study conducted by the UK Carbon Trust[10] looked at the different footprints created by a UK national daily newspaper when it used newsprint produced in Sweden compared to newsprint made in the UK. Because newsprint production is a highly energy-intensive manufacturing process and since most electricity generated in Sweden is from renewable hydro sources – unlike in the UK where most electricity is generated from coal or gas – the most sustainable manufacturing source was Sweden, not the UK!

Deliver

Clearly decisions on the mode of transport will affect the carbon footprint of a supply chain as will the extent to which transport capacity is efficiently used. However, the nature of the delivery network (i.e. the number, location and design of distribution centres, the use of hub and spoke arrangements, the extent of cross-docking, etc.) can have a wider impact on supply chain sustainability.

Many companies have used network optimisation models to help determine the shape of their distribution arrangements. However, these models tend to optimise on a narrow definition of cost rather than taking into account the wider resource footprint that is created by the network. A new generation of network optimisation tools is now emerging which take account of the carbon footprint as well as the more conventional costs.

Return

'Reverse logistics' is the term usually used to describe the process of bringing products back, normally at the end-of-life, but also for recall and repair. In the past, little attention was paid to the challenge of reverse logistics, often resulting in extremely high costs being incurred. Now, partly driven by increasingly stringent regulations – particularly on product disposal and reuse/recycling requirements – the issue has moved much higher up the agenda.

Essentially the challenge today is to create 'closed-loop' supply chains that will enable a much higher level of reuse and recycling. Clearly products must be designed with their end-of-life in mind, but also the logistics network employed must minimise the use of resources. Reverse logistics provides a major opportunity for companies to impact both their costs and their carbon footprint and should be viewed as an opportunity rather than a threat. Xerox is a good example of a company that actively seeks to design products and supply chain processes that enable a sustainable end-of-life recovery programme to be achieved.[11]

Reduce, reuse, recycle

The 3Rs of sustainable supply chain management – reduce, reuse and recycle – are now starting to receive much more attention in most companies today. There is a growing realisation that not only is a strategy focused on improving the environmental impact of economic activity good for all who live on this planet, but because such strategies consume fewer resources the overall profitability of the business should also improve.

Water: The next oil? As the world's population continues to increase and as climate change impacts on rainfall, there is an increasing mis-match between supply and demand for water. Supply chains are big consumers of water when all the different production and manufacturing processes involved from start to finish are considered. Already many organisations are actively measuring their 'water footprint' across the supply chain and are seeking alternative solutions to enable a reduction in the amount of water that is required to bring products to market. Water may indeed become the 'next oil' as shortages start to impact across a much wider arena.

Some examples of the water footprint of different products and commodities are shown below.

How much water does it take …

To make a cup of coffee?	140 litres
To make a litre of milk?	1,000 litres
To make a hamburger?	2,400 litres
To make a t-shirt?	2,500 litres
To make a pair of jeans?	10,850 litres
To produce a kilogram of beef?	16,000 litres

SOURCE: WWW.WATERFOOTPRINT.ORG

Many companies are now actively seeking to create marketing strategies that emphasise the 'greenness' of their supply chains. Whilst the more cynical observers may dismiss these moves as opportunism – what some have dubbed 'greenwash' – there can be no question that customers and consumers in markets around the world are starting to demand that suppliers reduce their various footprints.

Strong evidence is emerging that consumers are increasingly basing their purchasing behaviour on ethical and environmental criteria. For example, the findings of a recent survey in the UK are summarised in the box below.

In the next 12 months …

69 per cent of all consumers plan to buy *Fair Trade products*, 53 per cent currently do.

61 per cent plan to buy food from *farmers' markets*, up from 43 per cent who do so now.

54 per cent plan to buy *locally sourced food* up from 37 per cent

51 per cent plan to buy *environmentally friendly products* such as washing-up liquid, up from 34 per cent

SOURCE: HENLEY CENTRE HEADLIGHT VISION, 'WHO IS THE ETHICAL CONSUMER?', *MARKETING*, 11 JULY 2007

In some instances major retailers such as Wal-Mart and Tesco are seeking to improve their supply chain footprints and are demanding action from their suppliers to improve their performance on the 3Rs, i.e. to demonstrate how they are reducing the use of materials such as packaging and how they are designing products that can be reused or recycled. Both Wal-Mart and Tesco (and other retailers too) intend to provide information on the labels of the products they sell detailing the overall environmental impact of those items. To do this they are working closely with their suppliers to ensure that their supply chain arrangements are sustainable and that they continue to seek innovative ways to improve the end-to-end environmental footprint.

For example, Tesco recognised that glass bottles, because of their weight, add significantly to transport intensity and overall carbon emission. By working with suppliers to create lighter weight wine bottles, Tesco reduced its annual glass usage from one single supplier by 2,600 tonnes – a 15 per cent saving. Further savings were achieved by importing wines into the UK from Australia in bulk and then bottling them in lightweight glass in the UK.[12]

Further pressure on businesses to reduce their environmental footprints is coming from government regulation, often in the form of Emission Trading Schemes (ETS) or so-called 'Cap and Trade' legislation. For example, the European Union's Emissions Trading Scheme has recently been extended to cover a greater range of industries and is based on the principle that companies have a basic allowance for carbon emissions – if they go beyond that level they have to buy additional allowance from other companies who do not fully use their own allowance. Similar schemes are currently contemplated by governments around the world and in time their impact is likely to be significant.

Since, as we have noted, most of a typical business's total environmental footprint lies in its wider supply chain, particularly upstream of its own operations, the need for supply chain managers to become more involved in managing this footprint becomes apparent. Unless upstream suppliers are able to reduce their own footprint the additional costs that they will incur will inevitably end up in their cost of goods sold – and ultimately in the price of the products in the final marketplace.

The impact of congestion

One of the key issues when considering sustainable supply chain solutions is traffic congestion and the related infrastructure issues. In probably the majority of countries, developed and developing, the creation of logistics infrastructure has not kept pace with the level of economic activity. This is true for all types of infrastructure, including roads, ports and railways. Gridlock on motorways, container vessels waiting to unload at ports and bottlenecks on the railways are common occurrences in many countries and add to carbon emissions as well as adding cost to suppliers and customers alike.

There have been a number of causes of this problem, including increased global trade, lack of investment in capacity and the widespread adoption of just-in-time practices:

- *Increased global trade*
  With the growth in offshore manufacturing and the emergence of new markets, alongside the removal of trade barriers, the flow of products across borders has increased dramatically. At the same time the size of many container vessels has increased significantly – the new generation of container ships can carry upwards of 10,000 TEUs (20 foot equivalent), which if laid end-to-end would stretch for 60 kilometres or 37 miles! When unloaded each of these containers may need to be stacked on the dockside before being loaded out to trains or trucks, further adding to congestion. Furthermore, in recent years the increase in container security requirements has led to additional delays at both the points of origin and destination.

- *Lack of capacity*
  Paradoxically in some developed countries environmental concerns have led to unwillingness to build more infrastructure such as new motorways or port extensions. Also, there has been resistance in countries such as the UK to introduce bigger trucks which might actually reduce congestion, since fewer would be required. Equally in developing countries the sheer scale of the investment required to meet the demand is daunting. India is a good case in point where because of a lack of previous investment there is an overwhelming shortage of capacity on the roads, railways and at the ports – particularly in the face of burgeoning demand.

- *Just-in-time practices*
  As we have noted previously in this book, over the last 50 years there has been a significant uptake across all sectors and supply chains of the philosophy and practice of just-in-time (JIT). Essentially this has led to smaller but more frequent movements of products and materials. Even though many of those who have adopted JIT have attempted to mitigate its effects through aggregation and consolidation there can be no doubting that it has contributed to an increase in shipments and movements. In the past it could be argued that the saving in inventory holding costs more than covered the additional transport cost. However, now that concern with environmental issues has become much more prevalent, JIT in its crudest form will increasingly be questioned. The challenge for supply chain managers is to find a solution that enables the benefits of JIT to be gained without incurring the potential environmental disadvantages.

Road congestion in the UK

Total traffic in the UK is over 500 billion vehicle km per year. This is 80 per cent higher than in 1980, in line with the rise of GDP. Eight per cent of UK road traffic is now subjected to very congested conditions, which causes costs due to delays and unreliability. If unchecked, congestion is forecast to increase by 30 per cent by 2025 in England alone, costing a further £22 billion a year.

Moreover, slow-moving and stationary traffic emits increased amounts of CO_2 and other pollutants. The transport sector already contributes around a quarter of the UK's CO_2 emissions of which 93 per cent is from road transport.

SOURCE: UK PARLIAMENTARY OFFICE OF SCIENCE AND TECHNOLOGY, 'INTELLIGENT TRANSPORT SYSTEMS', *POSTNOTE*, NO. 322, JANUARY 2009

While congestion will probably continue to affect logistics management for many years to come, particularly as economic growth and development continue, there is likely to be some alleviation as a result of the application of what might be termed 'smart logistics' and 'intelligent transport'. The idea here is to combine the opportunities that exist for greater partnership and collaboration, both vertically and horizontally, in the supply chain with advanced information and communication technology.

Smart logistics works by aggregating and combining individual shipments into consolidated loads for final delivery. 'Cross docking' is an example of this idea whereby different suppliers ship complete truck loads to a distribution centre, typically with each pallet bar-coded or RFID-tagged with product and destination details, for re-sortment and consolidation with other shipments to the same final destination. The same principle can be used utilising 'logistics platforms' on the edge of large cities or conurbations to reduce individual deliveries to congested locations.

When advanced IT solutions such as dynamic vehicle routing and scheduling and intelligent agent modelling are used alongside these collaborative strategies, many things become possible – particularly enabling the better management of constrained capacity against a backdrop of uncertain demand.

References

1. World Commission on Environment and Development, *Our Common Future*, Oxford University Press, 1987.
2. Elkington, J., *Cannibals with Forks: The Triple Bottom Line for 21st Century Business*, Capstone Publishing, Oxford, 1997.
3. Stern, N., *Stern Review on the Economics of Climate Change*, HM Treasury, London, 2000.
4. Gore, A., *An Inconvenient Truth*, Bloomsbury, London, 2006.
5. Friedman, T., *The World is Flat*, Allen Lane, UK, 2005.

6. Botte, H., Meyer, T. and Stuchtey, M., 'An energy efficiency resolution in supply chains', *McKinsey Quarterly*, August 2009.

7. Holliday, C.O., Schmidheing, S. and Watts, P., *Walking the Talk: The Business Case for Sustainable Development*, Bennett-Koehler Publishers Inc., San Francisco, 2002.

8. Brickmann, C. and Ungerman, D., 'Climate change and supply chain management', *McKinsey Quarterly*, July 2008.

9. SAB Miller and World Wildlife Fund, *Water Footprinting: Identifying and Addressing Water Risks in the Value Chain*, SAB Miller, London, 2009.

10. Carbon Trust, *Carbon Footprints in the Supply Chain*, Carbon Trust, London, 2006.

11. Maslennikova, I. and Foley, D., 'Xerox's Approach to Sustainability', *Interfaces*, Vol. 30, No. 3, 2000.

12. Butner, K., Geuder, D. and Hittner, J., *Mastering Carbon Management: Balancing Trade-offs to Optimise Supply Chain Efficiencies*, IBM Global Services, 2008.

The supply chain of the future

14

- Emerging mega-trends

- Shifting centres of gravity

- The multi-channel revolution

- Seeking structural flexibility

- 2020 vision

In the relatively short time that companies have been focusing on managing supply chains, the world has changed dramatically. Over the last three decades or so since the phrase 'supply chain management' was first coined[1] we have witnessed a major trend to globalised supply chains, with activities that were once performed in-house now outsourced, accompanied by a dramatic increase in volatility in the business environment creating ever higher levels of uncertainty in both demand and supply.

There can be little doubt that these changes are only the precursor for the ever more seismic changes that potentially lie ahead. Because the development of supply chain strategy has to be contingent on the conditions prevailing in the wider business environment, it is increasingly important that supply chain managers understand what the future landscape may look like. So often in the past, organisations have made decisions on their supply chain networks based on the world as it then was. Sometimes those decisions led to a loss of flexibility which inhibited the company's ability to change quickly in response to changes in this business environment.

Whilst we cannot say with certainty what even the next few years will bring by way of change, there are some clear underlying trends which can provide some indication of the backdrop to the supply chain of the future.

Emerging mega-trends

Of the many emerging trends that will affect the shape of supply chains in the future, perhaps the most critical are those to do with demographics and changes in global spending patterns.

Some of these demographic and wealth redistribution changes include:

- A projected increase in the world's population from somewhere in the region of 7 billion today to over 9 billion by 2050. At the same time age profiles are changing differentially across countries and regions and this combined with cross-border migration means that some countries' populations will grow whilst others will shrink. As a result, spending patterns are likely to change, causing some markets to expand and others to decline.

- The United Nations reports that already today half of the world's population currently live in urban areas and by 2050 about 70 per cent will be city dwellers. The growth in the number of 'mega-cities' – defined as having a population of over 10 million people – will continue as the move from rural to urban areas accelerates. The challenge of serving these massive conurbations will require an increased focus on 'city logistics' with city-specific supply chain solutions.

- The trends towards a redistribution of wealth from the western world to the newly emerging economies will continue. For example, it is estimated that over the next 20 years the US's share of worldwide wealth will slip from 28 per cent to 24 per cent and that during the same time, Asia's share of the global market will almost double – meaning that it will account for over 50 per cent of the global economy by 2030. The middle classes in the emerging economies are likely to increase from 400 million in 2010 to over 1 billion by 2030.

The combined impact of these demographic and wealth distribution changes may well make existing supply chain arrangements less than optimal. Businesses that have established production and supply arrangements designed to serve the 'western-centric' demand patterns that prevailed in the past may need to substantially reconfigure their supply chain networks to take advantage of the rapidly developing markets of Brazil and India, for example. To illustrate the dramatic changes in global spending power already apparent, it is estimated that Asia accounts for around one third of worldwide retail sales, including 35 per cent of all car sales and 43 per cent of all mobile phones.[2] In addition, the geographical location of supply of many commodities could change as traditional sources may no longer be viable. For example, it is quite possible that because of climate change the patterns of global food production will alter quite dramatically. In other cases the relative costs of extracting and producing raw materials and basic commodities could change radically between countries, making some traditional sources uneconomic.

Shifting centres of gravity

All supply chains have a 'centre of gravity' determined by the pull of demand and supply factors. The relative costs and availability of materials and the costs of moving them to the point of final demand will determine where the optimal locations for factories, distribution centres and other value-adding activities should be.

Because of the uncertainties that surround the future patterns of demand and supply and the potential changes in input costs such as energy and other basic commodities, it becomes imperative that any decisions to redesign supply chains reflect the need to maximise flexibility. Ideally, the supply chain of the future will be capable of adapting quickly to any shifts that might occur on both the demand side and the supply side of the business.

Equally, with the continued volatility of many input costs, particularly oil and energy, many companies are already reviewing their existing supply chain strategies. For example, in June 2008, Keith Harrison, Chief Product Supply Officer of Procter & Gamble, was quoted as saying:

> Soaring energy costs are forcing P&G to re-think how to distribute its products ... A lot of our supply chain work was implemented when oil was $10 a barrel ... I could say that our supply chain design is now upside down ... What is our business going to look like in 2015?[3]

If the current conditions of turbulence and volatility continue then it may be that the supply chain solutions that served us well in the past may no longer be fit for purpose. As we have highlighted above, there is mounting evidence that because of major demographic changes and redistribution of wealth across the globe, the 'centre of gravity' in many markets will shift – causing a rethink of existing supply chain structures.

The shifting centres of gravity and the growing urbanisation of society are trends that are already evident and forward-thinking supply chain planners will already be factoring them into their strategy. The rise of mega-cities presents a particular logistical challenge. These cities are bigger in terms of population than many entire countries and are often characterised by inadequate infrastructure. In developing economies such as India, the challenge of serving massive markets with a wider range of products to cater for a customer with greater discretionary spending power will require innovative logistics solutions.

The use of logistics 'platforms' located on the edge of large cities is likely to increase to enable the consolidation of shipments for delivery into those cities. This will be accompanied by a growing number of collaborative arrangements amongst companies that will share logistics assets such as transport and distribution centres.

Whilst centralised production and offshore sourcing will still make sense for some product categories, there will be a need to bring supply much closer to demand. This change in thinking will be driven by the growing environmental concern over carbon footprints but also by cost considerations as transport costs continue to rise. At some point in the future no doubt new forms of energy may become available which could reverse this trend – but that is likely to be some years away.

Shifting centres of economic activity

The world is undergoing a massive realignment of economic activity, whose outlines are clearly visible in the changes occurring in the energy and materials sectors. Growth in demand for energy and basic materials (such as steel and copper) is moving from developed countries to developing ones, predominantly in Asia. Demand for oil in China and India, for example, will nearly double from 2003 to 2020, to 15.4 million barrels a day. Asia's oil consumption will approach that of the United States – the world's largest consumer – by the end of that period.

On the supply side, Asia's strong demand environment for energy and basic materials, coupled with its low labour costs, means that the region will increasingly become a global producer of aluminum, chemicals, paper, and steel. China, for instance, is adding steelmaking capacity so rapidly that its production will rise from 5 per cent of the worldwide total in 1995 to more than 30 per cent by 2015. In the process, it will become a leading exporter.

Over the next decade, resources (gas, minerals, steel, and pulp and paper, among others) will generally be developed and produced farther away from the points of consumption than ever before; Brazilian fibre, for instance, will be converted into paper products in China. In natural gas, the amount of indigenous production consumed within countries will continue to decline, replaced by cross-border flows delivered by long-distance pipelines and by ships carrying liquefied natural gas (LNG). Oil production too will increasingly switch to regions that are more and more remote (and often geopolitically unstable) as developed countries with dwindling reserves seek new supplies.

Important macroeconomic shifts are also occurring within regions. States in the Middle East are expanding their reach beyond oil, into new industries such as chemicals and metals. Dubai, for example, has emerged as a leading producer of aluminium, as a result of access to cheap energy (notably natural gas) and a proximity to markets in Asia and Europe. Qatar, in addition to being a major LNG player, is converting its cheap gas directly into high-quality diesel fuel and hopes to become a world leader in the emerging gas-to-liquids industry by 2010. Such activities could provide much-needed employment for the region's young and rapidly growing workforce.

To be sure, the rising levels of global connectivity required to meet the world's energy needs in the coming years will have positive economic effects, such as greater market liquidity and more globally priced commodities. At the same time, longer and more complex supply chains, combined with the mounting possibility that geopolitical events could curtail supply, will make prices more volatile.

SOURCE: BOZON, I.J.H., CAMPBELL, W.J. AND LINDSTRAND, M., 'GLOBAL TRENDS IN ENERGY', *THE MCKINSEY QUARTERLY*, JANUARY 2007

As well as these demographic and income distribution changes, other trends are reshaping the supply chain landscape. One trend in particular is the emergence of new routes to market and the adoption by many companies of what has come to be termed 'multi-channel' distribution.

The multi-channel revolution

Spurred on by the arrival of the Internet, there has been a dramatic growth in recent years of the use of alternative channels of distribution. Whilst the old routes to market may still be used, they have been augmented by these new channels which more often than not bypass traditional intermediaries and enable a direct contact between the supplier and the customer/consumer.

For example, many companies now offer their customers a range of options for ordering and for delivery/collection. Thus a retailer might offer the traditional 'bricks and mortar' outlets but also an Internet service for online shopping, a telephone ordering option and the possibility of home delivery or collection from the store. The challenge for logistics management is to ensure firstly that the customer experience is consistent across all the channels and secondly that the channels can complement each other to enable, whenever possible, the most efficient use of resources, e.g. shared distribution centres and single inventories.

In consumer markets there is growing evidence that the Internet is revolutionising both marketing and supply chain management. Statistics from the UK suggest that, at the time of writing, people under 25 are doing 40 per cent of their shopping online whereas the over 60s are doing less than 4 per cent of their shopping online. Hence the likelihood is that with each passing year the total percentage of all transactions that take place through the Internet will grow dramatically.

It is not only the sheer scale of this new channel that brings challenges to logistics management, it is also the fact that the Internet is likely to speed up the shift from a sellers' market to a buyer's market. In a way, the Internet 'democratises' the supply chain by placing the customer or consumer at the centre of the network. The customer can rapidly access information on alternative suppliers, they can make price comparisons (as shown in the example from Japan in the box below), they can assess delivery lead times and they can demand to have their own specific requirements catered for.

Web-savvy housewives sabotage efforts to save Japan's economy from stagnation

Japan's desperate fight with deflation – the policy battle that could decide the fate of the world's second-largest economy – is being undermined by a mobile phone application and an army of penny-pinching housewives.

Supermarket managers across the country describe themselves as powerless to resist the new downward pressure on prices because their once-loyal shoppers have harnessed the full power of social networking to get ten yen (7p) knocked off a litre of milk.

Equally the supplier can learn more about the customers and their buying behaviour and can tailor marketing strategies accordingly. One of the best examples is provided by Amazon which has developed powerful tools to enable it to target existing customers with product suggestions that match the profile of their previous purchases. At the time suppliers can use the Internet to better manage demand by steering customers towards products that are currently available from stock or even towards ones that have higher margins.

Associated with the rapid rise of Internet channels has been the growth of 'mobile' media, i.e. the use of mobile phones to enable a two-way communication channel to be established, particularly between suppliers and consumers – alerting them of promotional offers, for example. Consumers increasingly are using new generation mobile phones for Internet access to place orders but also to make price comparisons whilst on shopping expeditions.

An example of how mobile media is affecting sales is given in the example below from Domino's Pizza in Australia.

One of the advantages of having direct contact with the customer through online ordering is the dramatic improvement in visibility of real demand that it provides. For example, Tesco, one of the world's biggest online retailers (as well as one of the world's biggest bricks and mortar retailers), can see what its real product availability is because it is able to capture actual demand as it happens and is therefore able to measure on-the-shelf availability accurately. In the bricks and mortar business, even with sophisticated electronic point of sale (EPOS) data, the company cannot get the same level of accurate information.

From a logistics and supply chain management perspective, the multi-channel revolution has a number of implications. Ideally all channels should be served by the same logistics infrastructure, e.g. sharing distribution assets such as distribution centres, vehicles and, in particular, inventories. If this can be achieved then significant benefits can be obtained through gaining incremental revenue greater than the additional cost.

Often multi-channel operations imply an increase in home delivery as many of these emerging channels are primarily aimed at end-users who require delivery to a specific address rather than collecting it themselves. Whereas a bricks and mortar retailer has the 'last 50 metres challenge', i.e. how to manage the significant cost of getting the product from the delivery vehicle onto the shelf in the most cost-effective way, the online retailer is concerned with the 'last mile' costs. Because most home deliveries are for a single case equivalent or less, the problem is how to ensure that the cost of delivery does not erode profitability. With the advent of agreed delivery times and the use of dynamic vehicle routing and scheduling tools this problem should reduce.

The need for adaptability

Clearly markets and supply chains are always in a constant state of dynamic change and adaption. However, the evidence is that the rate of change has accelerated to the point where the business models that have served us well in the past may no longer work at all tomorrow.

Figure 14.1 highlights this challenge. We have moved from a business environment where the supplier held the power – often through their ownership of resources, technology and brands – to a situation where the customer, or even the consumer, is now in the driving seat. Where once it was a 'seller's market', today it is a 'buyer's market'. Simultaneously, the prevailing marketing philosophy has moved from the idea of mass markets serviced by mass production to the idea of 'markets-of-one' serviced by mass customisation.

Even though this fundamental shift has been observable for some time, it has not always been reflected in a similar shift in thinking about supply chain design.

The traditional supply chain business model was based around maximising efficiencies, particularly through the exploitation of the 'economies of scale'. So our factories were designed to produce things in large volumes and to maximise the use of capacity. This business model worked well in the conditions for which it was designed, e.g. the production of standard products designed for mass markets.

Figure 14.1 The supply chain of the future

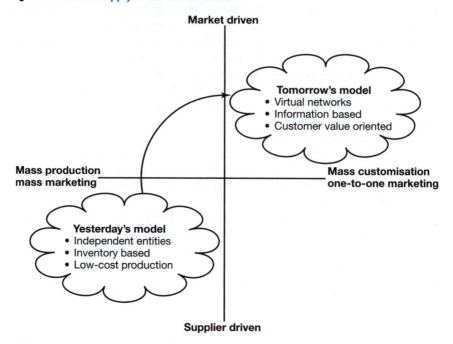

The problem now is that the context has changed. We have seen a move from the lower left-hand quadrant in Figure 14.1 to the upper right-hand quadrant and yet many companies have not recognised the implications of this shift for supply chain design. What is now required are supply chains that are far more agile and better able to cope with rapid change and higher levels of variety and even customisation.

Seeking structural flexibility

It has long been recognised that flexibility in operations and supply chain management is a desirable attribute. Generally flexibility in this context has usually been defined in terms of the ability to respond rapidly to demand changes in volume or mix for existing products. This capability might be defined as *dynamic flexibility* and it is linked to ideas such as set-up time reduction and the use of flexible manufacturing systems (FMS). However, in the world we have described earlier in this chapter, characterised by change which is discontinuous rather than incremental, a different type of flexibility is required.

In effect what is needed is something we might term *structural flexibility*. Structural flexibility reflects the ability of the supply chain to adapt or reconfigure its architecture in response to major changes on the demand side or the supply side. Supply chains with high levels of structural flexibility are well able to cope with the levels of volatility that are a feature of the twenty-first century business environment.

Equally, when fundamental shifts in the supply chain's centre of gravity occur they are capable of rapid adaptation to meet the changed conditions.

What are the key enablers of structural flexibility?

Perhaps the most critical enabler, but the one most difficult to achieve, is a corporate culture and 'mindset' that is open to change and is comfortable with frequent changes to processes and working practices. Also, because some of the enablers of structural flexibility – discussed below – involve much higher levels of collaborative working across organisational boundaries, there needs to be a willingness to actively create 'win-win' partnerships across the supply chain.

Given that this co-operative approach to working across the extended enterprise can be achieved, the main elements that underpin structural flexibility include:

- *Visibility and information sharing*
  The ability to see from one end of the pipeline to another is essential. It is important to be able to see the changes that are on the horizon both upstream and downstream. Information sharing provides a powerful platform on which to build collaborative working relationships across the supply chain.

- *Access to capacity*
  An important facilitator of adaptive supply chain management is the facility to access additional capacity when required. Capacity here refers not only to manufacturing but also in transport and warehousing. Furthermore, that capacity may not be owned by the firm in question, it could come from partners across the network, third-party providers or even competitors.

- *Access to knowledge and talent*
  Given the rapid rate of change in both markets and technologies, a major challenge to organisations today is ensuring that they have access to knowledge in terms of the potential for product and process innovation. Equally critical is access to people who are capable of exploiting that knowledge. 'Open innovation' and technology sharing agreements are ideas that are rapidly gaining ground. Once again, companies are increasingly turning to external sources of knowledge and talent to provide adaptive capabilities.

- *Inter-operability of processes and information systems*
  In an ideal world organisations would be able to alter the architecture of their physical supply chains in short time frames with minimal cost or disruption involved. Equally, as we noted earlier in Chapter 2, those same companies need the ability to manage multiple supply chains serving specific market segments. To enable this reconfiguration it greatly helps if the nodes and links of the supply chain are 'inter-operable'. In other words they can be plugged together in a variety of ways to enable specific supply chain solutions to be easily constructed. Standard processes and information systems help greatly in creating inter-operability.

- *Network orchestration*
  Because the achievement of higher levels of adaptability generally requires inputs from a variety of other entities in the wider supply/demand network, the need for co-ordination across the network arises. As supply chains become more 'virtual' than 'vertical' there is a growing requirement for orchestration. Whether that orchestration task is performed by the firm itself or by a specialist external logistics service provider or '4PL', the ability to structure appropriate networks and to synchronise activities across the nodes and links of those networks is paramount.

Structural flexibility is increasingly a prerequisite for doing business in a volatile and turbulent environment. What can happen when that flexibility is lacking is well illustrated by the example of the footwear fashion business Crocs (see box below).

Crocs: riding the fashion rollercoaster

Crocs is a North American based business that became famous for its iconic footwear that rapidly became a fashion item around the world. From its inception in 2002 until the end of 2007, the company experienced rapid growth and found it difficult to meet demand. In order to improve supply, Crocs significantly increased their production capacity, warehouse space and inventory. However, as sales peaked and declined, beginning in 2008, much of that additional capacity became redundant. The decline in sales continued as the global recession began to bite at the end of 2008 and into 2009. The company finished 2008 with a net loss of $185 million for the year. In quarter 1 of 2009 their revenues were down by 32 per cent compared to the previous year and the company reported a net loss of $22.4 million for the quarter.

Now Crocs was faced with excessive capacity with high fixed costs and was thus confronted with the need to consolidate their manufacturing and distribution operations. Starting in 2008 they shut down their Canadian and Brazilian manufacturing operations and abandoned specialist equipment and moulds that were used in the production of their unique product. As part of this process of retrenchment they consolidated their global distribution centres, cut their inventory by a half and reduced their global headcount by 2000.

2020 vision

In this age of uncertainty any attempt to develop a scenario of the future is fraught with difficulties. Nevertheless because there are already some observable trends and indicators it is possible to paint a picture of the challenges that lie ahead for supply chain management and also to suggest some possible ways of meeting those challenges.

'Doing more with less' will increasingly become the mantra of organisations that seek to survive in a resource-constrained world. Eco-efficiency considerations as we highlighted in Chapter 13 will drive many supply chain decisions, as companies seek to reduce both their use of scarce resources and their costs. These pressures will accelerate the move away from the classic large-scale, centralised manufacturing and distribution structures that tended to characterise the supply chain architecture of the past. Instead the focus will switch to what might be termed 'small footprint' supply chains which use less resources yet are more flexible and better able to serve local markets.

Already, new thinking and new technology is revolutionising manufacturing in many industries. A good example is provided by the steel industry, which in a way was a stereotype of the manufacturing model of the past. Driven by an inflexible production process and a search for economies of scale, massive integrated steel mills were built based on traditional blast furnaces. These facilities were capable of producing steel in a continuous process at a relatively low cost, but they had little flexibility. Today, steel-making technology is increasingly based around the idea of 'mini-mills', which are smaller and more flexible using electric arc furnaces and scrap iron as raw material. Consequently these new mills can produce steel both more eco-efficiently and can offer greater flexibility.

Another emerging technology that has the potential to enable more 'local-for-local' manufacturing is what is sometimes terms 'rapid manufacturing'.

Rapid manufacturing

One of the rapidly developing technologies that has the potential to transform supply chains is 'rapid manufacturing' (RM) – also sometimes termed 'digital manufacturing' or 'additive fabrication'.

The foundation for this technology is that products are built up layer by layer using laser-fused metal powders of polymers. Thus, rather than casting or machining a metal item or injection moulding a plastic product, this item is created from a series of very thin layers of material.

Whilst this technology has been used for some years to enable the production of prototypes, it is only recently that these ideas and tools have been applied to the manufacture or fabrication of end-use products. Boeing, for example, has used RM technology to manufacture parts for the F18 and other military aircraft.

The implications of RM for logistics and supply chain management are considerable: firstly, RM technology can enable local-for-local manufacturing to be achieved more cost-effectively; secondly, a much higher level of product customisation will be possible; thirdly, there is no need for inventory of finished product to be held; and, fourthly energy use and material waste are likely to be minimised.

It is not too far-fetched to envisage a world in which more customer value is created through late-stage customisation whilst the use of energy and resources is simultaneously reduced.

In the brief history of supply chain management we have already witnessed many dramatic changes in thinking and practice; however, in the next ten or so years we are likely to see yet further changes. One thing is certain, as supply chains become ever more virtual and network-based, and as global mega-trends reshape the business landscape, the role of logistics and supply chain management in ensuring a sustainable future will become ever more critical.

References

1. Oliver, R.K. and Webber, M.D., 'Supply chain management: logistics catches up with strategy', *Outlook*, Booz, Allen & Hamilton, Inc, 1982; reprinted in Christopher, M., *Logistics: The Strategic Issues*, Chapman & Hall, 1992.
2. 'East or famine', *The Economist*, 27 February 2010
3. Keith Harrison, quoted in Birchall, J. and Rigby, E., 'Oil price forces PLG to rethink its distribution', *Financial Times*, 27 June 2008.

Index

Page numbers in *italics* denote a table/diagram